GB
605
.A7
R45
2018

Reichert Powell,
Douglas, author.
Endless caverns

ENDLESS CAVERNS

Endless

CAVERNS

*An Underground Journey into
the Show Caves of Appalachia*

DOUGLAS REICHERT POWELL

THE UNIVERSITY OF NORTH CAROLINA PRESS

Chapel Hill

This book was published with the assistance of the
Fred W. Morrison Fund of the University of North Carolina Press.

Designed by Jamison Cockerham
Set in Arno and Warnock
by Tseng Information Systems, Inc.

Manufactured in the United States of America

The University of North Carolina Press has been a member
of the Green Press Initiative since 2003.

Jacket illustration: *Shenandoah Caverns Rainbow Lake, Va.*, 2012.
© Austin Irving, www.austinirving.com.

LIBRARY OF CONGRESS CATALOGING-IN-PUBLICATION DATA
Names: Reichert Powell, Douglas, author.
Title: Endless caverns : an underground journey into the show caves
of Appalachia / Douglas Reichert Powell.
Description: Chapel Hill : The University of North Carolina Press, [2018] |
Includes index.
Identifiers: LCCN 2017033406| ISBN 9781469638638 (cloth : alk. paper) |
ISBN 9781469638645 (ebook)
Subjects: LCSH: Caves—Appalachian Region. | Ecotourism—Appalachian
Region—History. | Appalachian Region—Description and travel.
Classification: LCC GB605.A7 R45 2018 | DDC 551.44/70975—dc23
LC record available at https://lccn.loc.gov/2017033406

MIX
Paper from
responsible sources
FSC
www.fsc.org   FSC® C013483

For

JAMES D. MOODY II

You can come out now

Contents

❖ ❖ ❖ ❖

Prologue   An Expedition into the Known   *1*

1   In the Intro Room: A Field Guide to
the Appalachian Show Cave   *11*

2   What Became of Grottoes:
The Stories of Grand Caverns   *30*

3   The Hall of Illusion:
Imagining Appalachian Caves   *48*

4   Constant Revision at the Cumberland Gap:
The Stories of Gap Cave   *62*

5   Total Darkness Demonstration:
Sympathy for the Devil   *84*

6   The Legacy of Gene Monday: The Stories of
Cherokee Caverns and Indian Cave   *102*

7   Adventures in Cave Development: Talking
Shop at the National Cave Association   *128*

8   Natural Wonders, Inc.:
The Stories of Endless Caverns   *158*

9   Last One Out, Turn off the Lights:
The Show Cave's Afterlife   *175*

Epilogue   Valley of the Badasses   *195*

Acknowledgments   *203*

Note on Sources   *205*

Index of Caves and Caverns   *209*

General Index   *211*

Figures & Map

❖ ❖ ❖ ❖

Figures

Dr. Stan Sides at the entrance to Bedquilt Cave 2

*During a Tour of Endless Caverns in Luray and
New Market, Virginia*, ca. 1920s 9

The Bride's Veil, Weyer's Cave Octo: 14th 1853 35

Map Showing the Location of Shendun, Virginia, ca. 1885 40

The Fugitive 55

Geology of the Cumberland Gap area 64

Alexander Alan Arthur, ca. 1885 69

General Oliver Otis Howard in 1900 75

Carter Saltpeter Cave 91

Photograph taken in Atomic Caverns, 1948 107

The baby in the path, Indian Cave 125

American Celebration on Parade, Shenandoah Caverns 148

The Stalacpipe Organ at Luray Caverns 151

The Endless Caverns sign on Massanutten Mountain 164

Entrance to Nick a Jack Cave Near Chattanooga, Tennessee 187

Walmart built on strip-mine bench 201

Map

Show Caves of the Great Appalachian Valley *xii*

ENDLESS CAVERNS

SHOW CAVES OF THE GREAT APPALACHIAN VALLEY

1. Appalachian Caverns
2. Bristol Caverns
3. Carter Saltpeter Cave (undeveloped)
4. Cathedral Caverns
5. Cherokee Caverns
6. Crystal Cave (closed)
7. Crystal Grottoes Caverns
8. Dixie Caverns
9. Endless Caverns
10. Forbidden Caverns
11. Gap Cave
12. Giant Caverns (closed)
13. Grand Caverns
14. Indian Cave
15. Linville Caverns
16. Lost Sea
17. Lost World Caverns
18. Luray Caverns
19. Manitou Cave (closed)
20. Massanutten Caverns
21. Melrose Caverns
22. Mystic Caverns (closed)
23. Natural Bridge Caverns
24. Natural Tunnel
25. Nickajack Cave
26. Organ Cave
27. Raccoon Mountain Cave
28. Ruby Falls
29. Russell Cave
30. Seneca Caverns & Stratosphere Caverns
31. Sequoyah Caverns (closed)
32. Skyline Caverns
33. Smoke Hole Caverns
34. Shenandoah Caverns
35. Tuckaleechee Caverns
36. Wonder Cave (closed)

KENTUCKY

TENNESSEE

Johnson City

Holston River

Knoxville

Niota

Tennessee River

Asheville

Chattanooga

GEORGIA

ALA.

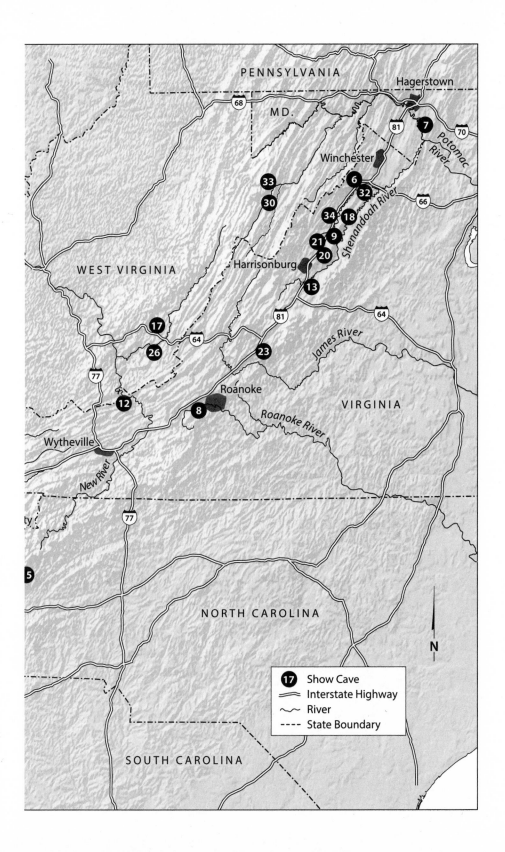

17	Show Cave
≈	Interstate Highway
~	River
----	State Boundary

Prologue

An Expedition into the Known

❖   ❖   ❖   ❖

I knew I was in trouble when I saw Dr. Stan's coveralls. He normally wore blue cotton, but today they were ripstop nylon, fire-engine red. Nine of us had walked a little over a mile through the scrubby second-growth woods of Barren County, Kentucky, the summer understory just coming into its own in late June. Now we were gathered in a small, natural alcove at the base of a hill, gearing up: donning helmets, checking headlamps, strapping elbow- and kneepads into place, taking one last trip behind the tree. Before us, a mossy rock outcrop formed a lintel over an opening four feet high, maybe ten feet wide. That was where we were heading, a cave named Bedquilt.

Dr. Stanley D. Sides, a tall, lean, gregarious, sixty-something cardiologist from Cape Girardeau, Missouri, was our leader, teacher and guide; he's also a cave historian and a caver of tremendous experience, acumen, and renown. I asked him what was up with his coveralls today.

"The nylon has a lower coefficient of drag," he replied with a hint of a grin. "By the way, Doug, I'd like you to be behind me today." Yes, I was in trouble.

When my eyes grew used to the dim light beyond the opening, I began to see why the friction of fabric was going to be a factor. We entered a sort of foyer, a room where we just had the space to sit up straight on a floor of jumbled cobbles. Stan crawled up a narrow passage in the back, then turned, and motioned for me to follow.

As the sunlight failed and the headlamps took over, the ceiling and the floor converged, and the cobbles turned to pebbles turned to silt. The passage remained wide but grew increasingly, almost intolerably low, up what (Dr. Stan pointed out) was a drain for some vast unseen space. Ahead of us somewhere was the former show cave known as Colossal Cavern, during its commercial run from 1897 until the 1920s. It was like entering a building through the plumbing.

I squirmed, then slithered, looking at the soles of Stan's boots, the cuffs of his red coveralls, my head pitched sideways when there was no longer

1

Dr. Stan Sides at the entrance to Bedquilt Cave. (2008 Karst Field Studies at Mammoth Cave, Western Kentucky University; photograph by the author)

clearance for my helmet, my gear bag dragging along beside me in the wide, flat crack. Stan's boot heels moved away in the darkness as my progress slowed. then stopped altogether.

A short distance ahead I could see that the crawl widened into a low room that by any other standard would seem claustrophobically small. But from my current vantage point it beckoned, spacious and airy in my headlight. Behind me, on the other hand, I could see nothing, lacking clearance to turn my head at all, much less look over my shoulder. I needed no visual information, though. I could feel everything I needed to know: my butt was in contact with the ceiling; my front pressed as flat on the floor as I could manage, and between me and the rock, above and below, there was room only for my jeans, with their insanely high coefficient of drag.

As seven other cavers piled up in the crawl behind me, I followed my first impulse, which was to shove myself forward with my toes while grasping for some purchase in the grit. No result. So I followed my second impulse: a surge of pure, bodily panic throughout my limbs. Then, a little more sensibly, I followed my third impulse, which was to call out to Dr. Stan.

"Stan, I'm stuck." I was shooting for nonchalant but had entirely too much adrenaline coursing through me to pull it off.

His headlight turned toward me. "Hold on, I'll be right there." I exhaled, tried to compose, to relax, as the cold water of the mud floor soaked through my clothes, and the weight of a central Kentucky hillside bore down on me with increasing urgency. How on Earth did I end up here?

❖   ❖   ❖   ❖

This book is, in a broad sense, the answer to that question. But in that moment, the answer was clear: I was here — clogging the drain a dozen yards inside the backdoor of Colossal Cave, part of the world's longest known cave system, the Flint Ridge–Mammoth Cave complex, winding beneath Barren County, Kentucky — as a researcher. I was participating in the 2008 Karst Field School hosted by Western Kentucky University and the independent Cave Research Foundation (CRF), taking a course called "Exploration of Mammoth Cave." The course consisted of a morning lecture followed by a day of caving, visiting all the caves that had been developed for tourism in the Mammoth Cave area (including various regions of Mammoth itself) in historical order.

Even though my self-appointed jurisdiction lay a couple of hundred miles to the east, I wanted this experience to provide me with some broad context for my own project. I had a chance to see the whole history of the show cave unfold in one site here in the rolling hills of central Kentucky. And only here could I get the opportunity to be led into these caves and taught about how to approach caving more broadly, in the company of the veteran cavers of the CRF. If I wasn't quite a real explorer, I was at least near them.

It was the CRF who undertook the persistent and determined expeditions in the 1960s and early 1970s that eventually linked the Flint Ridge caves with Mammoth Cave and established as fact that they were part of the same system, one whose total miles of passageway exceeded the world's other long caves several times over. Dr. Stan, president of the CRF during the project, was a close friend and colleague of the five men and one woman who found the linkage. On September 9, 1972, the final push, he was on the surface ready to provide medical support in the event of an emergency. That night, first wading, then crawling down a narrow waterway the explorers termed Hanson's Lost River, party leader John Wilcox slipped through a near-flooded passage into a vast chamber that was suddenly, unexpectedly familiar. Roger Brucker (another member of the CRF team) describes the scene in *The Long-*

est Cave: "Slowly his eyes became accustomed to the gloom. What was that gleaming, horizontal line against the far wall? Surely it was a pipe! Yes, a handrail! With vertical supports! John opened his mouth, knowing the effect it would have. He spoke slowly through an ear-to-ear grin. 'I see a tourist trail!'"

I had arrived deep in the Kentucky caves from the opposite direction: the old tourist trails had brought me by way of Mammoth to Flint Ridge. My research had taken me through dozens of cave tours in the company of car tourists and paid guides of all description. Over the past three years, I had traveled several thousand miles up and down the back roads of the southern Appalachian Mountains, visiting every show cave from Fort Payne, Alabama, northeast to the Pennsylvania line, thirty-seven of them altogether, including all thirty then open to the public.

My trail also led through the recesses of libraries and archives in Tennessee and Virginia to examine strata of old travel writings, brochures, business records, pictures, and surveys and into the homes and workplaces of the folks who keep the show cave industry going. I was gathering a lot of useful information about the broader history of show caves as an industry and an art form, but deep down I knew I was there just as much to fulfill a desire that every show cave visitor feels: to get beyond the rails and walkways and find out where all those little holes lead to.

❖   ❖   ❖   ❖

Now, stuffed into the crawlway of Bedquilt Cave, my wish was being granted. Dr. Stan came back to me, and spoke to me in a calm and clear tone honed by his profession. "OK, just back up a little. . . . Now move your arms like you are swimming underwater. . . . That's it . . . " Following instructions carefully, I shoved back a couple of inches of silt from the floor of the crawlway. That done, my body and my jeans scraped through the vise, and I emerged into a room where sitting hunched over, soaked to the skin, felt like luxury.

As much as I felt like the real deal in that moment, I wasn't really earning much caver cred. I wasn't so much training to become a caver as I was preparing to be a show cave guide in the pages of this book, a guide not to any particular show cave but to the phenomenon of the show cave more generally.

Real cave explorers often don't have a lot of use for show caves: they are apt to see them as cleaned-up, dumbed-down amusements for the herd. But the relationship between show caves and "real" cave exploration is more complicated than it initially appears.

After all, if it hadn't been for the commercial development of Mammoth Cave, the CRF would never have been able to launch its expeditions. It was building on a project begun in 1837 by Stephen Bishop, slave to Mammoth Cave's owners, first Franklin Gorin, then Dr. John Croghan. The foremost guide for visitors to the cave in the mid-nineteenth century, Bishop, legend has it, learned to write by tracing his guests' names on cave walls with a torch. Bishop later produced the first great map of Mammoth, forefather of the map CRF cavers endeavor to expand today. He also set an enduring precedent: that a cave is not truly known until it has been surveyed and mapped.

In the 1970s one of those cavers was Hal Crowther, a computer programmer who developed new software for the complex work of cave surveying and mapping. In one of the weird twists of history and culture that seem to proliferate around show caves, Stephen Bishop's map would lead to the creation of modern computer gaming. Crowther developed one of the very first games, the text-based adventure he named Colossal Cave in honor of the old show cave, to keep his kids amused and to share his enthusiasm for cave exploration during a summer spent surveying caves in the Mammoth–Flint Ridge complex. The opening moves of the game's map were modeled on none other than Bedquilt Cave, where I was stuck in the middle of what the game termed "a maze of twisty passages, all alike." Little did I suspect I would find myself here when I first explored this cave on my dad's Apple II, on a summer afternoon maybe twenty-five years before.

This moment encapsulates a lot of the reasons why I think show caves are worth an especially long look. Appearances notwithstanding, I wasn't embarking on an adventure into the unknown. I was crawling into a strange nexus of the known, coming into contact with the rough edges of a bunch of different ways we have inhabited, imagined, and represented the planet.

"Real" cavers are always in search of "virgin cave," finding a space where no man has gone before. What I was doing was seeking out these places precisely for the way they have been densely, promiscuously used. The beauty and knowledge you find there comes not from being unmarked by humanity but from being intricately overwritten by multiple generations. Show caves give us an opportunity to explore the ways we've related to each other and to the earth and to uncover cultural connections we've never seen before: who could have guessed that a map of Mammoth Cave would provide the missing link from chattel slavery to computer gaming?

The show cave's special function, I've realized, is to be able to illuminate all these convergences and contradictions in one space, pull it all together into one guided tour, and somehow transform a state of sustained cognitive dissonance into something fun. And all these weird, historical, cultural connections—they're real, they're part of a physical place where even the air has a distinctive smell and texture. You can touch it, you can crawl through it, get it on you, get stuck in it. Yet it is also a distinctive emotional state as well—one part romanticism, one part slapstick, and a lot of other parts thrown in for good measure. Show caves are a way of framing the complexities of the earth and our relationship to it in a way that is simultaneously fantastic and eminently, self-evidently real. They provide us with appealing points of entry to ideas that are often too vast, troubling, or difficult to think about.

❖　❖　❖　❖

I've spent two decades of studying the landscape and culture of the Mountain South, and two and a half decades before that living in it. At one point I played a little thought experiment: what is the most place-specific art form there is? The show cave emerged as a leading candidate. It really can happen only exactly where it is. But its implications, as it turns out, are as expansive as its emplacedness is specific. I went looking for some sites to study where I could test out some of my pet theories about place and region. In the show caves of Appalachia, I believe I've found more than that. I've come to think of Appalachia's show caves as a truly distinctive medium, little noted, perhaps, but influential and potentially enlightening, through which thousands of people every year are introduced to the story of the mountains.

The show cave is a genre with its own conventions, to be sure, but one that allows each show cave to adopt its own unique perspective on what kind of place, region, and world we are a part of and how it got that way. Some show cave tours are frivolous, others more self-consciously substantive and educational, and a couple, at least, are openly proselytizing for a particular point of view. But all cave tours require groups to at least temporarily travel together through this world of contradiction and illusion, enjoying it as much as we can, while sharing together a sense of amazement and even bafflement.

It's a resource we need to preserve, for its cultural as well as its scientific significance. It's a spot where you can truly be the cultural equivalent of a locavore, seeing something that can really and truly happen only here, though it may be prepared according to recipes and by techniques with which you are already familiar.

Will the show cave survive the enforced homogeneity of our Interstate Highway culture? Can it contend with the recreational-industrial complex of the Disney Era? I believe the answer is yes, and not just because the show cave has stubbornly outlived two hundred years' worth of mineral springs re-sorts, tourist camps, Wild West towns, and miniature golf courses.

The gift shop, the colored lights, and hokey lore are all part of an art form that persists. Why? Despite some appearances to the contrary, it achieves something significant. The show cave is a way of declaring "this place is im-portant," not only because it has things in it that you can't find anywhere else in the world, but also because it's bound up in the story of a restless, chang-ing earth on an unfathomable scale. A show cave tells a story of a place, of a world, that is unexpectedly scary, funny, weird, and edifying all at once, in a language almost anybody can understand. The practitioners of this art form, show cave builders, owners, and operators, are self-taught and self-supporting; their art is a complicated collaboration between the physical world and the realm of myths and dreams. The invisible landscape of stories and emotions that surrounds us in our lives on the surface world is, in the show cave, made visible to us. These caves aren't just natural wonders, his-torical landmarks, and vaudeville spectacles; they are the workings of a place opened to inspection.

As a result, seeing Appalachia, one of our nation's most complicated places, through the medium of the show cave is particularly revelatory. All across the Mountain South, the things that make the region distinctive struggle for viability in a changing world. The social fabric of household lore and craftsmanship that sustained generations is being unraveled by the global economy, as the expanding network of superstores and minimarts draws local economies into the same spiral of low-cost goods and low-wage jobs as everyplace else. Traditional arts are increasingly a province of con-noisseurs, removed from the working world that created them. Even the re-gion's folklore is challenged by the omnipresent media. And the landscape itself is leveled in the name of our society's appetite for timber, for coal, for power, for parking lots. All these practices are powered by a deep-seated single-mindedness, an assumption that a place can be only one thing at a time.

Show caves resist this trend. It's not that they don't change, but that they record all the changes, and present them to you simultaneously. The show cave tour is solemn, farcical, paradoxical, edifying, and menacing by turns, because the art of the show cave is to be all those things at once. At Oak Ridge, Tennessee's Cherokee Caverns, caretaker Jim Whidby can show you the hoofprints of a performing horse from the 1940s beside motorcycle tracks from the 1970s beside torch marks from thousands of years ago, all in mud deposited in a different epoch, when the entire cavern was part of the seafloor. Show caves remind us that, in the long run, the mall-ification of the Mountain South, leveling and segmenting the landscape into single uses, will likely be just another layer of the history and identity of the region etched into the walls of the cave.

In the southern mountains, show caves speak to us with a distinctive eloquence of a place in which today's conflicts and changes scribble a few small lines on larger patterns of transformation. They embrace that classic sense of the uncanny in Southern Gothic, the sense of being entangled with powers much vaster than one's self, rooted in the tangled haunting of conflicts past. But show caves add to this time-honored formula a humbler and more welcome sense of our place in a changing universe: even if we are stuck with our burdens and destinies, our part in the Big Picture that show caves make visible to us is very small — small, but enduring.

That's something that's worth taking stock of, so that's what I've done, even if it meant getting stuck underneath a hillside or two. I'd like to invite you on a tour of what I've found, one turn around the Appalachian show cave circuit. Show caves, while tacky and garish, are really and truly wondrous — and not just for the otherworldliness of the space, the freaky and astounding forms, but also for the cultural work they do. The space inside caves is by nature pure darkness, absolutely un-seeable. These show caves transform that space into a homespun visual spectacle, recording and dramatizing the evolving culture and condition of Southern Appalachia.

❖   ❖   ❖   ❖

So let's take a tour of this peculiar phenomenon as it occurs in this particular place at this time. I have structured this meta-tour of caves around the standard movements of the cave tour: an opening exposition followed by some combination of spectacles of illusion, tales of the cave's (and the show's) development from the dawn of time to the present, and the ever-encroaching darkness, which is both the cave's natural state and a powerful symbol of its legitimately dangerous appeal. It's customary, in the area where you wait for the tour to start, for a big map of the cave to be on display, so with that in mind, here's a quick survey of the trip ahead.

In the "Intro Room" of chapter 1, I orient you to the standard features of show caves, the traits that define the genre, one of which is to pause at the beginning of the tour to do exactly that. Then in chapter 2, I tell the story of Grand Caverns, the oldest and in many ways the definitive Appalachian show cave.

In chapter 3, I consider the ways the cave is used as a medium, archetyp-

During a Tour of Endless Caverns in Luray and New Market, Virginia, ca. 1920s.
(Courtesy of Norfolk & Western Historical Photograph Collection, Virginia Tech)

ally in that moment in the tour where cave formations are made to mimic familiar images: the Capitol Dome, Frozen Niagara, Cave Bacon. Chapter 4 ups the ante on this interplay between fact and fiction, the real and the imaginary, examining how the shifting identities of what's now known as Gap Cave, part of the Cumberland Gap National Historical Park, both reflect and helped to shape the character of the Appalachian region in the wake of the Civil War.

Chapter 5 explores what's at stake in the show cave's traditional demonstration of total darkness, a confrontation with mortality that evolves from dicier ways of having fun in caves. Chapter 6 pushes further into the darkness, examining what happens to two caves in East Tennessee, Cherokee Caverns and Indian Cave, when the lights fail and the cave starts to be reclaimed by darker forces.

Just as the show cave tour ends, inevitably, in the gift shop, chapter 7 returns to the surface with an examination of the business end of show caves. Visiting the gathering of show cave owners and operators at the National Cave Association, I learn as much about the culture of cave owners as I do about their trade secrets. In chapter 8, I track the fate of one of the classic Shenandoah show caves, this book's namesake Endless Caverns, as it achieved the height of accomplishment, failure, and reclamation, only to be acquired by a mall builder and converted into a NASCAR-themed RV park.

Visiting a series of closed show caves in chapter 9, I learn some things worth knowing about what remains after the show is over: the geologic charisma, the earthy meanings that draw us to these sites over and over again. A final ride through a ragged edge of Appalachia in eastern West Virginia considers these caves as a line of defense against the cultural leveling of our time, against erasure of memory, of the facts and the mysteries of existence.

In what follows, I want to think a bit about how and why show caves work. I will show you show caves at work, taking you through the histories of some of the Great Valley's most significant sites. And since show caves always seem to connect, through whatever labyrinthine logic, to other stories, other ideas, and broader landscapes, we'll see what we can learn through this distinctive perspective about Appalachia, the South, America, the globe.

This kind of reflection is, for me, the finest and most significant contribution of the show cave to culture at large: in our increasingly subdivided culture, the show cave remains the rare medium that makes a group of strangers' encounter with uncertainty, multiplicity, and ambiguity into a convivial, enjoyable experience. In *Endless Caverns*, my job as your guide is to lead you into this phenomenon, to shine a light on this unusual formation, the Appalachian show cave, and to tell its story.

ONE

In the Intro Room

A Field Guide to the Appalachian Show Cave

❖   ❖   ❖   ❖

My own introduction to world of show caves really came via the Lost Sea in Sweetwater, Tennessee. It wasn't the first cave or even the first show cave I ever visited, but it was the first one that really awakened my attention to the show cave's artful embrace of simultaneity, contradiction, and confusion. It made sense to head back there at the very beginning of this project.

Lost Sea represented the Cadillac of all scout trips for Troop 33 in my hometown of Johnson City, about three hours away. Some chilly spring weekend we'd load up in station wagons with sleeping bags and flashlights and old clothes and head for the caverns for a trip, which included the commercial tour, a wild cave tour, and then an overnight stay in one of the cave's largest rooms. In 1978–79, for an eleven-year-old, this was the experience, the one that kept you going during the low moments of mandatory attendance at city council meetings to satisfy requirements for Citizenship in the Community merit badge. Hang in there, the cave trip is coming: real knowledge and real wonder all at once.

Flash forward almost thirty years: it's 2005, and I'm back, alone, on a slow early summer weekday, getting a much more workaday behind-the-scenes, matter-of-fact once-around of the cave of my well-remembered dreams. It is the second day of my first trip up the show cave trail, from the rental pickup at the airport in Chattanooga to the drop-off at Dulles International. In between, I was visiting upward of a dozen show caves, driving a couple of thousand miles on back roads all the way.

Lisa, the manager, chats politely with me in her cinderblock office just off the gift shop. New to the whole interview thing, I try to get some subjective impressions, a peek behind the curtain, but it's nothing doing. She's used to giving this kind of informational-promotional interview to travel sections and regional publications, so it's straight press-packet stuff. Not that there's anything wrong with that, especially since they're kind enough to take me around free of charge.

J.J., my guide, meets me at the end of the artificial tunnel with a vintage Cold War feel to it that leads from the gift shop to the top of the commercial tour. It empties not into the nuclear missile command post you'd expect if, like me, you'd grown up on late Cold War movie staples like *War Games*, but into a spacious, majestic cavern. J.J. and I shuffle down the graded trail past the exhibition moonshine still and the anthracite chamber to the dock on the shores of the lake from which Lost Sea takes its name. There, J.J.'s coworker, Troy, sits beside a small podium, half-interestedly reading an old pamphlet about this very place. He's about the same age as J.J., late teens, white kid, kind of country, identical green polo shirts and slacks. J.J. is the taller and stockier of the two, Troy being a little more of the wiry type.

J.J. has already explained to me on the way down here that they are both seasonal workers, local high school students, and that this is generally considered a pretty sweet gig. Troy seems less convinced of that at the moment. He looks up, looks at J.J., says, "What's the deal with him?" Meaning me.

"Oh, he's a reporter," J.J. replies. (Close enough.) "I'm taking him out solo." Troy seems underwhelmed. "Man, I ain't seen anybody all day. They won't even let me have my phone. Not like I get any bars down here — but I could at least listen to music." We walk out on the metal deck, floating on pontoons; J.J. points out a set of submerged cleats where the dock could be secured if the water was lower, during dry stretches in the late summer.

We cast off our glass-bottomed boat. J.J. fires up the electric motor, and we quietly troll out toward the middle. I ask about the floodlights shining up from below.

"Naw, they're not on the bottom, they're just a few feet below the surface. No one knows exactly how deep it is here. We have one person who's a scuba diver, but we mostly use him to change the lightbulbs and help stock the fish."

As I look back across the lake, dappled green by the random field of submerged floodlights, I feel a pleasant, lazy confusion, like, I imagine, the plump, pale rainbow trout feel as they pass below the glass beneath my feet. But the mood is tinged, continuously, with an awareness that here, if the lights go out, J.J. and the guy with the pamphlet and I are all screwed. Somewhere above my head it is a sunny June day in East Tennessee. But we are adrift on the Lost Sea, the world's second largest underground lake, 300 feet beneath the foothills of the Smokies, in the limestone karstlands of the upper Tennessee Valley.

❖   ❖   ❖   ❖

A Field Guide to the Appalachian Show Cave

Even in J.J.'s relatively unromantic presentation, I was feeling that weirdness, that uncanny blend of pleasure and threat, a tension between ignorance and mystery, that is the signature emotional state of the show cave: that sense of convergence. It's why people go see the show. And Lost Sea's caverns are a fine representative example of the genre. The earliest known explorer was a Pleistocene jaguar, whose fossilized paw print represented the climax of the Wild Cave tour for scouts, the lone print at the end of a remote crawl, evoking the vision of a living creature of power and strength far surpassing its kind today, nonetheless powerless, wandering in the absolute dark ever farther from the land where status as an apex predator is meaningful.

Humans, too, have known of the cavern for centuries, judging from indigenous artifacts found in the cave. Pine torch stubs, potsherds, mining equipment, moonshine stills, dance floors, civil defense supplies, and other paraphernalia precede the show cave trappings of today. This series of long, rambling underground rooms offers encounters with natural marvels through multiple and conflicting layers of human usage.

The Lost Sea's own history supposes that the cave was once known as Craighead Caverns in honor of the Cherokee luminary Chief Craighead, a prominent area landholder before the Cherokee Removal of the late 1830s. And it's been an active part of the local economy since at least as far back as the Civil War, when the cave served the Confederacy as an important source of saltpeter; smoke-written names and dates testify to the presence of soldiers and workers, and reconstructed leeching vats (which likely would have been outside the cave during the actual mining) provide the occasion for a quick lesson on the extraction of nitrates from the soil on today's show cave tour.

Once the war and its resource demands ended, local guides gave informal tours of the cave, and local folks explored it, culminating in the discovery, in 1905, of the massive underground lake. A teenager named Ben Sands, whose father had on occasion led tours of the cave, squirmed through a tight, muddy crawl into the lake room, returning to report that, unable to see the extent of the water, he threw mud balls as far as he could in every direction but heard only distant splashes.

Ben's crawlway, besides being tight, also flooded seasonally. It would be some years before the lake could be made accessible to the general public. In the meantime, in 1915 owner George Kyle installed a wooden dance floor in the cavern's "Big Room," which became an area destination for dancing, drinking, and cockfighting (the losers thrown in a ninety-foot pit in the corner). With the advent of car tourism, Craighead Caverns capitalized on its site adjacent to the Smokies and just off main tourist routes to Florida from the Northeast and Midwest. In 1927 the caverns were opened as a full-blown, electrically lighted roadside attraction, though that effort was quashed by the advent of the Great Depression two years later. Various schemes for putting the developed cave to productive use—mushroom farming, another round as a speakeasy called the Cavern Tavern, and a stockpile for civil defense supplies—came and went through midcentury. Fortified crackers, 17.5-gallon tins of water, sanitary napkins, and first aid kits were stacked in rows by the old mushroom beds and the splintered, rotted dance floor.

It's a ready-made show cave setup, a southern mountain hat trick: Indians, Hillbillies, and Confederates all at once. Throw in the threat of nuclear annihilation, and there's something for everyone; add a natural wonder or two and a few thousand light bulbs, and you've got a tour ready to roll. Just add guides and gift shops.

And sure enough, there came the dawn of the Interstate age in the form of I-75, sweeping down from the Midwest to the Deep South, passing a mere eleven miles away. Local entrepreneur Van Michael teamed with veteran cave developer Roy Davis, fresh off his successful domestication of middle Tennessee's Cumberland Caverns, and in 1965, The Lost Sea, which at that time could still bask in the glory of being the World's Largest Underground Lake, opened for business. Its subdued, midcentury-modern visitor center and gift shop are built atop the sleek tunnel providing more leisurely access to the cave's marvels than the Cavern Tavern's 200 steps, which were slippery, uneven, and exhausting, leaving overserved patrons passed out in the old foyer.

Now that drainage and blasting controlled the water levels and the routes to the lake room, the standard tour culminated in glass-bottomed boat trips across the unfathomed depths of the Lost Sea itself. The old cockfight/dancehall/mushroom farm/bomb shelter, once the main attraction for the locals, was now no longer on the commercial tour. Instead it became the campsite for scout, church, and other youth groups to spend the night on the Wild Cave tour, where in the late 1970s I had the first inklings of the idea behind this book. And thus it came to pass that I drifted across the lake with J.J., blissed out with the weirdness, and the lights stayed on.

❖　❖　❖　❖

It isn't all about the wonder, the illusion and confusion, the fear and awe. That's the primary product they're selling here. But it gets made through a very labor-intensive process. Woven through the metaphysics of the experi-

　　　　　　　A Field Guide to the Appalachian Show Cave

ence is a rival spectacle of the technical achievement involved in making the show cave happen. Even the most low-tech, old-timey show cave involves a tremendous amount of raw physical work: blasting and paving and lighting and wiring. You can't ride on the boats in the Lost Sea without wondering, at some point, how did they get the boats down here? And the answer is, with a lot of work.

And here we're just talking about the challenges involved in the infra-structure of the cave, such as needing a scuba diver to change underwater lightbulbs. Thanks in part to the Lost Sea, "subterranean boat wrangler" is an actual job description. But there's a whole other realm of bureaucratic work involved as well, which doesn't make for nearly as interesting a stop on the tour but has complexities all its own: the layers of insurance involved, of regulation and inspection and permitting, the revolving door of seasonal labor, the boat wrangler who wants permission to listen to music on the job. All make for a bureaucratic labyrinth with leads trailing off in all directions.

Dealing with the tourists is equally complex. According to J.J. (who gives me some of the behind-the-scenes stuff Lisa studiously avoided), the cave-loving public can include crystal-powered earth worshipers hoping to bathe in sacred streams or enter the cordoned-off "Cherokee Council Room," hyperventilating claustrophobes just barely holding together after their friends or kids or friends' kids convinced them it couldn't be that bad, a bevy of ankle-sprainers and complainers and self-appointed experts and intensive parents and lax parents, and road-weary and rowdy and sullen and irritating and ingratiating kids. It's a remarkably challenging business envi-ronment, especially when you consider that the whole model hinges on de-livering a certain state of mind: that uncanny fun.

❖　❖　❖　❖

That's where the cultural work of the cave kicks in. To get to the Big Feel-ing that makes all the logistics worthwhile, there's a whole layer of artfulness about the way this drama plays out. The show cave, like any other kind of art form that's been around for a few millennia, has developed some gen-eral features as a genre, some reliable formulas for eliciting that signature response. There are some conventions to the way the caves as a group go about presenting themselves, the equivalent of the shadowy confrontations of film noir, the meet-cute of the romantic comedy, the Act Five bloodbath of Shakespearean tragedy.

So let's talk about the "ground rules" (so to speak) that govern the genre (and making as many cave-related puns as possible is most definitely a ground rule). I've boiled it down to three basic things pretty much every show cave is built from: illusion, darkness, and development. Put these three notions together in an illuminated walk of about three-quarters of a mile underground, and you've got the fundamentals of the genre.

What follows is a kind of mash-up, an amalgam of some typical pieces of the show cave experience, a meta-tour not of any given cave but of show caves as a genre. You might call this Composite Caverns — Appalachia's Most Typical Show Cave. We need to move toward the back of the gift shop, where there's a teenager with a big flashlight and an ill-fitting blazer waiting to open a door that looks like it could lead to a utility closet, but instead, on the other side, there's a staircase down into the mouth of an actual cave. And just inside that great stone mouth, if the pattern holds, there will be a wide spot to gather up the group and give the first major installment of the Guide Spiel. Let's call this the Intro Room.

❖   ❖   ❖   ❖

I've lost count now of the times I've stood on a wet, sloping path in the antechamber of a cavern, shoulder to shoulder with a group of strangers, getting the quick briefing on cave formation and description. It's usually being conducted by someone who has done it so many times that it takes on the quality of a catechism: What is it called when it hangs down from the ceiling? A stalactite. Why? Because it has to hold on tight to keep from falling. And if it is on the floor? A stalagmite. Why? Because it might reach the ceiling one day.

Well versed, I can speed the litany of the Intro Room along if I'm alone on the tour (as sometimes happens) or a little bored or pressed for time, snapping off the responses in rapid succession to supply the missing canonical information. The three colors of the cave are white for calcite, black for magnesium, and red for iron. The green of cave algae is banished from the trinity, an intrusion caused by the unholy union of warmth of the lights and the spores carried on visitors' clothing. I can recite the basic processes of cave formation: the rainwater becometh mildly acidic and findeth its way through the smallest of fissures dissolving the space in which we stand today. This litany includes some thou shalt nots, as well: the pernicious effects of hand oils on living formations is roundly denounced, and unsanctioned touching prohibited. Photography, on the other hand, is invariably encouraged, the cave gods apparently untroubled by the making of images.

From this level we descend into areas of doctrinal as well as physical difference. Richly decorated caves will take the opportunity to introduce a

A Field Guide to the Appalachian Show Cave

standard typology of formations — dripstone, rimstone, flowstone, and when possible the crowd-pleasing ribbon formation, aka "cave bacon." Caves with a longer history of human occupation might note evidence of indigenous use, or later industrial use for mining or moonshining.

Some caves take this opportunity to impart a scientific narrative of the Earth's formation, while others demur on the numbers a little bit, leaving it an open question whether all that water trickling through the rocks came from an inland sea several orogenies ago or a more recent massive global flood. A couple of caves even take more ardent creationist positions. All are in the service of laying out some of the broad backstory of development, answering the question where do caves come from but, in the precise nature of the answer, constructing context for a lot of the ideas to follow.

The one thing they all do have in common, though, is that they tell their own story — the development of the show you are seeing now. It's an almost triumphalist note: what you see now is what this cave was always becoming — even though in the same breath the guide will attribute the actual making of the cave to a god or a physical process on a scale that truly humbles the human presence.

See, we're just barely inside the front door and the complications and contradictions are already coming fast and furious. The facts, like the caves themselves, unravel in all directions. But it makes it that much more remarkable that there is so much in common from cave to cave.

❖   ❖   ❖   ❖

For example, the next stop is almost certain to involve looking at something that looks like something else. Having dispensed with some exposition in the Intro Room, we turn quickly to the more amusing world of illusion. The guide brings the group into a cluster in a space that might be called the Menagerie or the Gallery or the Hall of Statues and starts tracing out the patterns with the flashlight, George Washington in profile, Snoopy in silhouette, and for the best examples there's always that pregnant pause in between the moment when the guide points the flashlight beam at the rock in question and when the first "oooohhh yeaahhhs" come back from the group, scattered at first then multiplying like corn starting to pop.

On reflection, that little moment is surprisingly complex. If you're like most people, you're already experiencing a little bit of visual overload — the low light making your irises strain to take in all the information they can, about a setting that seems like it must be artificial, a set, a bit of Imagineering. Despite the fact that none of this was made to human specifications, you're now seeing in this alien place images as familiar as Snoopy. And that transformation of the natural world comes through human intervention — through stories, through suggestion, through imagination, through artificial light.

Exactly what you see depends, of course, on the cave: a sweeping flowstone formation might evoke Niagara, a rounded stalagmite the Capital Dome. Clusters of stubby stalagmites in mud flats inevitably call to mind groups of people, and whether it's the Holy Family or One Direction depends on the disposition of the cave owner. I have a particular liking for the reflections — a still shallow pool of water transforms a cluster of stalactites above into 3-D renderings of Manhattan or Pacific Island chains. Ice cream cones, castles, dogs, presidents, horses, armor, fugitives, tacos, all are traced in the crevices and protrusions of the walls and ceiling; dragons, dinosaurs, and other giant reptiles are special favorites.

Using caves as a canvas is, of course, an old, old artistic tradition, maybe even the oldest. The earliest surviving examples of figurative art in the world are cave paintings, the believed-to-be-oldest a 35,000-year-old rendering of a pig in a cave on Sulawesi, an island of Indonesia, the best-known the 15,000-year-old bison depicted on the caves of Lascaux in southern France. Rediscovered by a group of boys in 1940, Lascaux became a show cave almost immediately, welcoming 1,200 visitors a day until the traffic and lighting began to take their toll on the paintings and indeed the whole cave ecosystem.

Here in the Appalachian Valley, caves whose location are a carefully guarded secret of the archaeological community house some of North America's oldest surviving artwork, the eponymous mud glyphs of the Mud Glyph Caves. Down in the dark zones of at least a score of caves scattered mostly across East Tennessee, artists from Late Archaic period, maybe 5,000 years ago, began galleries of work etched in the soft surfaces of the walls of the rooms.

Curiously, though many of these caves had been used for burials or mined for mineral resources such as chert, which made the best tools and spear points, many more appeared to have been used just for the art. Which means that somebody went to the trouble to find, explore, light with pine torches, and then improve the cave, for no other apparent reason than to make the space more interesting. This pattern of going to a lot of trouble just to put on a show in a cave goes way, way back. The anthropologists and archaeologists continue to develop their theories of the ritual significance of these spaces, but with what I've seen, I wonder, What if they were doing it for fun? What if they were producing, in their own way, that same uncanny experience you can pay for at Lost Sea today?

Of course, if the pattern holds, one day future explorers will be rediscovering these show caves and speculating on what the ritual significance of this space might have been. And what would the answer be?

What, for example, is the significance of the moment when the guide gathers the group for a pop quiz? "How tall do you think that stalagmite over there is?" the guide demands at Tuckaleechee Caverns in the foothills of the Smokies. He indicates a formation across a broad, capacious room. The crowd, sensing a trap, clams up; a kid blurts out "a hundred feet!" Ice broken, a couple of guests try a more calculated guess: "Twelve feet." "Twenty-five feet." The answer is, of course, either much greater or much smaller than any guess ventured. A trick of forced perspective and the non-Euclidian architecture of the space have turned the scene we're looking at, the visual data themselves, into an illusion—an illusion of the thing we're actually seeing. And the quiz, which usually we use to demonstrate what we know, is instead used to get us to demonstrate what we don't know.

In some of the finest examples of the genre, this all culminates in the light-and-sound show—the Money Formation. Ruby Falls, in the side of Lookout Mountain overlooking Chattanooga, is probably the best known. Its eponymous waterfall is illuminated from different angles and in multiple colors, including Ruby—the name coming from discoverer Leo Lambert's wife. The falls, which shower down on the center of the room from a crevice at the ceiling 150 feet above, are atomized by the lights, moving constellations of colored crystals.

At Endless Caverns in the heart of the Shenandoah, this climactic scene is a bit more romantic. A time-worn Schubert recording plays over the speakers in the Cathedral Room, while layers of lights, down a corridor rimmed all around with formations, play with your sense of the depth of field. Receding concentric circles of floodlights shine separately, then together, then in unison, revealing at last a fabulously decorated chamber. It's simple but effective, really lovely in an antique, almost steampunk way—an old-fashioned seduction. The guide, a college-age kid with a kind of a soccer dude thing going on, seems not too enthused about hearing the Schubert piece again today, having seen plenty of these seductions go down: "They've got a light show for you," he undersells and withdraws discreetly to wait in the corridor by the control panel.

At Front Royal, Virginia's Skyline Caverns, so-called for its prime location at the north end of the Skyline Drive of the Blue Ridge Parkway, the tour culminates with a more dominant vibe. A booming tape-recorded voice, attributing the formation of the cavern to God himself and urging us to reflect prayerfully on that fact at a formation called "The Shrine." (Before activating the recording, the guide, a youngster choking on his necktie and drowning in his blazer, gently cautions the group that it's "kinda religious.") The lights above glow and expand and combine to transform a dripstone formation overhead into a massive eagle, its wings spread imperiously above our craning necks. I think they're going for totemic, but it comes off a little Reichstag for my tastes. I come away from the gift shop with a "Skyline Caverns is for Lovers" T-shirt nevertheless.

All along the length of the Appalachian Valley, the makers and operators of show caves are carrying on the ancient tradition of creating subterranean illusions. The collaboration between cave and artist continues, producing a potent mélange of the freakish and the familiar, which, at its best, can be a springboard for imagining more fantastic versions of the way things actually are.

❖   ❖   ❖   ❖

At some point, however, the whole presentation will switch gears and get us thinking about what isn't there, what we don't have—underscoring that, even though we're in this space voluntarily, in a controlled environment, carefully herded along, we're in a different place, a potentially dangerous place, and not coincidentally the place where our physical remains have traditionally been put when we die. We're all here for a good time, yet at any moment, should we exhaust the goodwill of this person we'd normally expect to see taking tickets at the multiplex, who knows what could happen?

Maybe that's why guide humor centers on jokey threats. When we meet another tour, one guide is liable to quip to the other some variation on, "Hey, you brought 'em all back this time!" What authority guides don't accrue through sheer charisma they get back when you are reminded, while standing in your herd of twenty-odd summer tourists in a damp, narrow space somewhere below the parking lot, that only the guide knows the route of the tour and how to summon help if any one of the many catastrophes you can imagine were to come to pass. And, most important, your guide knows where the light switches are.

It is at that light switch where the guide enjoys the most remarkable demonstration of his or her power. Clearly, you can't have a show cave without lights, whether they are the naturalistic, energy efficient LED lighting schemes of the more environmentally sensitive operators of today or the incandescent fairyland spectacles of the holdouts tracing their roots to an earlier generation of tourist tastes. More than just illumination, light is a key component of the medium: if the cave is a canvas, lights are the brushes, used to create contrast and perspective and depth and emphasis.

But the light could not make its contributions without the underlying fact that the default condition of the cave is complete and total darkness. The lights are the only line of defense between us and the shortcomings of our design as creatures. No cave that humans explore beyond its threshold can ever truly be said to be in its natural condition, because without artificial light, you literally cannot see anything: you cannot see your hand in front of your face, not even if you have the night vision of a Pleistocene jaguar. This fact is dramatized at a pivotal moment in almost every one of the caves I have visited, when the guide gathers the group, issues a mild disclaimer about what is to come, and turns off the lights.

The darkness truly is total. Thick, velvety. Not every group can take it—sometimes spoilsports illuminate watch faces, camera LCD screens, cell phones, and in the rich humid dark these small lights seem like beacons. But guides never leave the lights down for long, anyway. Sometimes they bring them up gradually, illustrating how the cavern would look by candlelight, by lantern light, by flashlight, before restoring our full ration of incandescence. One joker—a sweet-natured country girl at Virginia's Natural Bridge Caverns who had earned my respect for her patient way with the big day-camp group on this tour—tells us that there's an "Indian legend" that if you wave your hands in front of your face and cross your eyes you'll see a bright light; then she snaps the lights back on to reveal a room of waving, eye-crossing tourists (myself included).

But the tow-headed young man, surely no more than fourteen, who was leading the tour at Shenandoah Caverns had some real deadpan fun, sitting silently in a corner as a giggling group with more and more of a "this ain't funny" attitude stewed in our pitch-black chamber. When he finally did illuminate the room, he revealed to us that we had been standing there for exactly one minute, and with a sly smile, asked us to imagine hours, days, in this inky void. The group tittered, regained a bit of its bravura, but got the point, and moved a little closer together.

When you ask people, as I often do these days, if they've ever been in a show cave, this is the thing they remember most distinctly. I admit I've become a kind of connoisseur of the darkness demonstration—for me, the longer, and the more solemn, the better. A half-hearted blackout is the number one sign that the guide is phoning it in that day.

If they give you the time to savor the darkness for a few moments longer than it takes just to say you've done it, you really do begin to feel your whole perception shift, feel your irises strain to open wide enough to find some kind of data, feel your ears searching through a newly realized audio complexity, both in the exaggerated sounds nearby of corduroy rubbing and noses whistling and feet shifting and in the drippy sound of a living cave, all fleshing out a tremendous sonic depth of field, the damp, fecund smell becoming richer and more pervasive.

But that sensory intensification is accompanied by a deep, surging awareness of your own near helplessness — maybe the light from your phone would be enough to find your way back up the tourist trail. Or would it? When was the last time you plugged it in?

For the show cave visitor it's more like a reminder: there are still some places where your digitalia won't do you a lot of good. You get off the grid down here, and no matter how much electric light we pour across the surface, that darkness is awaiting, unfazed. The lighting system that so triumphantly creates illusion suddenly seems like a very fragile skein draped across the surface of something so ancient the entire history of artificial light is an insignificant fragment of this place's existence. You? You're a millisecond, you're nothing. Wait, I paid fifteen dollars for this?

❖   ❖   ❖   ❖

Yes, you did, you parted with actual American currency to see a show that reminds you, at least for a moment or two, of your fragility, your mortality, your relative insignificance. Why not just watch the evening news? Here's a couple of theories. First, the encounter is stage-managed for you. Show cave promotional materials often emphasize the safety, the excellent maintenance, the solid and well-designed infrastructure — the kind of preventative reassurance that backhandedly admits to potential danger.

Plus, the rest of the show cave provides a context that takes the edge off. You're entirely likely to get this dose of existential angst coming off a light display that transforms your ancient, surreal surroundings into different flavors of ice cream, from vanilla to tutti frutti, gathered together with like-minded strangers by a teenage protector.

Second, unlike the random, pervasive threats of daily life, show caves always balance the seductive lunacy of illusion and the menace of the darkness by putting it all firmly in some kind of story of development. Even if the messages show caves send are not always amusing — that's why show caves are categorically different from amusement parks — these elements are all

A Field Guide to the Appalachian Show Cave

part of a larger pattern of succession. The tour's emphasis on development insists that no matter how strange or disturbing things can get, you have to take a longer view: the way things are now is not the way things are going to be, or have to be. Where amusement parks try to construct an eternal present, show caves make patterns of change a part of the fun.

Constant self-reference is one way the tour does this. Part self-promotion and part documentary, the show cave always tells the story of how the cave became a show. Unlike theme parks, where concealment of the artifice is one of the core principles of theming the environment, the tour lays out the history of the event you're seeing as you see it, from the moment a local farmer saw a mysterious cloud of fog around a rock overhang on a winter day, or crawled through a crevice in search of a coonhound or whatever, to not just the present but the present moment itself, since, well, here you are.

Probably you'll get your first dose of development backstory standing in the Intro Room, but then other nodes and landmarks in the history of the making of the show cave will thread through the rest of the tour: here's where the cave's developers picked their way from the surface into the vast, lavishly decorated underground chamber. Here's where the old tourist path went up and over the blasted-out tunnel we just passed through, a steep, tight, slick trail taken by gentlemen in homburg hats and ladies in skirts and button-up boots. Here's the high-water mark of the flood that tried to wash away the whole operation a few years back. Here's where church services were held, where the band played for square dances, where the largely forgotten celebrity once stood to address the crowd, where the calcite-encrusted urn caught the steady drip off the stalagmite above to provide a drinking water stop. We're surrounded by previous versions of the show cave itself. It would all seem really postmodern, except it isn't.

We're in a space that remembers everything that's been done in and with and to it — when you leave your mark here, it stays marked. So the tour tells us not just about what's been done with the cave in terms of fixing it up for the tourist trade, but a broader story about the ways humans have used caves that ties in the story of the caves to a lot of other stories and other places. A show cave like Lost Sea is a veritable anthology of forms of human behavior and misbehavior, from indigenous ritual practice to resource extraction to illicit recreation to Cold War paranoia to contemporary car tourism.

The surface of the cave itself, absent all signs of human use, tells a story of its own, about development on a scale so vast that disagreement about what that story ought to be is one of the defining cultural rifts of our time. Religious and scientific explanations of the earth's origins come into direct contact in the show cave, with both guests and show cave operators taking a range of positions in the debate.

Here the cave again shows its typical flair for accommodating contradiction. Roger Hartley, the owner-operator of Appalachian Caverns in Bluff City, Tennessee, takes a diplomatic approach to his creationist beliefs: "If God really is all-powerful, then he could make a 500-million-year-old cave appear one day 6,000 years ago," he reasons. So the cave really is 500 million years old, the scientists aren't wrong, it's just that God made it that way, 6,000 years ago? It's kind of a brilliant way of begging the question, I tell him. "Exactly, it's not a point I'm argumentative about."

So even though it's a known fact that many of their visitors and, as the case of Roger Hartley shows, some of the operators as well don't really accept the validity of those numbers, numbers abound. There's a certain kind of pleasure taken in the act of measuring things, even when, perhaps because, you ultimately run into the unmeasurable: down 118 stairs, under the 212-foot-tall dome, by the 40-ton boulder which fell from the ceiling 18,000 years ago, is the hole that leads to the river whose origins and destination have never been determined, despite years of scientific investigation!

Personally, I don't have any problems with the general contours of the scientific explanation: that 750 million years ago, give or take a few tens of millions, the entire area that is now Appalachia was submerged in an inland sea. The layers and layers of sediment gradually transformed into sandstone, and the ever-growing deposits of organic matter mixed with the calcium of the exoskeletons of early life forms, becoming (eventually) limestone. Over the next few hundred million years, mountains would rise and fall in major seismic events called orogenies, as the separating continents careened off each other in their ongoing journeys across the Earth's surface. The mountain chain's present shape looks suspiciously like the coast of West Africa, which hit and ran somewhere around 250 million years ago. The remaining seawater drained out of the Great Valley over the course of the next couple of hundred million years, and the limestone eroded (and continues to erode) to produce the richly decorated chambers we visit today.

Thinking about time on this scale, though, can be the intellectual equivalent of the sensory experience of total darkness: mind-expanding, but shot through with a big dose of perspective about your place in the universe. Whether you see it as the unfolding of a divine plan or the outcome of ongoing physical processes or you just don't want to be argumentative about it, you're in a space that visually, that physically puts you in the context of a narrative that goes back well beyond what anyone can even begin to imagine as the dawn of time. I mean, the insane architecture of the space came into being through a process that began even before the rocks you see now were plants.

❖   ❖   ❖   ❖

Lest the whole thing seem too fatalistic, however, the existence of the show cave itself is a kind of assertion that, however insignificant our role may seem in the overall sweep of time, humans have the power to transform these ancient spaces. Often the signature motif of the development story show caves tell about themselves is the individual visionary, the explorer/creator/caretaker/entrepreneur who, through whatever gap-ridden logic he might be using (and it's almost invariably a he), it was worth going to all that trouble and expense to make it possible for people to taste the complicated pleasures of the underground. Let's call him the Cave Man.

In keeping with the long tradition of caves and their resident hermits, many of these caves have some individual enshrined in their lore who personally authored the cave's final, decisive chapter of development into the showplace you are visiting today. The Cave Man may not be the discoverer or the original owner, necessarily, or the first to turn the lights on, but at some point most of the caves acquire a familiar spirit who remains present in the show cave trappings of today.

The archetype here is Leo Lambert, a young man from Gas City, Indiana, born in 1895. He moved to Chattanooga in 1915 following after a pretty girl, Ruby Eugenia Losey, the very Ruby for whom he would soon name a waterfall deep beneath Lookout Mountain. He discovered quickly, in that cave-rich area, that he not only enjoyed exploring caves but could envision them becoming, with some human intervention, something people would gladly pay to see, and he turned out to have a gift for talking investors into buying into this vision.

What he didn't have was much luck with the timing. He sank the elevator shaft that would transport tourists to the path to the falls in November 1928, using limestone from his excavation to build the Cavern Castle, a charming entry hall modeled on a fifteenth-century Irish fortress, designed to host a restaurant and nightclub with live music, cocktails, and dancing to go along with the subterranean wonders.

Lambert forged ahead with his plans even as he watched the economy crater on the eve of their completion. The caverns opened for business in December 1929, after the Great Depression commenced in October, and by March 1931 the investors Lambert had charmed before had lost patience with him and fired him as manager, selling the operation by August 1932. Undaunted, Lambert explored caves on the other side of the valley beneath Raccoon Mountain, rounded up another band of investors, and opened Tennessee Caverns (now Raccoon Mountain Caverns) in June 1931.

But it was, to say the least, a tough business environment for tourism at a time when most folks who were out on the road were searching for work. By 1932 this cave changed ownership, and in 1934 Lambert returned to the staff of Ruby Falls. He still had enough in the tank for one more go, though. In 1938 Lambert was opening up Nickajack Caverns a few miles farther down the Tennessee River. But in 1947 he was back at Ruby Falls, where he worked until his death in 1950. Leo's darling Ruby, whose trail he followed into the cavern that still bears her name, his one and only wife, followed him into the dark in 1951.

It's hard to know what gets into a man's system that gives him the mind and the will not just to try this implausible scheme but to try it again and again. It's typical of the Cave Men that they've been responsible for more than one cave in their career. Colonel Edward M. Brown, a golfing buddy of Woodrow Wilson's and veteran of the Philippine Insurrection, used the proceeds from his New York printing business to buy first Endless Caverns in 1920, then, over the course of the next decade, Melrose Caverns (which he renamed Blue Grottoes) a few miles down the road; and then a set of limestone outcrops near Mt. Solon, Virginia, which he called the Cyclopean Towers, and some sort of water feature (records of what exactly this was get sketchy) called the Sapphire Pool. Finally, he embarked on the creation of a regional geology tourism empire called Natural Wonders, Inc. Many of the signature lodge buildings Colonel Brown designed, elegant and rustic and entirely built from blue limestone quarried onsite, still stand, reminders of a show cave artist with resources and a broader vision.

Other repeat offenders in the show cave game have reasons that are a little more obscure. Colonel Brown's contemporary Hunter Chapman owned and operated both Indian Cave in Tennessee and Shenandoah Caverns in Virginia supposedly because he enjoyed the novelty that both caves were by small towns named New Market. Knoxville, Tennessee, real-estate speculator Gene Monday later obtained both Indian Cave and Atomic Caverns near Oak Ridge, seemingly less for their investment potential than for their spiritual significance. He leased both caves to independent churches free of charge, encouraging them to use the show cave as a revenue stream to support their ministries.

You're hard pressed to find one example of anybody who's just in the

A Field Guide to the Appalachian Show Cave

show cave business for the money, drawn to the siren song of get-rich-quick. It isn't quick, and rarely does anybody get rich. More representative is the experience of Cave Man Jacob "Jay" Gurley, a photographer for the Redstone Arsenal's Guided Missile Laboratory in Huntsville, Alabama. In 1952, the twenty-nine-year-old Gurley explored what was then called Bat Cave but was soon renamed Cathedral Caverns (his wife's pick of potential names), as Gurley bought the 160 acres of land above the cave and set to work preparing the cave for its show cave debut, the home of Goliath, (probably) the world's largest column at 45 feet high, 40 feet wide, and 243 feet around.

Living with his family on site, often working alone, having left behind a job and a life in Huntsville, Gurley poured everything he had into making the cave presentable. The cave poured everything it had into flash floods that occasionally wiped out Gurley's work, sending him back to the drawing board to come up with more flood-proof routes and designs. He built bridges and blasted tunnels and parted the way through breakdown piles, extending the tour ever farther into the cavern's huge forests of stalagmites and stalactites, always with the most careful touch even on the most elaborate projects to avoid damaging any of its wonders while providing careful, safe access.

Despite all this effort, and the staggering beauty of the cave itself, its vast rooms filled with sweeping flowstone and bristling dripstone, Cathedral Caverns never did build up much of an audience. Tucked away in a lovely but off-beat patch of northern Alabama, business was slow even in the summer months, and life was tough for the Gurleys. Investor relations were not good. By 1977 Cathedral Caverns was closed, Gurley's work washed away this time by the waves of economic turmoil that accompany the show cave trade. The cave remained in a kind of developmental limbo for the next decade, when the state of Alabama was finally convinced to buy the property to create a state park.

Like Leo Lambert returning to Ruby Falls for the twilight of his career, Gurley was brought on as a special adviser to the operation, but the state dithered and bickered until it was too late for Gurley to see it happen. Cathedral Caverns State Park opened for business in the year 2000, but Jay Gurley passed away in 1996. A friend eulogized him on line, saying "Those closest to Jay would probably say that his lifelong passion for the caverns, followed by a decade of frustration at the state's bureaucratic slowness, finally broke his heart."

This level of devotion, extraordinary in itself, is not unusual among this fraternity of show caves. Out of all of them, though, Bradford Cobb, the gentle cave-o-phile who took over Massanutten Caverns in the early 1960s, comes closest to being a latter-day hermit.

Cobb took over the caverns in 1955, long after its decline and fall from pre-Depression resort splendor. The lodge once hosted auto shows and weddings and even a Fourth of July Klan rally, and the grounds included a landing strip, an Olympic-sized pool, and a golf course, but by 1955 all were parceled out, returned to pasture. Nevertheless, one day Cobb quit his job in data processing in New York City and relocated to Keezletown, where he ran the cave as a one-man show, living in a little shack on site that you can still see today.

He was New York born and raised, a Harvard-educated man, and a World War II veteran, and I guess nobody will ever really know what bonded him so strongly to that cave. For decades he sold tickets, gave tours, kept up the maintenance, and explored the cave, pushing leads off the tour route into the darkness. The cavern, tucked away in a quiet vale on the side of Massanutten Mountain inconveniently distant from the Interstate, is now locked up tight, with Brad Cobb's ashes secure inside it since his death in 1991. Like the indigenous developers of the mud glyph caves, Cobb used the cave as an economic resource, as a cultural medium, and, finally, as a burial site.

Probably every one of these guys could be labeled eccentric, each in his own way, and yet their eccentricities share a common theme, some kind of particular bent for using the cave as a medium — for making money, yes, but for a lot more than that. It's worth saying again: this is just too much trouble to go to for money alone, especially when the money proves so elusive — indeed, it's part of the trouble more often than not.

❖ ❖ ❖ ❖

Maybe it's appropriate, then, that show cave tours invariably draw to a close by plunging the visitor with baptismal vigor back into the world of commerce.

If the show cave knows how to send you out from here to eternity, it also knows how to reel you back in: pass the collection plate. "Gratuities Accepted" reads the sign by the gate where the guide makes the valedictory comments, thanking one and all, asking for an autograph on the guest register, and then getting down to business: enjoy our gift shop, consider stopping in one of our secondary attractions, and help us get the good word out there, tell your friends. Do you need a Coke for the road?

You pay to get in, you pay to get out. In between, you encounter vast spaces filled with stuff nobody made, a world filled entirely with things

A Field Guide to the Appalachian Show Cave

organically recording the whole of history, phenomena that could only happen in this very spot. Then you emerge into a sea of stuff that it is sometimes hard to believe anybody made, rooms filled with things that seem to have no past or future, washed in from all over the world: the polished minerals from South America, the T-shirts from Bangladesh, the army men from Taiwan all destined to be found under a seat cushion by the guy fixing up the used car for resale, to be ground into the plastic undergrowth of a house full of kids, to be tossed in the bag headed for Goodwill. A few collectors will hold on to some of the weirder pieces of bric-a-brac but for most of us memorabilia is really an orderly way of forgetting, of dispersing experience into the universe of things, every bit as ephemeral as the show cave is indelible. And yet the one helps pay for the other.

The exit through the gift shop asserts conclusively that the show cave isn't just otherworldly; it's also very much connected to the rest of the world. Each cave tells the story of a broader region, of its people on the move and its landscapes changing, and with them the needs, the demands people make of the subterranean world.

❖   ❖   ❖   ❖

Put the stories of many caves together across a swath of terrain like Southern Appalachia, one that has a lot of qualities of history and culture that give it a distinctive character, and the whole is greater than just the sum of its parts. The precise ways the show caves tell their own histories, the peculiar ways they share and adapt their shared conventions and customs, scattered across a particular patch of karstlands, create an offbeat composite portrait of a region and its people. Every show cave is about itself, but no show cave is ever just about itself: the issues and the concerns and the conflicts and concepts that converge there always telescope out to the region, the nation, and the world.

Every cave is really and truly unique: it can happen only where it is. You can't move it, not one inch. But the ways we interact with caves, the reasons why we're willing to risk the darkness, are part of broader patterns of history and culture, and it's all written there on the surface of the cave, in the graffiti of lonely soldiers and drunken teenagers, in the paths and pipes and lights and rails and stairs of the tour, and the story that gets told.

TWO

What Became of Grottoes

The Stories of Grand Caverns

❖   ❖   ❖   ❖

Illusion, darkness, development, and the labors of the cave men all devote themselves to the creation of a distinctive space where visitors can dwell for a time in an agreeable state of paradox that both heightens and humbles human imagination. Though each one is unique, caves draw on their common aesthetic, historical, geographic, and geologic storytelling practices, genre conventions that not only have a history but make that history a part of the narrative. So, to better understand the history of this genre, we must begin where the Appalachian, and very likely North American, show cave as we know it was born.

Nowhere is the show cave's complicated theater of convergence more fully realized than in the multifaceted history of our nation's oldest show cave, Grand Caverns in Grottoes, Virginia. This cave exemplifies in many ways the patterns of the show cave genre—it ought to, since it started some of them. It's a story of illusion, of the power of representation to inspire the imagination to visions. It's a tale of the vagaries of development, of how the show cave both records and is part of a bigger story of a place, what it's been and what it could be. And it's a history that, for all its tourist frivolity, includes persistent reminders that the mood can always take a darker turn.

Most of all it is a story of how all these different aspects of the show cave intersect—for that convergence of disparate themes and ideas is the show cave's real cultural signature, the friction that produces the cave tour's trademark brew of excitement and unease. And, fittingly, it all converged for me on January 17, 2008.

❖   ❖   ❖   ❖

On a blustery gray January day, Grottoes, Virginia, is not really much to look at—just a wide spot alongside US 340, zooming south, or "up the Valley" as they say around here, the back way from Elkton to Waynesboro. I was en route from Harrisonburg, where I'd been plundering the archives of the James Madison University library for old pamphlets, and was heading over to do more of the same at the University of Virginia in Charlottesville and the Library of Virginia in Richmond, where I was also looking forward to seeing the records of the Geological Survey. This trip was devoted to pushing leads in libraries, not caves—the tourist season was about as low as it gets, and I was squeezing in a little research time between semesters—but I at least had to swing by Grand Caverns, underneath Cave Hill just south of Grottoes proper, just for ceremonial purposes if nothing else.

It turned out to be quite a bit else, a quick little stop that would trigger a whole chain reaction of connections, drawing me into reconstructing the lives and careers of three men—David Hunter Strother (aka Porte Crayon), Major Jedediah Hotchkiss, and J. W. Rumple, Esq.—all of whom helped document and popularize the cave and found their own fortunes reshaped as a consequence. Tracing the linkages of their experiences in and around the cave is an object lesson about how the concerns folks bring into these caves can often telescope out from individual emotions to most sweeping and vital conflicts of history.

This is where the American show cave was really born: it began in 1804, when hunter Bernard Weyer discovered what would soon be known as Weyer's Cave as he searched a hillside in the Shenandoah Valley of Virginia for a missing animal trap. The owner of the cave entrance, a farmer named Matthias Ament, came to take a look and saw lavish formations and dollar signs. By 1806 he had built a gate and a small building over the entrance to the cave, given names to formations and rooms like "The Bridal Chamber" and "The Enchanted Moors," and launched a sidelight selling tickets for tours led by Leonard Mohler, an area man whose family would take care of the caverns on behalf of its various owners for decades to come. By 1807 an anonymous author proclaimed that "all agree it is one of the most extraordinary caves which have ever been discovered in America, and when illuminated by the light of candles one of the most magnificent specimens of nature's productions which they have ever beheld." Thus the show cave was born in North America, replete with entrepreneurs, artificial light, overheated promotional writing, and, of course, a lovely, otherworldly cavern.

The show cave had been up and running for a generation by the time, in 1837, William Barton Rogers, state geologist and professor of natural philosophy at the University of Virginia and namesake of Mount Rogers, Virginia's highest peak, began his comprehensive survey of the state's geologic structure and mineral resources. When Rogers needed visual aids for his reports to the state legislature, he didn't go for the meticulous charts and maps he prepared from the field reports of his team members; instead, he had a Philadelphia set painter named Russell Smith go out to Weyer's Cave in 1844 and reproduce some of its most striking interiors. Rogers was not just a scientist, he was a science communicator, canny enough as an organizer and rhetorician to know that if he needed to play on people's curiosity to get their money, the show cave was a good way to go.

It seemed appropriate to stop by here, as if to get the blessing of the show cave gods on my research, as they had once blessed Rogers's. Besides, a lot of that research was going to focus on this landscape — it would be good, when reading about it, to be able to picture the spot clearly in my mind's eye. And I knew I was going to be reading about it because Grand is one of the best documented of the show caves in the Appalachian Valley, and not just because it is the oldest.

❖   ❖   ❖   ❖

As I combed the archives during this trip, it turned out that, unlike almost any other show cave on my travels, I would often run across images of the interior of Weyer's Cave from the days before photography — apparently it was worth it to go to a fair amount of trouble not only to make a show cave but also to depict it. Multiple images of Weyer's Cave were included in Edward Beyer's popular 1858 *Album of Virginia*, the centerpiece of a set of meticulous illustrations that focused primarily on the landscape and life of the burgeoning mineral springs resorts of the day. Travel accounts of visits to Weyer's Cave like the ones quoted previously were a staple of family magazines of the day; authors would try to do (and outdo) in words what the cave did with lights and stories, confronting the limits of their art.

"How can mere words portray scenes which have no parallel among the things of upper earth?" wrote a Virginian named David Hunter Strother, whose description of an 1854 visit to Weyer's Cave has been published and republished, quoted at length, and openly plagiarized over the years. Born in 1816 of a prominent family in Berkeley Springs on the (now West) Virginia border with Maryland, Strother took the Grand Tour of Europe to study art and architecture. When he returned to the states, he was soon hailed as a master draftsman, noted for his remarkable powers of first-person perception and the depth and quickness of his observation as he drew subjects from life.

Strother developed a garrulous, self-deprecating style as a writer of travelogues, draping light comedy over his sharp, concise descriptions. Strother coupled his two enthusiasms to become a tremendously popular writer for *Harper's* under the modest pseudonym Porte Crayon (French for "pencil holder"). It was perhaps his misfortune to excel in two genres —

illustration and nonfiction—that received little critical appreciation in subsequent generations, and his cultural and racial insensitivity justifiably limits his relevance to a contemporary readership (i.e., it's pretty racist). But his *New York Times* obituary in 1888 proclaimed him a "household name" of the antebellum era. Whatever his blind spots, though, his descriptions of what he could see are remarkable.

Virginia Illustrated, his account of travels across the state, including "The Adventures of Porte Crayon and His Cousins," appeared in 1857, after its tremendously popular serialization in *Harper's* in 1855. The cousins in question were three young ladies from his extended family—Fanny, Minnie, and Dora, each charming in her own special way—who convinced him the girls deserved adventures, too. So they packed up their things and took along their hideous racial stereotype of a coachman, "Little Mice" (who is, of course, comically huge), and away they went up the valley like a nineteenth-century reboot of Charlie's Angels and Bosley (and their slave). For a party in search of a quality introduction to adventure, Porte Crayon knew just the place for their first stop: Weyer's Cave.

Even in this very early version of the show cave trade in North America, all the pieces were neatly in place. Illusion is truly the hallmark hook of the tour: "At every step strange and beautiful objects flash into being," he writes. "In the midst of her sublimest passages, Nature will sometimes step aside to play the *farceur*." "The Cataract," "The Hall of Statuary," and "The Oyster Shell"—all are stops on the tour much the same as today.

And fear has its part as well: all the members of the party feel the dread sweetly expressed by Minnie (with her endearing lisp): "The idea of going in at all confuses me so. Then the thought of a place where the moon don't shine, nor the sun—it's horrible! It never struck me before!"

Even after they get comfortable with traveling underground, panic is never far from the surface. Strange noises in the cave convince them they are about to be attacked by a bear, which proves only to be the set-up for some more broad racial humor at the expense of "Little Mice," who has blundered down into the cave behind them and nearly gotten stuck in a narrow crawl. "Oh, Mistis," he declares, "now I believes dere is a torment, sence I seen dis place."

Crayon even includes what may be the earliest documentation of the blissful menace of the darkness demonstration in the American show cave, as the guide proposes that they "put out the lights, that they might enjoy the poetry of darkness and silence for a while." When the lights went out, "Porte felt his arms simultaneously pinched by three little hands, and at the same time a huge grasp took him by the boot-leg. The silence was only broken by the suppressed breathing of the company, distinctly audible, and the not unmusical tinkling of water dropping far and near, ringing in the darkness like fairy bells."

Finally, the cave tells the story of its own development. Even in 1854, a visit to Weyer's Cave could be nostalgic. Crayon himself worried out loud that the excitement of the cave visit might not rival his experiences visiting the cave as a boy; he "supposed the keenness of my appreciation of its wonders would have been blunted by that circumstance, as well as by the years of travel and adventure that have followed. I was gratified to find I was mistaken. It seemed, rather, that time and cultivation had mellowed the sensibilities and increased the power of the vision." Crayon's tour already includes tales of traditions of previous generations of visitors, like the now-discontinued mass candlelight illuminations, which drew crowds but stained and marred the walls and ceilings.

True to form, the living memory of all this info was maintained by Weyer's Cave's very own Cave Man, Mr. Leonard Mohler, who, Crayon notes, had "some time since surrendered the office of guide to his son, a likely and intelligent lad, thirteen or fourteen," but "he on this occasion agreed to resume it, in special compliment to the party." In this family, the title of Cave Man was hereditary: no matter how many times the cave changed hands over the years, the men of the Mohler family were there lighting the candles, practicing their arts of illusion, telling the story of the space.

The special relationship David Hunter Strother had with this place in his guise as Porte Crayon would, as it turns out, have significant consequences. For one thing, the cave just about drove him crazy with the desire to make art: "So different from what we are accustomed to see, so infinite in its variety, every flash of light developing some new field wherein the imagination might revel, every change of position suggesting some new theme for the fancy to seize upon . . . I arranged my candles and rearranged them. I ran up and down. I could not choose, and was frequently forced to laugh aloud at my own absurdity." Crayon, now in full-on philosophizing mode, recognized that a bigger story was being told here too: "Canst thou read, O philosopher, what is written on these eternal tablets? The percolation of water through limestone strata for ten thousand years — and nothing more?"

Little could Strother have suspected what consequences the dispositions that Weyer's Cave so awakened in him and the knowledge gained in his travels would have. When the Civil War broke out, Strother, his artistic background tending him toward more progressive views than you might guess for

The Bride's Veil, Weyer's Cave Octo: 14th 1853.
(Drawing by David Hunter Strother ["Porte Crayon"]; courtesy of West
Virginia and Regional Historical Art Collection, West Virginia University)

a young man of an old Virginia family, or for that matter judging just from
his unreconstructed representation of slaves and slavery, volunteered his services to the Union army as a civilian cartographer.

But when the Union forces faced Stonewall Jackson in the legendary
Shenandoah Valley Campaign of 1862, the staff of Major General Nathaniel

Banks, tasked with tracking down the elusive cavalry commander and bottling up his forces, felt Strother's demonstrated acuity for the valley's landscape and his firsthand knowledge of the terrain made him a valuable tactical adviser. How strange it must have been for Strother to find his oh-so-jolly adventures with his precocious nieces and shambling blackface sidekick pressed into the service of a war machine — one that would forever transform the culture that Strother explored and documented so fondly, especially the part about shambling blackface sidekicks. Strother would help create a culture that would eventually, and rightly, disavow some of his own work.

◆　　◆　　◆　　◆

Meanwhile, across enemy lines, the Confederates had their own local landscape expert and cartographer, Jedediah Hotchkiss, Strother's mirror image. Strother was a bit more interested in the landscape as a place to play, but Hotchkiss was a man who could figure out how to put the land to work.

Hotchkiss was born of an established Upstate New York family and excelled in studies of natural philosophy, especially geology and botany, though he never formally pursued an advanced degree. He was also a mostly self-taught engineer and learned to see the landscape with a careful, utilitarian, but ingeniously detailed eye, conducting scrupulous, ongoing surveys of the topography and ecology of his home.

Hotchkiss emigrated to Virginia with his wife (a cousin of Harriet Beecher Stowe) to open an academy called Loch Willow in Churchville. Like Strother, Hotchkiss volunteered his services to the armed forces, but in this case the Confederates. The amazing maps of the Great Valley from Winchester to Lexington he created for Stonewall Jackson, which are credited by historians for giving Jackson a significant tactical advantage, not only are meticulously detailed in terms of both the natural landscape and built environment but are elegantly, warmly realized.

They provide military intelligence worthy of the name (for once) — albeit in the service of preserving slavery, even though Hotchkiss did not initially support secession. Though he was apparently accorded the rank of major as a member of Jackson's staff, Hotchkiss never wore a uniform or considered himself a professional soldier — more of a consultant on matters topographical, even if that meant leading columns of troops to their targets while himself under fire. It was all about understanding how the place worked, and he was really good at it.

If the results are any indication, he certainly outperformed Strother. With Hotchkiss's help Jackson's army was able to cover great distances and take up superior positions in a now-legendary sequence of military tactics. The outmaneuvered Banks, routed at Front Royal and Winchester, withdrew down the valley, northward toward the Potomac, in disarray, fearing Jackson might make a play for Washington. Strother's wartime diary (which became a postwar bestseller) captures the chaos and confusion of an army in a just-barely controlled retreat.

Meanwhile, the climactic battle of the campaign took place practically in the shadow of Cave Hill, as Strother's playground become Hotchkiss's weapon. At the adjacent villages of Cross Keys and Port Republic, the out-manned, outgunned Jackson brilliantly played multiple Union armies off a set of bridges and fords—utilizing the knowledge Hotchkiss provided him to beat back attacks, prevent advances, and then spirit his own force away across the Blue Ridge to reinforce Lee in the defense of Richmond. Hotchkiss found the perfect site from which to watch these battles play out. As he wrote in his journal for Sunday, June 8, 1862, "We could see the battlefield quite plainly, with the aid of my field glasses, from Cave Hill." He returned in November to map the battlefield and stayed with the Mohler family while he did so.

The cave, recorder of the development of the area that it is, has absorbed these events into its own mythos. Major speleothems were renamed; Stone-wall Jackson's Horse is to this day a featured formation. The graffiti of sol-diers from both Union and Confederate armies, over 200 of them, line cer-tain rock faces—because you may have to execute maneuvers that go down in military legend and help determine the fate of a nation, but why not take a minute to check out the local attraction? (Surely the geologically minded Hotchkiss was unable to resist?) Some of them might even have recognized it as the cave they read about in *Harper's*, by that hilarious Porte Crayon.

The local legend goes that Stonewall himself, asked if he wanted to take in the sights, replied no thanks, he'd be underground soon enough. He was dead within the year, mistakenly shot by his own pickets, an incident Hotch-kiss witnessed. Who knows the fate of all those young men, taking in a last moment of wonder and of humorous, harmless fear, before going out to kill and die just downstream, leaving their permanent mark in the show cave's organic archive? Before it was over, 3,000 of them and their friends and their enemies lay dead within a five-mile radius of Cave Hill.

❖   ❖   ❖   ❖

I emerged from the cave tour that January day having seen those same for-mations Strother described more than 150 years ago, which those Civil War soldiers saw, and like Stonewall's army I'd be moving quickly on, across the

Blue Ridge, thence to Richmond. It was a day for walking in other's foot-steps. Turning my collar up against the wind, I wandered up on Cave Hill in the patchy winter sunshine, taking in the view of the valley below, perhaps following the very trails of Porte Crayon and his cousins and/or Jed Hotch-kiss and his surveyors.

After the war, Strother returned to his Martinsburg, (now West) Vir-ginia home, eventually spending his later years as consul to Mexico, writing and drawing all the while. Hotchkiss, on the other hand, returned to this area, the scene of his tactical and topographical triumphs. He took up residence at Staunton, twenty miles or so away from the cave, and became a freelance engineer and surveyor, mineral and property speculator, cartographer, and historian.

A winter's day, with the leaves off the trees, is a particularly good time to appreciate Hotchkiss's mark on this place, or so I learned on my stroll. Jutting up 200 feet above the river bottom, the hill is cratered with sink-holes and faults, and especially steep on the side facing town. From there, I looked to the north and east, and there it was, like a city planner's take on crop circles: the tidy parallels and perpendiculars of the street plan of the town of Grottoes—a plan Hotchkiss drew up and rolled out. Hotchkiss's Confederate affiliations had given him the skills, experiences, and personal connections he needed for the job, but the project he piloted at Grottoes, constructing not just a new town but a new kind of town, was a marked de-parture from the rural nostalgia of the cult of the Lost Cause.

Strother had stood somewhere around here and tried to remember, to preserve what would already be, by the time he published his stories, the way things used to be. Yet less than a decade later his encounter with the cave would help lead to his role in dismantling this way of life gradually but per-manently. In the process, incidentally, he would settle the score from the first Shenandoah Campaign, serving on the general's staff on the other side from Hotchkiss when the Confederacy was conclusively defeated in the Shenan-doah Valley at the 1864 Battle of Cedar Creek. It's as if he wanted to write it all down before he signed up to help destroy it.

Hotchkiss, on the other hand, stood here and saw the future. He had seen the destruction of the old ways of the valley firsthand, but he had al-ready started to think about what could come next. Cave Hill and its envi-rons inspired not just the battlefield he designed here but a vision of a town that wasn't here yet, streets leading right up to the entrance to the cave, rail bringing in tourists from the Northeast who would be amazed not only by the wonders of the cave but by the town's orderly grid, the way its clear and deliberate zoning defies, even ignores, the more sinuous, improvisational patterns of local roads and settlements. The order of these roads came from an idea that was then written on the earth much like a cave guide etching a crocodile's face on an outcrop with a beam of light.

❖   ❖   ❖   ❖

In 1888 Hotchkiss again rode in the vanguard, advancing on Cave Hill. But this time, instead of riding with Stonewall's artillery brigades, he was in the company of a band of investors. These were men of the New South, engineers more than cavaliers, bankers more than swains—quite a few of them, Hotchkiss included, were from New York. The Shenandoah Valley Railroad had unveiled a plan that would take it right by the mouth of Weyer's Cave, and the site that is now Grottoes would have the latest transportation infrastructure, proximity to what Hotchkiss believed to be rich iron ore deposits along the base of the Blue Ridge, and, the kicker, that crazy, magical, historical, famous cave, providing a kind of seal of approval, certifying, by its very existence, that this place was right for making new versions of the world.

Or so thought the members of the Grottoes Company, who arrived to create the City of Shendun. Even the name, taken from the industrialized city in China, represented a decisive break with local heritage, underscored by its master-planned layout so foreign to the settlements organized around churches and gristmills and crossings of cattle paths, laid out along lines of least resistance. In a similar vein, the cave at this time became known as the Grottoes of the Shenandoah, a more ambitious yet more generic name erasing the local connections in favor of a broader regional focus and a reminder of the company name.

Then they threw open the doors to New Southerners like themselves, who wanted to make a killing transforming a place. Hotchkiss went out on the lecture circuit, appearing before civic clubs and other gatherings of money and ambition. Like many real-estate schemers of the early 1890s, and there were many, many of them, the members of the Grottoes Company made it their business to place puff pieces in newspapers and journals across the country. Shendun's promoters proclaimed it pretty much all things to all people, underpinned (literally) by the enduring marvel and revenue stream of the show cave.

Here's some typical copy from an article unsubtly titled "The New South," in a February 7, 1891, issue of the *Tribune* (Cambridge, Mass.): "The attention of investors had been turned toward the Grottoes as a particularly favorable field for speculation before the engineers laid out the present city

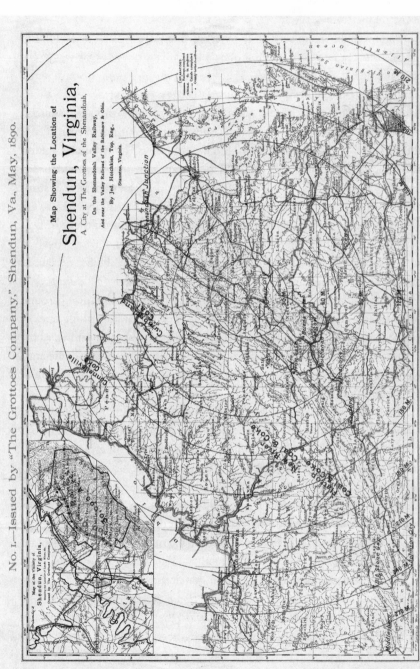

No. 1.—Issued by "The Grottoes Company," Shendun, Va., May, 1890.

Map Showing the Location of

Shendun, Virginia,

A City at The Grottoes of the Shenandoah,

On the Shenandoah Valley Railway,

And near the Valley Railroad of the Baltimore & Ohio.

By Jed. Hotchkiss, Top. Eng.,

Staunton, Virginia.

site, for it has long been known as a most delightful retreat both in summer and winter, while there is also great mineral wealth in the immediate vicinity. . . . The thousands of visitors who pay to enter these beautiful caves provide a constant source of revenue to the company. . . . The future of Shendun is already an assured success. No more attractive spot for a city than the Grottoes site can be found in Virginia today. The population is noticeably increasing. Investments are also increasing and confidence is expressed on every side."

As I look to the north and east, I can tell there was supposed to be more of a town here than there is now. Clearly, I am not gazing out at Shendun, "the jewel of the Shenandoah Valley and the future Metropolis of Southwest Virginia," as it was described in the company's house organ, the *Shendun News*, in 1890. The 2000 census put the population at about 2,000, and the town wears Hotchkiss's ambitious street plan like a suit a few sizes too large—the density is not quite high enough to really fill out the grid.

Fittingly, you can't really understand this from down on ground level: passing through on the highway, it just feels oddly spread out. You've got to see it from Cave Hill to really get it. The town itself has become something like a show cave formation. If you look at it from just the right angle you can see a different shape, one left there by a previous generation, making the terrain reflect its values.

❖ ❖ ❖ ❖

So what happened to Shendun? Where'd the rest of the town go? It turned out I'd find the answer to this puzzle the very next day at the ironically named Small Library, the rare books and manuscripts division of the University of Virginia libraries. I set up shop at a table in the reading room under the watchful gaze of a bust of William Barton Rogers to read through the sizable collection of materials on Virginia tourism—mostly pamphlets and postcards and the like. This is what I thought I was really after. Mixed in with this stuff, though, was a large bound volume tightly filled with onionskin pages, carbons of mostly typewritten correspondence, the Letterbook of the Grottoes Corporation, 1892–1895.

It reads like an epistolary novel about the collapse of the Shendun scheme. We join the story already in progress; I'm plunged straight into a dense thicket of bargaining and legal and political maneuvering and bill-collecting as the corporation spun out of control, unable to collect on pledges to purchase stock and thus unable to pay on the mountain of debt you incur when you try to start up a city from scratch. It's safe to say it generates a lot of correspondence.

Hotchkiss has been deposed as president by his impatient investors, as the mineral resources and the industrial development have proved less fruitful than expected, and the corporation leadership, while excellent at convincing people to promise to buy stock, was not nearly so good at convincing them to actually pay for it.

The successful insurgents name as their president a young man from North Carolina, J. W. Rumple, of the Cabarrus County Rumples, a would-be up-and-comer from a family of clergy and educators. He was arriving in town with freshly minted degrees from Davidson College, where his father Jethro was chair of the board of trustees, and some ideas about how to make his fortune. Rumple was a young, educated, white man with professional ambition but an upper-middle-class belief in meritocracy (and a cultural tendency toward white supremacy). He was part of the new generation that had no direct experience of the Late Unpleasantness — the very image of the New Southerner who would populate the New South Hotchkiss had imagined.

And yet, how must he have looked to "Stonewall's Mapmaker"? Rumple could look at this landscape and not see it littered with thousands of the dead, had never studied its contours to see how it was set for fighting. The advantages he sought upon it now seemingly had so much less at stake.

Though Rumple and his allies among the shareholders felt they had scored quite a coup when they wrested control of the company from Hotchkiss, the wily tactician may have outmaneuvered them in the end, handing them a colossal mess, their problem to solve now, as he withdrew to a fortified position in his Staunton mansion, "The Oaks," leaving Rumple to preside over the decline and fall of Shendun.

❖   ❖   ❖   ❖

Much of Rumple's early correspondence is an effort to reckon with the scope and the intractability of the problems they face, fairly pleading with stock subscribers to pay for their shares: "In fact we have arrived at a place where we can get no further indulgence from our creditors, so that either we must have these monies or we must suffer proportionately."

The cave pops up at regular intervals throughout the missives dedicated to office politics and financial ruin, the author suddenly cordial, straightening his tie and patting down his hair to answer inquiries about the cave from potential guests and the occasional collector or quasi-scientific investigator. Hard-core cave trivia folks will want to know that pioneering speleologist Horace Carter Hovey (author of the 1896 *Celebrated American Caves*) shows up at one point, as does the US Geological Survey, hoping to collect upward of 200 stalactites to distribute as specimens to colleges and universities around the country (a request that was flatly denied).

As I drift through the Letterbook I suddenly realize I'm in the neighborhood of this very day: I wonder what fresh fiscal Hell confronted the Men of the New South exactly 115 years ago? I flip through a few pages to find January 17, 1893, and, to my considerable surprise, not only was there correspondence that day, but correspondence that provided the crux of the answer to the question of "Where did Shendun go?" A letter on that date to Messers Griffith & Co., Insurers, of Philadelphia, states flatly: "The Grottoes Hotel has been totally destroyed by fire. The fire was discovered at about half past eight o'clock. . . . It was located in the rear of the buildings near the kitchen."

Suddenly my walk on Cave Hill the day before took on a new, slightly eerie sheen—it's weird to learn about a coincidence like this after the fact, as if somebody or something had set me up. On that day, January 16, exactly 115 years ago, J. W. Rumple could've looked out from that same spot on the brow of Cave Hill, in the footsteps of Strother and Hotchkiss, and seen that mostly vacant grid powering a vision of a "New South" through the billowing smoke of its last chance. He was seeing a new kind of conflict play itself out, one conflagration in a global financial collapse.

Though Rumple's suffering no doubt seemed to him unique, he was in fact part of a broader historical moment of which his experience was symptomatic, almost typical. The economy was even more hollow and fragile than Cave Hill. The rapid expansion of the railroad in the post–Civil War era had led to a massive bubble, not only inflating railroad stock but also leading to rampant real-estate speculation (and, Rumple learned the hard way, an epidemic of insurance fraud).

When the air came out in the Panic of '93, presaged by a bank collapse or two and a sudden curtailment of the credit supply, major projects all across the nation went under. The biggest price for all this irresponsible economic misbehavior was paid, of course, by the ordinary people swindled and pushed out of work and into a world of hurt. Little did I know there on Cave Hill at 2008's outset that by year's end that particular economic environment would be all too familiar to me, the newspapers filled with updated versions of the story of the Grottoes Company on an almost daily basis, leaving the fringes of cities and towns across America with their own versions of Hotchkiss's empty grids.

What follows in the Letterbook is a flurry of onionskin, the withered husk of an utterly doomed effort at damage control. Of the six insurers who had underwritten the various facets of the hotel operation, one could not be found, two refused to reply, one went out of business, one had moved, apparently to Toledo, and one simply refused to accept the telegrams. Mixed in is an angry rebuttal to an editor at the *Shenandoah Herald*: "The Shendun Hotel was not in the position of a 'Boom Town' hotel," Rumple fumes in response to the implication that they had torched it for the insurance money. The fact that they couldn't get any insurance money suggests this accusation either was not true or was the worst plan the Grottoes Company had come up with yet. "I make no suggestion as to what you should do with what I write to you," Rumple concluded snappishly, "Being a gentleman, you are perfectly competent to do that for yourself."

Losing the hotel was like losing the queen in this big chessboard Hotchkiss and the boys had spread out on the valley floor. Even though it was only a tourist diversion, humble in comparison to the industrial empire the Grottoes Company intended to raise on this site, it was the hook to get folks to take a look at the site in the first place. The expansion of the hotel and the improvement of the boulevard leading to the cave entrance, where the Mohlers still maintained their dynastic hold on the guides' work, were Phase One of the project. Losing the hotel meant not just losing their investment in the tourist economy; it meant losing their showroom, the stage for unveiling the bigger vision of the potential of this place. Like Rogers before them, the Grottoes Company recognized that if you want to get people to put their money behind their curiosity, the show cave had a special appeal.

The end came fairly quickly after the hotel went up in flames. Letter after letter chronicles the disintegration of the entire operation. Staff cuts began even before the hotel fire, as Rumple bemoaned that "I have not even a stenographer, but have had to write each letter of the many that go out from this office." It's easy to imagine a dapper young Victorian getting increasingly disheveled, alone in the office, laboring over letters selling off the broom factory and the brick factory and the other nascent industries, stripping the townscape for parts—like the phone system, the boilers, copy presses, streetcars, all the stuff you might have laying around if you thought you were going to build a town and then you didn't. I half expected to see the bill of sale for the very typewriter it was written on as the final entry.

In fact, the final entry in the Letterbook is a note to Mr. J. W. Wilson, Fairfield, Virginia, August 21, 1895, coordinating a visit for a party of fifteen, arriving by train. Throughout this chronicle of the turmoil this scheme visited upon the place they renamed Shendun, the cave remained a small but constant presence, really the only revenue stream fully up and running before they got here and the only one to withstand the disastrous attempt at devel-

The Stories of Grand Caverns

opment. Its mysteries proved to be the only thing they could count on: "The caves have paid a considerable item," Rumple notes in a December 1892 letter otherwise filled with bad news. In the midst of the Great Shendun Rummage Sale in late '94 and early '95, there's a bill from the Electric Construction Company in Richmond, for an order of over 200 lamps. While all else failed, the cave would still return a little bit on investment.

So I knew checkmate was a very few moves away when, in March 1894, a set of handwritten letters appear in which Rumple begins casting around for a potential cave buyer. At the Letterbook's conclusion there are two potential buyers lined up, each holding an option to purchase the cave for $12,500.00. And thus, I literally closed the book on the Grottoes Company and turned to a bound volume of vintage pamphlets.

But I suddenly realized that something else has disappeared from the story along with the phones and the tools and the surplus brooms — Mr. J. W. Rumple. I flip back to find a letter by Rumple and start working toward the end again, trying to figure out exactly when, in my skimming, he dropped out of the story. By sheer coincidence I land on a letter about what might have been Rumple's last happy moment as Grottoes president, the birth of his son in October 1893. From there, as the pieces and parts of the enterprise are sold off, the signature morphs from "J. W. Rumple, President" to "Rumple and Blackburn, Receivers" following March of 1893; Blackburn, we learn, is Hotchkiss's son-in-law, brought back aboard to help broker the dissolution of Shendun. Soon Rumple is just another spare part, and on April 18, 1894 — not long after the search for a new cave owner begins — he writes a note that states, tersely, "This will formally indicate my desire to resign as one of the Receivers of the Grottoes Company."

At this point Blackburn, a much more colorless writer, takes over, and I again thought, The End. But then one of Blackburn's next letters caught my eye because I saw Rumple's name. A company attempts to return a check it found in its records made out to Rumple, and Blackburn concisely replies that "Mr. Rumple has died, and I have been appointed by the court as his successor." Later he mentions that Rumple's death was in July 1894. Unlike both Strother and Hotchkiss, who were shaped by that view from Cave Hill, if Rumple ever looked out from that hilltop with the cave beneath his feet, he was seeing the place, and the chain of events, that would claim his very life.

It's a strangely chilling moment in the warm, wood paneled confines of the Small Library — a little injection of mortality not unlike the darker moments of a cave tour. I've done quite a bit of digging since then to try to figure out what happened to Rumple, and the best I've been able to find is a single line in a biographical sketch of his father Jethro from the State Library of North Carolina, noting his son "James Wharton Walker, who became a lawyer and was drowned in the Shenandoah River, Va., in 1893." They don't even get the date right.

Which leaves me plenty of leeway just to wonder out loud. Did presiding over the disintegration of Shendun break Rumple, leaving him convinced he was just another surplus piece to be disposed of? Could it be that a man in his position made some enemies, the kind who would recognize he was cut off from reinforcements with his back to the river? The darkness intrudes — the cave witnesses another death — but from where we stand now we can no longer see but can only sense disgrace, despair, destruction, maybe even self-destruction.

❖ ❖ ❖ ❖

Like any good show cave story, this one starts out with the facts and moves inexorably toward a dark, unsettling void at its core, ending nonetheless on matters of commerce. However mundane the situation, the stakes, as always, can suddenly and without warning ratchet up to life and death. Fortunately, the fortunes of the town, the place, haven't been quite so dire. Kind of a funny thing happened, actually. After the Grottoes Company collapsed, the name Shendun stuck around for a while, but folks started referring to the town by the name of the caves instead of the exotic name manufactured for the "Jewel of the Shenandoah," the new thing that never really happened. But it was the newfangled name for the caverns, the Grottoes, that hung on, building that memory of the corporate experiment into the landscape. The cave, as ever, faithfully, if obliquely, records the changes going on around it.

The caverns puttered along in various private owners' hands for decades but was eclipsed by Luray Cavern's showy formations and much more convenient situation relative to Washington. Grottoes was bypassed first by the Lee Highway and then by Interstate 81, both of which run along the western side of the valley ten to fifteen miles away. It has never done a lot more than just keep on keeping on, even with the change of name to the more billboard-friendly Grand Caverns in 1926. By 1974 the cave was acquired by the public Upper Valley Regional Parks Authority, and in 2009 the Town of Grottoes acquired the property. It feels almost like full circle: the cave's owners once sought to control the town; now the town controls the cave, its modest but reliable trickle of revenue channeled toward the public good, one more peculiar little convergence in this place that has seen so many.

So maybe that's the quietest but in some ways most crucial thing you can learn here, the thing I probably should have thought about more often as fall of 2008 arrived and the bubble burst and the economy cratered once again: you may never fill out your most grandiose version of yourself, but there's always another way that things can be. The valley's, maybe the country's, oldest show cave has written and overwritten that notion on this corner of the Upper Shenandoah, in ways you might encounter on any given day without even knowing it.

THREE

The Hall of Illusion

Imagining Appalachian Caves

❖   ❖   ❖   ❖

When a show cave is really sticking to the genre conventions, very soon after the Intro Room the tour will feature something that looks like something else. The comparisons vary from cave to cave, since it all depends not only on the shape of the rock in question but on the angle of the light shone on it as well. But that moment when you make out an alligator or a taco or John Lennon in the rock face sums up an important aspect of the show cave experience. The cave gives a unique shape to the things we project there. Our imaginations reshape the way we see the cave, but the reverse is also true: the cave reshapes the way we see the world, teaching us that the Earth is underpinned by some pretty fantastic weirdness.

Among the many wonders you can see in the Gatlinburg area is the rural traffic jam. On a hot day in the summer of 2006 I was stuck in a pretty good one on US 411 east of Sevierville, Tennessee. I was headed out on a trip to take in some of the east side of the Great Valley, landing at McGhee-Tyson Airport south of Knoxville, piloting the rental toward tourist destinations in the Smokies and the High Country region of Western North Carolina, taking a roundabout way to get to Johnson City to see my folks and do some writing. For now, though, it was stop and go, staring out the window, the thick, humid sunlight intensifying the mottled green of English Mountain, part of the chain of Smokies foothills paralleling the road just to the south. Extra bad sign: nothing was coming in the westbound lane. The air was wavy with heat and fumes as a column of semis, campers, trucks, cars, and cycles idled then crept, idled, then crept.

There was no way of knowing what the problem was ahead: a wreck, a lane closure, a slow-moving tractor hauling a big wagonload of hay bales? Maybe a camper dropped a wheel off the shoulder and got sideways? Could be anything, given that the volume of traffic clearly overwhelmed the design of the road, two lanes threading through what is still mostly agricultural land. The irony is a good many of us probably came this way, as I did, hoping to avoid an even worse traffic nightmare on the main artery connecting Interstate 40 with the hillbilly Vegas that is Pigeon Forge.

I couldn't help but think that being stranded in this column of cars was an inconvenient but appropriate part of the trip: Forbidden Caverns is truly Pigeon Forge's show cave. Traffic tie-ups come with the territory.

Forbidden Caverns has been known of for a long time, up in a holler behind a mill that's been there for centuries. White settlers called it Blowing Cave, just like they did many other caves up and down the valley—any cave big enough to vent cool air in the summertime. It's the "John Doe" of cave names. The cave formed via a sinkhole on the side of English Mountain, water finding its level down through several stories' worth of hillside to an underground creek powering a robust spring above the mill.

People found their way down that sinkhole too, making all the usual uses of the cave from chert mining to moonshining. It wasn't until Memorial Day 1967 that Forbidden Caverns became a commercial operation, after the success of Gatlinburg's Myrtle-Beach-in-the-Mountains spilled out into the valley floor and Pigeon Forge began to grow out into a broad swath of amusements and attractions.

As a result, Forbidden's tour has a stronger dose of tourist schmaltz than almost any other cave in Appalachia. It's heavy on the colored lights shining on formations with spooky and/or kooky names: the "Ice Cream Parlor," the "Grotto of the Dead," "Grotto of Evil Spirits," "Ledge of the Gargoyle," the "Lucky Fried Egg." In the Intro Room you hear an "Indian Legend" of star-crossed lovers that gives the cave its name (you can fill in the blanks). At the far point of the tour you admire a reconstructed moonshine still to layer on the hillbilly shtick. True to form, they boast a textbook Money Formation, a light-and-sound show dramatizing the "Indian legend" in shadow play.

The guides seem to put a special emphasis on the corny jokes, and the tour group seems especially receptive to them, and to keeping the proceedings light on the environmental education or the history lessons, heavy on the mass appeal. My group that day was made up of the kind of cross section of white middle America that you'd be immersed in at any of the outlet malls or go kart tracks or helicopter rides that line Pigeon Forge's main drag. (A small cluster of Latinos was the extent of cultural diversity.) The group kind of revolved around a young and very newlywed couple—perhaps freshly minted at one of the area's many wedding chapels. Their honeymoon ardor was cute at first but they eventually got so handsy in the moist semi-darkness that they pushed the boundaries of what the crowd was willing to consider appropriate, much less adorable.

Forbidden Caverns is a beautiful cave, carefully and diligently maintained, and well worth a visit—but it feels like a cultural time capsule from an earlier, goofier, more gas-guzzling age (not that we weren't guzzling plenty of gas sitting there in the rural traffic jam outside of Sevierville). Even in the digital age, the caverns' website anachronistically boasts of the excellence of their "stereophonic sound" like an album cover from the days of hi-fi. It feels like *Petticoat Junction* meets *Land of the Lost*, the colors all supersaturated, the sets all stylized, the content denatured, the frights all safely cartoonish.

❖   ❖   ❖   ❖

Don't fall for it, though. This show cave from the Hanna-Barbera Era may well be deeply connected to some of the most ambitious and disturbing representations of East Tennessee and Southern Appalachia that have ever been made. During the years Forbidden Caverns was being developed and getting its show under way, a young author was living with his wife in a cabin in Blount County south of Knoxville, not all that far from the airport, and he was dreaming up some really weird, visceral images of life in this area. The author was Cormac McCarthy, and the book he was working on was 1974's *Child of God*.

Child of God culminates in the surreal and terrifying scene of an underground cavern that has become the necropolis of the victims of perhaps the craziest hillbilly ever, Lester Ballard: "Here the walls with their softlooking convolutions, slavered over as they were with wet and bloodred mud, had an organic look to them, like the innards of some great beast. Here in the bowels of the mountain Ballard turned his light on ledges or pallets of stone where dead people lay like saints." Ballard uses the cave to escape the reach of the law literally and figuratively, "down narrow dripping corridors, across stone rooms where fragile spires stood everywhere from the floor and a stream in its stone bed ran on in the sightless dark." It is a primal place where Ballard can indulge his most base and amoral impulses. Forbidden Caverns is to *Child of God*'s cave as *Hee Haw* is to *Deliverance*.

But maybe Forbidden Cavern's and Ballard's caves aren't as different as they initially seem. Curiously, even though Blount County's got plenty of caves, McCarthy didn't use his immediate surroundings as the setting for his novel. Instead, he located it in the area around Forbidden Caverns—Sevier County and English Mountain are mentioned by name. McCarthy's description of a cave entrance at the bottom of a sinkhole, leading to a series of rooms descending to running water, is generally consistent with Forbidden's larger cave network; Lester's necropolis even matches the shape of the deep, spacious room that features Forbidden's reconstructed still.

I can't prove anything here, and the notoriously reticent author isn't supplying any answers, but the circumstantial evidence strongly suggests that at some point in the early 1970s, McCarthy might have been making the same drive over from southern Blount County that I was in 2006, probably muttering under his breath about how the growth of the tourist trade was tying up the highways, too.

A visit to Forbidden Caverns and its garish grottoes might well have helped move McCarthy toward his own more grotesque and disturbing visions of evil spirits and the dead hidden away in the literal and figurative guts of the Appalachians. Isn't it something to picture Cormac McCarthy, chronicler of the grim, violent underbelly of American mythology, tagging along in a tour group of school-age kids and grannies and newlyweds, doing a little location scouting for his Appalachian underworld, maybe picking up some homemade fudge in the gift shop for the ride home?

❖   ❖   ❖   ❖

In situations like this one, show caves haven't just recorded images of Appalachia, they have shaped them—the relationship between show caves and the broader culture is a two-way street. The way show caves are made and the way visitors experience them are influenced by the preconceptions, beliefs, fears, and notions that surround caves in our collective culture, but show caves also have the potential to influence the way we think about that world below ground and above, in a startling variety of ways.

The saying goes that no one ever really encounters *Hamlet* for the first time. By the time you see or read the play, you've heard of it, heard it quoted, heard references made to it so many times that even if you've never consciously known one thing about the play, you nod knowingly when you hear "To be or not to be, that is the question."

So it is with caves: barring, I suppose, very small infants and people raised by wolves—the exceptions, I'd argue, that prove the rule—nobody ever comes to a cave without having pictures in their head of what caves are, and what they are like.

When we bring our images and ideas about caves to the show cave, we have a unique opportunity to compare those caves of fantasy to the real thing—except the real thing, in the show cave, turns out to be fantastical, too. The experience of seeing an actual cave through the cultural lens of the cave tour encourages the imagination rather than limiting or correcting it. Flash photography is welcome (even though you realize later that your flash has washed out the shadows that made the scene photogenic in the first place).

So, when we're talking about the network of show caves in the Appalachian Valley, we're not just talking about a slice of terrain but also a swath of culture. Show caves provide an unusual opportunity to witness the give-and-take of stories and images, the circulation and transformation of ideas, that keep the places the caves are part of in a constant state of change — much like the caves themselves, where every drip from the ceiling contributes to the cave's gradual, perpetual reshaping. The illusions spun in the show cave, even the most frivolous and the most modest of them, can have surprisingly far-reaching consequences.

❖   ❖   ❖   ❖

The caves of Western North Carolina make for another interesting case in point. Or so I learned when my route on this 2006 trip took me from Forbidden Caverns and greater Pigeon Forge up the French Broad River, reverse-following the route of one of the first real roads across the Blue Ridge into the Great Appalachian Valley. Heading upstream, at the North Carolina line the French Broad valley narrows to a gorge by which the river descends from the high valley of Asheville and its environs.

Just across the line in a broad spot at the mouth of the gorge sits Hot Springs, North Carolina, the gateway to an area along the Blue Ridge in Western North Carolina its promoters have tagged as "the High Country." It's a different brand of tourism from what you find on the other side of the ridge around Gatlinburg and Pigeon Forge, and Hot Springs makes for an apt point of entry to it. Known for its bold mineral springs for pretty much as long as humans have been in this area, Hot Springs is on at least its second time around with tourist development, American style. If you know what you are looking for, you can read the transformation of the whole area in the bend in the French Broad where, today, scenically sited open-air hot tubs offer hourly rentals to the weary traveler, tense from battling rural traffic jams all morning.

As relaxing as those tubs are, this site has been busy for several centuries now: a retreat for indigenous hunters and travelers; a roadside inn for white settlers, drovers, and wanderers; a retreat for ladies of gentlemen of fashion in the Antebellum era. In the midst of the present-day rent-a-tub, the ruins of a once-elegant and spacious Georgian brick bathhouse attest to this earlier high-water mark of the tourist trade. After the decline and fall of the mineral springs resorts in the late nineteenth century, the operation transformed in the twentieth century into a World War I German prisoner-of-war camp, to an abandoned ruin frequented by partiers, to the contemporary operation that's rising on the site. The cabins and spa buildings have a low-key rusticity that's of a piece with Western NC's more earth-friendly, asset-based ethos of development, literally rising from the ruins of the area's history.

Where Pigeon Forge replaces the local landscape with tourist attractions, Hot Springs is working on making the local landscape, including its previous generations of tourist culture, the attraction. If Pigeon Forge is an outgrowth of Car Culture, Hot Springs is a Trail Town: the Appalachian Trail runs right through the center of town, and the shape of tourism in Hot Springs today definitely bears its imprint in its emphasis on a closer relationship with the details of the place. Where the rest of the valley is organized around Interstate 81, the High Country centers on the Blue Ridge Parkway, every turn framing a view that looks a lot like the Appalachia of a second-home real-estate agent's dreams. What the High Country promises with its emphasis on being attractive (rather than hosting attractions) is something more like authenticity, a chance to come into real contact with the Mountain South, to be a part of its story.

There's a complicated irony at work here: when people come looking for "authenticity," more often than not they're actually seeking the version of the place that they already have in mind, looking to become a part of the story they believe in. The terrain of the High Country becomes a space on which to project on these fictive, idealized versions of the Appalachian experience, another illusion traced onto the bedrock. Meanwhile the arrival of the newcomers transforms what the "real" culture of the place actually is. The goods and services, the jobs, the infrastructure shift to fulfill the newcomers' vision of the place. The rising property values drive out longtime residents, the very ones celebrated in the versions of heritage that attracted the newcomers in the first place. Where Pigeon Forge provides the opportunity to experience the pastoral traffic jam, the High Country offers the chance to witness rural gentrification.

However, it's a mistake to think this is a new thing. Western North Carolina's whole tourist culture is so old: Americans have been visiting here just to see the place, just to enjoy it, longer than Americans have been living in most of the rest of the continent. Plantation gentry had summer getaways on the headwaters of the French Broad when settlers in Gatlinburg and Pigeon

Forge could still remember fighting Indians. The second-home tourism of the High Country today isn't destroying its history, it is part of its history. Generations of tourists and the beliefs they projected on this place, the various authenticities they came looking for, are an important part of the High Country's story.

❖   ❖   ❖   ❖

It just seems like it ought to have caves, and not just any old caves, but the caves that shelter and preserve the culture, magic caves where this region is more fully itself than anywhere else — the region's secret heart. The problem is, those caves just don't exist — at least not in the ground. In this storied region, the imaginary caves are more famous than the real ones.

North Carolina's imaginary caves are a prime example of how the stories people bring to the Mountain South about what Appalachia "really" is can have real-world implications. In 1998, for example, the full paramilitary force of the federal, state, and local law enforcement, joined by the flotilla of satellite trucks that mark the eruption of a media spectacle, was brought to bear on finding a cave that was purely a product of our collective creativity.

They were all pitching in on the manhunt for Eric Rudolph, the extreme right-wing terrorist who set off bombs at the '96 Olympics and at Atlanta-area abortion clinics and gay bars, killing two people and injuring more than 120 others. In 1998, Rudolph, tipped to the pursuit by CNN, fled his home near Andrews, North Carolina, into the Nantahala National Forest. In the media circus that followed, news outlets and infotainment like *Hard Copy* and *People* magazine had almost no actual developments to report, so they killed time inventing (with plenty of encouragement from government spokesmen) a fabulous narrative of Eric Rudolph's cave, the hideout where, with the supposed aid and assistance of sympathetic locals, he lived in relative ease and comfort. As novelist and essayist Denis Johnson wrote in 2001, "The cave . . . where Rudolph lives now with (according to the Federal Bureau of Investigation) half a year's supply of BI-LO California raisins, BI-LO Harvest Choice Cut Green Beans, BI-LO Old-Fashioned Oatmeal, Planters Peanuts, and StarKist Tuna: if anybody but Rudolph knows its location, nobody's telling, not even for one million dollars.".

I've always thought this myth of the cave was fascinating as a kind of stand-in for the larger region. The land itself takes Rudolph, its native son, into its womb; the order of nature itself suggests this place is inherently conservative, even ahistorical in character. Denis Johnson quotes anthropologist Jean Gebser: "The cave is a maternal, matriarchal aspect of the world. . . . To

Imagining Appalachian Caves

The Fugitive. Illustration by Tim O'Brien, 1998.
(Originally published in *Time*, July 27, 1998; courtesy of the artist)

return to the cave, even in thought, is to regress from life into the state of being unborn."

It's an apt hideout for a pro-life terrorist. But as it turned out, this idea of Rudolph ensconced in his subterranean fortress of solitude really is and always was a myth: Rudolph was captured five years later by a rookie local cop, when Rudolph was dumpster-diving behind a grocery store. (The media was long, long gone by that time, and only a skeleton crew of the original manhunt team remained on duty.) Turned out Rudolph was camped in a hobo jungle behind the junior high and, by his own account, was living off leftovers from Taco Bell.

Rudolph got along more like an ordinary homeless man than a survivalist mastermind in a cavern lair. If you think about it, how hard is it really to disappear in America today? There are plenty of people, tens of thousands, living hand-to-mouth in the vacant lots, back alleys, and, indeed, National Forests of the United States; normally, they're just called "the homeless." But there was something appealing about the idea of Rudolph's cave for all these media types, and for the locals who dutifully led them to cliffs and rock shelters and gave them quotes about how the area was rotten with caves.

Maybe it's somehow comforting to think of Rudolph as a kind of elemental force, an outgrowth of the strange landscape into which he later vanished, a boogeyman, rather than some really mean guy picking through the leavings of the global food industry, another one of the thousands of homeless veterans (Rudolph learned to handle explosives during a stint in the Army) camped out in our national forests. That way, he's a freak of nature, the product of a freaky place, instead of a part of the world the rest of us have to inhabit—a real life Lester Ballard, ensconced in his necropolis, the kind of (un)natural man Forbidden Caverns may have inadvertently helped Cormac McCarthy imagine.

But that myth is, oddly enough, the very reason Rudolph ended up living there in the first place. He wasn't a native son of the mountains: his family moved around a shady network of white-supremacist communities before his mother moved to western North Carolina from Florida, precisely because of the reputation of the mountains as being hospitable to fringe white nationalist political beliefs. Now Rudolph's escapade helps keep that self-fulfilling prophecy fulfilling itself.

❖   ❖   ❖   ❖

The cave, then, is one element of the larger reputation of this region as being a place apart, famously termed "a strange land and peculiar people" by nineteenth-century local colorist Will Wallace Harney. But it isn't always a bad thing to be a space outside of the world. This idea of the cave as the place where you're closest to being in touch with some kind of Appalachian essence turns up in a very different way in Charles Frazier's *Cold Mountain*.

Maybe it's not just coincidence that Frazier's narrative also features a richly imagined subterranean landscape. Most significantly, at least in terms of *Cold Mountain*'s plot, the Shining Rocks—an actual mica outcrop near Cold Mountain's summit—figures into the novel as a mythical, mystical gateway to a better place, the paradise of the region's Native Americans and protagonist Inman's last fallback plan to escape the spread across the landscape of modern war, its mindset, its aftermath. Near the end of the novel, Inman not-very-facetiously suggests to his true love, Ada, that "as a last resort, they could fast for the prescribed number of days and wait for the portals of the Shining Rocks to open and welcome them into the land of peace."

But there's a little more, shall we say, earthbound cave in the novel, a cave a lot like the one we collectively imagined for Eric Rudolph, where "outlier" fugitives from the war live amid their plunder from area gentry, "Table set with Wedgwood and silver, though many of them had eaten all their lives from table service made entirely of gourd and horn." Here the novel's most no-account character, Stobrod, joins forces with a simpleton named Pangle to reinvent traditional music. Pangle, the narrator notes, was drawn to the cave purely by animal instinct: "In the winter he took instruction from toad and groundhog and bear: he denned up in a cave, scarcely moving during the cold months."

The cave proves for Pangle to be more than just a place to hibernate, but a place where even a simple person like himself can get in touch with deep cultural impulses. Sleep is not the only instinctive behavior here; when Pangle hears a tune played by Stobrod, who has become a sort of savant himself on the fiddle, he "get[s] up and stomp[s] out a dance of great mystery, ancient Celtic jerk and spasm." When Stobrod gives him a banjo from a looting expedition, Pangle instantly transforms into an upbeat revision of the albino banjo-picker from James Dickey's *Deliverance*.

The music Stobrod and Pangle learn to make in their cave gives the two of them, outsiders and losers even by the standards of the novel's landscape of misfortune, a higher purpose, a moral seriousness. Even *Cold Mountain*'s villain, the heartless Home Guard officer Teague, declares of them, "Good God, these is holy men. Their mind turns on matters kept secret from the likes of you and me."

I am intrigued by the fact that two such different imaginary places as Eric Rudolph's cave, in which the Appalachians nurture an extremist murderer, and Charles Frazier's, where the core of the mountains protects a transcendent cultural legacy from the ravages of "a terrain of violence," come along at almost the same time. Frazier's novel appeared in 1997, after the Olympic Park bombing but before the 1998 manhunt, and rode the crest of its popularity through the height of the Rudolph media circus. Frazier himself was often sought as a kind of "expert witness" about the contemporary culture of the region. But these caves share something—if not a common feeling about the mountain region, then a sense that hidden somewhere in this mountain fastness is a place outside of history, a place that, for better or worse, takes care of its own.

❖   ❖   ❖   ❖

The thing is, there just aren't that many caves in North Carolina. The conservative estimate of the state's official geologic survey is less than a dozen. Of those, most are what's called crevice caves, formed by the splitting of rock, or talus caves, formed by gaps in a heap of boulders. These are very distant, undecorated cousins of the solution caves of the valley, which were formed by the much more gradual and subtle seepage of mildly acidic groundwater through limestone. The geology just isn't right over on the east side of the Blue Ridge, the rocks less porous, the mountain's steep slopes draining water too quickly for it to filter through the fissures of the bedrock.

The closest we've got is Linville Caverns, a low-key tourist operation that's content to let us go just a little ways beneath the surface. Linville Caverns is a small, wet, and quite pretty cave that's been making a go of it in a holler up above Marion, North Carolina, just a few miles away from the Blue Ridge Parkway and a traditional detour for travelers on that route. And here again the show cave reshapes the culture, in its small and persistent way. Linville Caverns shows us how these caves can not only project fantastical versions of the region but also bring them back down, as it were, to earth. There aren't really any magical storehouses of local culture in these caves, the womb of the mountains' essence; there's really just this one little cave. But whatever the cave lacks in depth or majesty, its cultural resources are robust. Just like its more flamboyant cousin Forbidden Caverns on the other side of the Blue Ridge, it's helped make stories about the region that are circulated around the globe.

The state's lone show cave is also its most extensive solution cave, period: its record-setting 1,200-foot labyrinth of stream passages make up the thirty-minute tour. With the exception of one deep seam filled to the level of the show cave passage with water, all the leads have been pushed, and only a little bit of cave even lies outside the range of the tourist trail.

A small parking lot and a single gift shop building are the only amenities on the surface. They're not going for the gusto with the ziplines or gemstone mining. The whole thing has been a family business since the day it opened in 1939 — developed right alongside the Blue Ridge Parkway, to which Linville Caverns is linked much as Forbidden Caverns' fate is tied to Pigeon Forge. A portrait of Mrs. Ellen Townsend, who began work in 1947 and stayed with it for the next forty years, hangs above the register; she worked for the Collins family, who employed siblings, children, nephews and nieces, cousins, and a lot of local kids.

From what I can tell they've trained them up right, because the darkness demonstration here is first rate. The guide lights a dim little electric lantern, then kills the masters, and tells a story of two boys back in the early twentieth century who lost their one and only lantern while exploring. Extinguishing the lantern, the guide describes to the now absolutely dark room how the boys had to find their way out in the pitch black and the bone-chilling water—the latter of which also proved their salvation since the current led them back to the entrance. In a way the story doesn't even have to be well told—the crowd in the dark is nothing if not suggestible—but the guide not only hits his mark but lets the darkness linger an extra second or two for emphasis. Even this little cave could kill you if it wanted.

The story that really makes my ears prick up, though, comes when we stop in front of the formation called The Fireplace, where we learn that this spot, an alcove at a junction of two passages, was the home and workshop of some Civil War–era deserters who sat by the fire and made shoes, which were sold in the area markets. Local folks discreetly brought the deserters food and other supplies, or so the story goes, until the fugitives were given away in the end by the smoke from the fire they kept going in the namesake formation—plumes of smoke in the winter forest gave away their location to the Home Guard.

Fun to imagine, but I'm not buying it. Just look around: there's no way anybody was really living here: I'm visiting in a dry spell, and there's still water from the cave's stream flowing through this supposed campsite. It's as farfetched as the oft-repeated notion that Eric Rudolph was living off salamanders—as if he'd spend all day every day grabbling in a frigid stream when the Taco Bell dumpster beckoned.

There's no place you could lie down on that cold wet floor wrapped up in an old wool blanket (the space is barely big enough for a smallish cave tour group to stand shoulder-to-shoulder) without finding yourself hypothermic before too long. I could see maybe hiding out for a few hours, waiting for some kind of trouble to die down, but the mountains offer so many superior long-term hiding places—ones where you could run away if discovered, for example. And, of course, ones that won't kill you with their chill and damp. Spending the night here is a stretch, much less cheerfully whiling away the winter months mastering the fiddle.

The folks who run Linville Caverns seem to know this, too: the story has been taken off the cave's skeletal website, and in the official history of the cavern available in the bookstore, revised and expanded in 2005, authors Cato and Susan Holler include only a truncated rendition of the story, minus the treacherous campfire smoke and the implied tragic conclusion. It's still a featured point in the tour, though, alongside the cave bacon and the Gator's Head and Frozen Niagara. Clearly, the rules of historical accuracy don't apply quite the same in this context: the show cave not only preserves stories; it also makes new ones.

It's hard not to notice some of the close correspondences here among the Eric Rudolph cave story, Charles Frazier's, and the stories of Linville Caverns. In the case of *Cold Mountain*, the idea of the cave as hideout for outliers parallel's the Linville Caverns legend pretty closely, up to and including the capture of the cave dwellers by the Home Guard. The Eric Rudolph story not only borrows the cave-as-hideout motif but also picks up on the idea that locals supported fugitives, discreetly delivering food to the subterranean lair.

And as with Cormac McCarthy and Forbidden Caverns, the authors of these fictional caves had plenty of opportunity to visit Linville Caverns. Part of the marketing of *Cold Mountain* was to note Frazier's long residence and deep roots in the mountains of Western North Carolina—it seems likely he would at least have heard of, if not visited, Linville Caverns, the mountains' only real cave. And picturing all those reporters loitering around Andrews waiting around for something new to write about after weeks of covering the fruitless search, it's easy to imagine that some of them might have roamed up the Blue Ridge Parkway in search of a sidebar or some local color piece and found themselves stopping in, like so many others, to see the show cave.

Then they went on to add their mark to the dense layer of narrative draped across the High Country, joining Linville Caverns and Hot Springs and the Blue Ridge Parkway and the Appalachian Trail in helping write the history and the mythos of the region. They went with the magic cave angle mostly, and I guess that's to be expected. But you know, looking at Linville Caverns, they could've taken another story away. Linville Caverns tells us of the staying power of something lovely and modest and a little understated, the dedication and work that has kept this place an active part of the complex cultural processes of imagining Appalachia.

So, in a sense, whatever the contrasts between Forbidden Caverns and Linville Caverns, however stark the differences between Pigeon Forge and the High Country, they're all connected, not just by the shape of the Great Valley but as a part of a larger network of images and ideas. These show caves provide a special perspective on how the making of a place works, how stories combine and conflict, shaped by their surroundings and reshaping them in turn. America went on from the days of Rudolph and *Cold Mountain* to imagine new fugitives hiding out in new caverns following 9/11. To what extent were we using the stories we made in Appalachia when we pictured Tora Bora?

FOUR

Constant Revision at the Cumberland Gap

The Stories of Gap Cave

❖   ❖   ❖   ❖

Nowhere is the complicated interaction between fact and fiction, truth and illusion more intricate than at Gap Cave, lying just south of the Cumberland Gap in the slim wedge of the state of Virginia that intersects there with the boundaries of Tennessee and Kentucky. The Cumberland Gap is a site rich not only with history but with historical imagery and symbolism. The Gap District, as some folks still call it, is a real place with a story of its own, but it is also a place often used in constructing stories about the region and the nation, and one that has been shaped by stories as well—especially those that cling to the surface of Gap Cave's chambers and formations.

At Forbidden and Linville caverns you can see how show caves are part of a complicated give and take among a range of images and texts that shape the identity of a place. But a lot of the connections there are speculative or serendipitous. We may never know if Cormac McCarthy visited Forbidden Caverns while working on *Child of God*, for example. The story of Gap Cave, on the other hand, shows the cave being transformed on purpose, as a part of a plan to intentionally change the identity of the place—not just once but several times, including a project that's ongoing right now.

I first came here in the spring of 2006, when I took the official tour and chatted up the rangers that guide the way now that the cave is a part of the Cumberland Gap National Historic Site. But I've been back here again and again—as a tourist with my family and parents on a camping trip; in my (slightly) more official role as a writer and researcher to plumb the archival resources preserved at park headquarters; and again and again as an ordinary traveler. When you live in the Midwest (as I have for most of the past twenty years) but your people are back in East Tennessee, the Cumberland Gap still fulfills its ancient role in providing the best way to get from the Great Valley into Kentucky and the Ohio Valley beyond, and back again.

And as many times as I've been through there, I still stop every time I can somewhere along the string of towns that today make up the Gap District: Middlesboro, Kentucky on one side of the tunnel and Cumberland

Gap and Harrogate, Tennessee. on the other, just to poke around a little. It is just a really interesting place: a place that's been recognized as an iconic landscape, embodying values and ideals held to be central to regional and national identities. And yet that iconic status is not static. Beneath the monumental veneer, the story of the Gap District is one that illustrates how our control over the meanings of these icons is the object of continuous struggle. And—of course—the local show cave is all wrapped up in the heart of that struggle, recording it, reshaping it.

◈　　◈　　◈　　◈

A lot more than just the state lines converge here. The Gap has long supplied American culture with a place where we can see multiple pasts and futures bumping up against each other, a pattern of worlds colliding written deep into geology of the Gap's terrain. Powell Valley, running through Tennessee and Virginia on the Gap's southern flanks, represents the contact zone between the Great Valley's petrified seafloor limestone and the coalfields' sedimentary shales. Just north of the Gap in Kentucky's Yellow Creek Valley, the town of Middlesboro is built in the crater of a 300-million-year-old meteorite strike.

From the Gap's highest point, a rocky outcrop called the Pinnacle, looking north, you can see the entirety of the three-mile-wide flat spot that meteorite made when it hit, an anomaly in the wrinkled topography of southeastern Kentucky. Looking the other way, you behold the receding waves of the valley and ridge province—Powell Mountain, Clinch Mountain, then the valley floor rolling away toward the Smokies, the 350-million-year-old limestone washing up against the Pine Mountain thrust, lunging from Kentucky into northeast Tennessee.

And there in that last band of Greenbrier limestone, its beds tilted in collision with the Kentucky sandstone beyond, is a complex cave network surveyed at over fourteen miles. At least six natural entrances lead into an intricate maze of shafts and pits and passageways, all descending to a robust spring pouring down the mountain toward Powell Valley, having dissolved its way over the course of a few million years down through the cracks.

The story of the Cumberland Gap as it is typically told doesn't reach back quite that far. Instead it centers on two of the most canonically significant phenomena of American history: first, the conquest of the western frontier, then the Civil War. Daniel Boone's 1775 expedition through the Gap was the sociohistorical equivalent of a meteorite impact, the blow that breached the last remaining barrier between the inexorably, increasingly

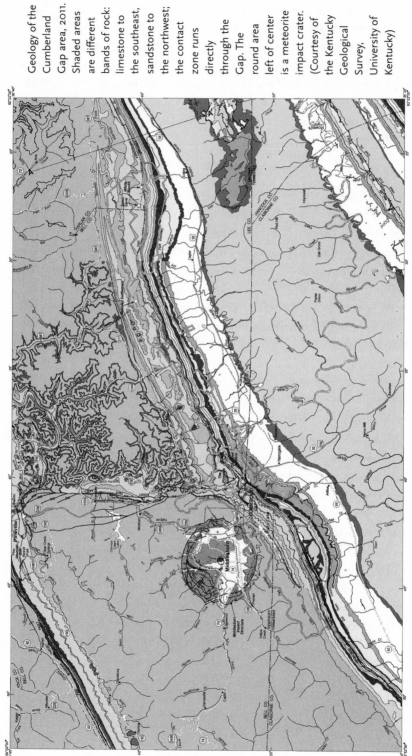

Geology of the Cumberland Gap area, 2011. Shaded areas are different bands of rock: limestone to the southeast, sandstone to the northwest; the contact zone runs directly through the Gap. The round area left of center is a meteorite impact crater. (Courtesy of the Kentucky Geological Survey, University of Kentucky)

Anglo-European east coast and the North American interior. The next thirty years saw more than a quarter-million migrants, including uncounted slaves, pass through the Gap in Boone's wake.

Woven through the tale of this mass migration (much as it is through the limestone of the Gap itself) is Gap Cave, which was first documented by white settlers in 1750 by the explorer and speculator Dr. Thomas Walker. There's no way of telling how many travelers watered themselves and their livestock here, the last pit stop before making the short, steep climb to the saddle and down the other side into Kaintuck. Gradually the small town of Cumberland Gap, Tennessee, grew up just below the spring, the cave providing its water supply, the passing column of fortune seekers providing its commerce.

The social and cultural significance of this site in national expansion coupled with the rugged beauty of the place that became known as the "American Gibraltar" quickly earned it a role in the iconography of a young nation looking to define its central myths. At the turn of the twentieth century, the renowned frontier historian Frederick Jackson Turner declared that at Cumberland Gap you could "stand . . . and watch the process of civilization, marching single file."

Turner's vision of the Gap was no doubt filtered through the lens of George Caleb Bingham's 1852 *Emigration of Daniel Boone*, which is to this day an almost inevitable part of any public presentation of information about the Gap, the Parks Service's visitor center being no exception. The painting's orderly pyramidal composition of Boone and his compatriots draws light and order into the center of a painting whose landscape is otherwise cast in a twisted and ominous twilight receding to a menacing darkness. Any resemblances between the depiction of Boone leading the mule upon which rides his wife Sarah, demure beneath her shawl, and the Holy Family are totally not coincidental. Bingham carefully renders the actual topography of the Gap, but in a way that adds a moral character to the land and the changes these new arrivals were bringing to it.

❖　❖　❖　❖

But the domestic tranquility that American civilization supposedly brought to the Gap was short-lived (if indeed it ever lived). By the Civil War the Gap embodied the nation's strife, an embattled symbol of an embattled people, changing hands four times in a region unstably divided in its loyalties. The Gap was again the frontier, but here in its older sense of being a borderland among separate nations, a landscape befitting the "brother versus brother" narrative of the War Between the States. Like much of the southern mountains, the Gap was a place where both strategic positions and political loyalties were very much up for grabs.

Now instead of providing an emblem of national unity and shared purpose, the Gap was a theater of national uncertainty. Those folks who remained in the Union needed to be able to imagine that somehow, that space was still a symbol of the Union, regardless of how the boundaries were drawn. You could occupy the national icon, but you couldn't keep it from still representing the nation. And when folks need to imagine the heart and soul of the Mountain South, they can't seem to help imagining a cave.

❖   ❖   ❖   ❖

At least, that's how I explain the popularity of John Townsend Trowbridge's 1864 smash hit novel *Cudjo's Cave*: it's yet another example of our culture's affinity for tales of caves as hideouts for fugitives and sanctuaries for nonconformists and of our penchant for looking to the Southern Mountains to preserve something we're in danger of losing. Trowbridge, a journalist, novelist, poet, editor, and self-described hack, wove a tale set among runaway slaves hiding in a cave identified in the novel as being near the Cumberland Gap. In a story described as "a mixture of war-time propaganda, romance, and adventure" the cave becomes a meeting place of Quakers, Unionists, and other fringe types, a space where an alternative community could escape from and resist the Confederacy's politics and culture.

Cudjo's Cave is now little-remembered outside of Appalachian literature scholarship. In contemporary papers such as the *New York Tribune*, however, critics claimed that "the story will retain a durable hold on public interest by reason of its earnestness, vitality, and truth to nature." And in 1864, it was a huge best seller—in the North, anyway. Advertisements boasted of multiple print runs and gushed that it must be "a work of rare merit," while a theatrical version was staged by P. T. Barnum. And Trowbridge's novel was not completely without staying power. In 1898 the *New York Times* reported that *Cudjo's Cave* was included on a list of the twenty-five most important American novels. The *Times* columnist sniffed, however, that "an ephemeral romance of the early days of the Civil War looks strangely in company with Hawthorne's books."

Cudjo's Cave is, if nothing else, a ripping yarn, centering on the struggles of a young Quaker named Penn living near the fictitious Gap District settlement of Currytown. Penn's decent treatment of others, especially the African Americans, slave and free, that he heretically treats like human beings, quickly runs him afoul of the local secessionist militia. He flees into the mountains, where he is taken in by two escaped slaves, the kindly Cudjo and the more militant Pomp. With the eponymous cave now serving as a refuge, Penn begins reaching out to like-minded friends and neighbors and a local loyalist militia, and pretty soon our heroes fall into a lengthy succession of arrests, near executions, and hair's-breadth escapes, returning time and again to the cave with a new twist in the plot to ruminate briefly before venturing out again. Though most of the principles eventually flee to the North to join the war effort, Old Cudjo is killed in the climactic assault on the cave, tumbling into the darkness but taking his abusive master with him.

Despite the celebrated "truth to nature" of his novel, there's no evidence that Trowbridge ever visited the area. The general shape of the cave matches the layout of Gap Cave, including a detail figuring in several plot twists that the cave had a natural exit out a mountaintop pit that connected to the very top of the cave. Throughout the Civil War, however, Gap Cave was a terrible hideout, right by the main road, the water supply, cold storage, and recreational getaway for whatever army was occupying the Gap at the time. But Townsend was a propagandist, drawing on and adding to the myth of the place—there was no need to get too distracted by the facts.

Townsend was correct, however, in his understanding that the area was turbulent and violent—perhaps he wanted to suggest that the scourge of secession and slavery were reverting one of the great emblems of American virtue to its precivilized state. In fact, social conditions in the Gap District had been on a downward slide since well before the start of the Civil War, even as the sanctified imagery of the Gap in paintings like Bingham's were taking root in the public imagination.

In the vicinity of the actual Gap, Turner's stately "process of civilization" actually stumbled a bit. The first obstacle was the opening, in 1825, of the Erie Canal, which gave travelers from the Eastern Seaboard a much less strenuous route to the Ohio Valley. The once-vaunted Wilderness Road became a rutted, neglected mess. Resource extraction replaced playing host to the emigrating masses at the heart of the local economy. The cave was put to work throughout this period, its spring powering sawmills, gristmills, and a blast furnace instead of watering cattle. The country became starker, harder.

Then the Civil War brought violent chaos from which the area, some might argue, has never yet fully recovered. Near century's end the Gap, bypassed by railroads, no longer a thoroughfare but a hinterland, had a lawless reputation. At this point in history, Gap Cave, ever the leading cultural indicator, was known as John A. Murrell Cave, commemorating a notorious

West Tennessee outlaw who supposedly ambushed a Virginia merchant at the cave spring (though whether this was a cautionary tale or an early attempt at promotion is lost to history). The saddle of the great Cumberland Gap itself, that national icon, was known as "Hell's Half Acre," a tiny sliver of Virginia renowned for vice of all kinds. In 1888 Charles Dudley Warner, a travel writer for *Harper's* in the tradition of Porte Crayon, traveled "the now neglected Wilderness Road" and described how "this whole valley, lying very prettily among the mountains, has a bad name for 'difficulties' . . . where in recent times differences of opinion had been settled by the revolver."

Warner continued, more optimistically, "This sort of thing is, however, practically over." On the north side of the Gap, Warner noted, "is the site of a great city, already plotted, which the English company are to build." On the south side, the "new English hotel" provided a sign that "Cumberland Gap is full of expectation." All this optimism sprang from the efforts of a Scotland-born Canadian lumberman, Alexander A. Arthur, lionized in the press as "the Cecil Rhodes of the Cumberland," a speculator and developer with an inclination to dream big.

❖   ❖   ❖   ❖

Alexander Alan Arthur speculated and developed his way across the Tennessee Valley, arriving at the Gap, mineral and timber scouts in tow, in 1885. A pioneer of global capitalism, Arthur was, like Boone before him, a sojourner, always intensely devoted to transforming the place he was in but always on the lookout for a newer, bigger, more lucrative challenge. The cave itself issued an omen of the changes to come: Cumberland Gap historian Robert Kincaid notes that Arthur and a group of friends — mostly young British men on the make, with names like Otway Wheeler-Cuffe (the third baronet of Lyrath) and Colonel Chester "Cocky" Master — were camped at the Gap on the night of August 31, 1886, when they felt tremors from an earthquake that was at that moment devastating Charleston, South Carolina. Arthur and his buddies ran down the hill to Gap Cave and, Kincaid reports, discovered that "huge boulders had tumbled down from the ceilings and covered the floor of the cavern with jagged rock."

Arthur apparently interpreted the sign optimistically and formed Gap Associates from among his fellow campers; he soon became a principal and agent for the American Association, Ltd. Arthur had a lot going for him: deep pockets and good connections in the form of a group of English investors that included the Duke of Marlborough, and an engineer's technical knowledge and technocratic aspirations, not to mention a taste for Prince

The Stories of Gap Cave

Alexander Alan Arthur, ca. 1885.
(Courtesy of the Alexander A. Arthur Family Papers, Archives and
Special Collections, Lincoln Memorial University, Harrogate, Tennessee)

Albert coats and a truly luxurious set of whiskers. "He rode," novelist and historian Wilma Dykeman wrote in *The French Broad*, "lord and master, on a shiny black stump-tailed horse over his domain, never settling the bulk of his weight into the saddle, but always standing in the stirrups as if personally overseeing in the wilderness the birth of empire."

From his vantage point in his English saddle, Arthur saw the whole mountain south as ripe not just for resource-extractive industry but for wholesale social reorganization. In true imperial fashion, Arthur refused to curb his ambitions at merely colonizing the region's natural resources. He saw the landscape not just in terms of raw material but also in terms of real estate and human resources. He would not be content with mills, factories, and foundries: Arthur sought to reinvent the place itself, dreaming up modern, model communities, platting new street plans, and reorganizing land and people into a more coherent, legible, manageable form.

One would be tempted to label Arthur a unique figure in the history of the region were it not for the fact that, in this tour of Appalachian show caves, we've already met another such figure in the person of Jedidiah Hotchkiss, whose plan to create a New South starting with the city of Shendun, Virginia, was rolling out almost simultaneously. The wave of real-estate speculation over the new lands made available for development by the proliferation of railroads, at its giddy prime, the bubble fully inflated, meant there were plenty of people willing to offer capital to somebody willing to really go for the gusto.

Arthur found a bold venue for his ambitions at the Cumberland Gap. In the meteorite crater's anomalous expanse of relatively level ground high in the mountains, Arthur saw a blank canvas for an even larger grid than the one Hotchkiss deployed at Shendun, with a diverse economy centered on processing the timber and ore he and his scouts surveyed in Yellow Creek Valley. In the broad, rolling pastoral slopes on the south side of the Gap, Arthur envisioned Harrogate, a classic tourist resort and enclave of the soon-to-be Middlesboro elite. Arthur would bring hospitality in the fine tradition of the Greenbrier, complete with a show cave to rival newly opened Luray in beauty and the more established Mammoth in historic significance. The area's reputation for lawlessness came with a level of permission to establish order, and with its cultural heritage came a sense of possibility, of potential, of this being the right place for something new to happen.

Here at the Gap, rich with the resonance of frontier conquest, Arthur had found a mythic tableau against which he could unfold his ambitions with dramatic panache. The *Knoxville News-Sentinel* declared it "thrilling as any novel," and indeed, the plot, filled as it is with what the *News-Sentinel* summed up as "Romance, danger, and the thrill of seeing the rise from the wilderness," certainly rivals that of *Cudjo's Cave*. Arthur realized, just as Trowbridge did, that this was a place that could sell a melodrama, though the trappings of imperial leather (rather than humble buckskin) made this a different kind of set piece. In any event it was a good enough story to sell to Arthur's English backers, who proceeded to pour $25 to $30 million into Arthur's plan.

Work commenced on foundries, mills, power plants, business districts; modest home lots were platted, sold, resold, facing streets named Winchester, Exeter, Rochester, Dorchester, surrounding the hilltop mansions of Arthur Heights; a beltline railroad and a canal system ringed the whole plan, and beneath it, a sewer system. Planners agreed the Yellow Creek Valley could sustain a city of a quarter-million, which would bear the name of a Yorkshire industrial center then enjoying great prosperity and growth.

Gap Cave received an exotic, romantic makeover during this time. In 1890, a Mr. G. B. Cockrell of the East Kentucky Land Company purchased the cave property alongside Arthur's Four Seasons Resort, in a kind of symbiotic relationship: the resort would supply the life blood of tourists, and the resort would draw on the cave's water supply. A cultural exchange was afoot as well. The cavern, decked out as "King Solomon's Cave," injected an exotic note of orientalism by tying into the literary popularity of H. Rider Haggard's bestselling tale of imperial fearlessness, *King Solomon's Mines* (1885). Early promoters proclaimed that "sightseers who miss this extraordinary freak of nature are omitting from their lives the opportunity of seeing one of the greatest wonders of the world." A tour, which included a boat trip up the now-dammed creek, became a regular stop for potential investors and local dignitaries being squired around Arthur's invisible cities.

The whole scheme relied on the completion of the railroad through a tunnel beneath the Gap, connecting Middlesboro to Knoxville. Arthur's backers, incorporated as the American Association, Ltd., funded the Knoxville, Cumberland Gap, and Louisville Railroad as the association itself bought up nearly 100,000 acres of land in Bell County, Kentucky. In 1889 the Gap's first railroad tunnel reached completion, and Middlesboro sprang to life, transforming the Yellow Creek Valley into a regional center with a population that immediately shot past 10,000. Modern industry arrived in the Gap district much as Daniel Boone had: the vanguard of a new order to society, opening the Gap to the movement of people and materials, redrawing the map and resettling the people on the other side, to a chorus of mythologizing cheerleading for the twin projects of Manifest Destiny and civilizing the natives.

Apparently, the earthquake's first ill omen wasn't obvious enough. The next one was a little more direct. Promoters staged a gala outing for Knoxville's elite on the ceremonial first train on the new line, planning a celebratory picnic at the Gap—perhaps including a trip through the Gap's scenic caverns. But, the *News-Sentinel* recalled, "the party which had started out so joyfully returned saddened by tragedy." The train derailed, killing nine and injuring 27, among them, Arthur himself, who was confined to a wheelchair for a long convalescence and hampered by the pain of his injuries the rest of his life.

The wreck foretold how the entire development scheme, like many burgeoning schemes across America during the boom years of the early 1890s, would jump the track before it really even got started. Arthur's railroad- and town-building schemes ran slightly ahead of the larger trend in the United States, so the collapse of the Middlesboro plan was a bellwether. Like Boone, Arthur was in the vanguard of a massive movement, a wave of socioeconomic change now known as the Panic of '93, which scuttled a lot of model-town dreams, including Shendun further up the valley.

But even before the Panic fully struck home in the Gap, Arthur's industrial-imperialist project and the American Association's capital were in severe jeopardy, leading the charge into the frontiers of insolvency. In a harbinger of the inevitable, broader economic collapse, the Barings Bank of London, overburdened with losses from railroad and real-estate gambles, became insolvent in November 1890. The shockwaves this event sent through the nascent global economy ended any hope for a continuation of English investment in either Middlesboro or the Four Seasons resort.

The boomtown of Middlesboro went bust very thoroughly: the area's iron ores proved to be of poor quality, meaning the steel mills intended to be the economic engine for the community went undeveloped, and thus the workforce drawn by the prospect of those nonexistent jobs unsettled the town. The downtown shopping district even suffered a devastating fire.

By the time the vaunted million-dollar hotel opened, Arthur had already been removed from his position by the directors of the American Association, and he had retired to his home on the grounds of the Four Seasons to sort out his affairs. Instead, he got a front-row view as the resort proved so unprofitable that it not only was closed but was sold as salvage for $9,000 in 1895, less than three years after its much-publicized gala opening. Ever the optimist, Arthur tried the "model town" gig one more time, slapping a

The Stories of Gap Cave

little grid around a whistle stop down the valley and naming it (what else) "Arthur." When his town proved no more successful than its namesake, Arthur shipped out again, finding his way eventually to the 1897 Alaska Gold Rush—ever the economic frontiersman.

Yet, in all his subsequent wanderings, Middlesboro was never, it seems, far from Arthur's thoughts. Years later, his health broken, Arthur returned to the "Magic City" that was his most ambitious project shortly before his death in 1912. Middlesboro's population eventually stabilized, and the town gets by today as a local shopping hub, rather than standing astride the mountains like the colossus Arthur envisioned. Instead, Middlesboro gained a reputation through the first half of the twentieth century as a wide-open border town with vice as a major industry—still a social, legal, and some would say moral frontier.

❖　❖　❖　❖

But at the Cumberland Gap, for every frontier, there is a frontiersman, ready to make this iconic landscape play a part in the enactment of his vision of what this place should stand for. In this case, another man with deep pockets, great connections, and a splendid set of whiskers. But to up the ante a little bit, let's give this character just one arm. And let's make him not only a man possessed of a sweeping social vision, and an old-school chivalric bearing, but complete the picture with military regalia. This man is General Oliver Otis Howard, and he comes to the Cumberland Gap a tourist in 1895, visiting Civil War sites en route to a tour of battlefields where he held a commanding role, to find one final mission waiting for him in the ruin of Arthur's failed experiment.

Howard was born 1830 in Leeds, Maine. Before the Civil War, Howard had distinguished himself primarily as an exceptionally pious man who contemplated leaving his position on the mathematics faculty at West Point to become an Episcopalian priest. Instead, he found himself a colonel commanding a Union brigade at Bull Run. He soon rose to brigadier general but almost as quickly suffered the loss of his right arm at the battle of Fair Oaks in June of 1862. He famously joked to General Philip Kearney, whose left arm was lost in the Mexican-American War, that they should shop for gloves together. Amputation notwithstanding, he resumed his command a few months later. Howard served out the remainder of the war as a top-ranking officer, first in the Army of the Potomac and later in William Tecumseh Sherman's Army of the Tennessee.

In truth, though Howard's strength of character has never been called into question, his enduring reputation as a military commander is mixed at best. He was roughly as effective a tactician as Alexander Alan Arthur was an urban planner. Sherman nevertheless kept him close, and Howard proved highly effective as a wartime administrator, moving 80,000 men, their supplies and weapons on the March to the Sea.

Howard was deeply, if paternalistically, devoted to the welfare of his soldiers and became known as "the Christian General" for his insistence that drinking and swearing and other profane behavior, the sort romantically associated with generals like Sherman and Grant, would not take place among his ranks. Furthermore, he was one of the few voices consistently raised against the deliberate infliction of property damage and suffering on the civilian population, an argument it would seem he increasingly lost as the war drew toward its conclusion. Howard's sense of purpose, his dedication, and even to some extent his idealism assured him of the kind of service record that made him indispensable once he found his niche.

Howard's skill at administration coupled with his tenacious conscience led him into a postwar career centered on doing the kind of high-minded work that nobody else wanted to do. Most notably, Howard was the head, in the Reconstruction Era, of the Freedmen's Bureau, which he seems to have approached with the same kind of straight-laced sincerity he brought to much else in his life. Howard failed to grasp, however, that despite the war's outcome, few white Americans had any real desire to welcome African Americans as equals.

Howard has been faulted by historians for his naiveté, for believing that the declaration of equality by statute would force the kind of cultural change necessary to truly guarantee enfranchisement for the former slaves and their descendants. He seems not unlike Alexander Alan Arthur in thinking that you could simply rewrite a place, that changes in society would inevitably follow upon changes in the structure of a society. If you declare that freedmen can vote, that black testimony carries weight in court, that former plantation owners will pay a certain level of wages, then it will be so. Of course, this is a man who, as a general, believed you could prohibit foot soldiers from swearing.

Howard's tool of choice for rewriting the sociopolitical landscape, however, was not industry but education. One strong and enduring commitment of the Freedmen's Bureau was to the development of higher education for blacks; the bureau provided seed money and often bankrolled the construction of buildings on the campuses of what are now known as historically black colleges and universities all across the South. In the District of Colum-

General Oliver Otis Howard in 1900.
(Courtesy of the Photograph Archives, Archives and Special Collections,
Lincoln Memorial University, Harrogate, Tennessee)

bia, Howard personally helped find funds, materials, and faculty for the institution that still bears his name, Howard University, which he served as president from 1869 to 1874.

After serving in the campaigns against the Native American tribes of the West (where, once again, his most-remembered works center on treaties rather than pitched battles), Howard returned east to become a philanthropist, humanitarian, and public speaker. Traveling through the Cumberland Gap district en route to a tour of Chattanooga battlefields in 1895, Howard found himself in the still-fresh ruins of Arthur's development scheme, which had left the communities around the Gap in even more dire economic straits than before.

The town of Cumberland Gap, for example, had benefited during the boom from the opening of the area's only high school, the Harrow School, run by Reverend A. A. Myers on behalf of the American Missionary Society and endowed by some of the more broad-minded elites who enthusiastically but oh so briefly enjoyed the pleasures of the Four Seasons. When the hotel disappeared, so did the Harrow School's financial underpinnings, at just the moment when education and vocational training was most desperately needed. "Friends," Howard proclaimed to the school's supporters gathered there that evening, "if you will make this school a larger enterprise I will take hold and do what I can."

Here was a task that gave Howard the opportunity to put the full range of his abilities to work: his skill at organization, his passion for education, and his strong moral sensibilities. And it didn't hurt, since so much of his commitment was to fund-raising, that he was a real-life Civil War general whose commission was signed by Abraham Lincoln himself. Once again the power of American mythos would be invoked to change the landscape and culture of the Cumberland Gap. Howard once again took to the boards on a speaking tour, but this time, instead of reminiscences of his Civil War service or his view of the Indian Campaigns, Howard invoked national memory, of the Great Emancipator and of the national symbolism of the Gap.

Howard's standard speech centered on a meeting he had with Lincoln as they planned the campaigns to take Tennessee. At one point Lincoln gestured to the Cumberland Gap on the map and proclaimed, "They are loyal there, they are loyal!" As they parted, Lincoln spoke personally with his general. It's easy to imagine the dramatic appeal of the scene for an audience of potential benefactors, the silver-bearded, one-armed veteran describing how the Martyr of the Republic looked him in the eyes and said, "General, if you come out of this horror and misery alive, and I pray to God you may, I want you to do something for those mountain people who have been shut out of the world all these years. I know them. If I live I will do all I can to aid, and between us perhaps we can do the justice they deserve."

The list of donors was long and influential, starting with Andrew Carnegie and Theodore Roosevelt. Who could refuse this upright, principled man when he enlisted your aid to fulfill a promise to Abraham Lincoln?

The humble Harrow School became "Lincoln's Memorial in the Mountains," eventually Lincoln Memorial University: an institution of higher education dedicated to providing access for the people of the mountains. Howard himself assumed the leadership of the university as managing director from 1897 until his death in 1909, when he collapsed in his Vermont home after a strenuous speaking tour.

In this final great project of his life of great projects (with decidedly mixed outcomes), Howard literally succeeded where Arthur had failed. He realized, in a sustained way, a tangible manifestation of his vision of the world in the very ruins of Arthur's hubris. The school rose from the pleasure spa—the last vestiges of the Four Seasons Hotel became LMU's centerpiece, Grant-Lee Hall. And it still stands today, contributing to the economy and culture of the Gap District more that Arthur's gospel of wealth ever did.

From the beginning, the relationship between Howard's project and Arthur's was openly adversarial. The founder of the Harrow School, Reverend A. A. Myers, was a roving evangelist who, witnessing Middlesboro's boomtown greed and vice, preached against the avarice of the enterprise. Howard opted out of Myers's more brimstone-scented approach and instead appealed to the idea of the innate virtues of the loyal mountaineer, a kind of Christian populism. From those premises he took the measures designed to make his assumptions, his narratives, become facts.

In the early 1920s the university acquired another important piece of the Gap when it purchased King Solomon's Cave, primarily to protect its water supply. (This was a serious concern: a typhoid outbreak killed five students and sickened fifty in 1924.) Before this acquisition, the school's official view on the show cave appears to have been dim. A student identified as K. S. Clark opens his account of a 1915 tour in the university's official publication, the *Mountain Herald*, by noting that "an ambitious land company, seeing an opportunity to rake in a few shekels, purchased or in some way obtained right and title to one of God's wonders." Reaching the large hall called the Ballroom, once electrically lit for the benefit of Arthur's guests, K. S. offers as an interpretive note: "Here a rich man who used to control the cave, when the Four Seasons Hotel was in its 'heyday,' actually held parties for the idle rich, and here many scenes were enacted of which the people here are not glad."

So, what is a socially conscious institution to do when suddenly it obtains right and title to one of God's wonders? And that wonder is decked out kind of tawdry, hanging out by the side of the road in Hell's Half-Acre, giving the old come-hither with promises of revealing nature's secrets and enacting scenes in the Ballroom? That air of worldliness in the very name recalls foreign literatures about distant, decadent lands. Even upright students like K. S. Clark could get a little flustered: "The faint murmur of the waters, the blackness of the distant tunnel and the stillness give one strange sensations, and one finds his companions apt to be rather untalkative . . . lest they awaken—what?"

In this situation, you've got to get yourself a new narrative. Or, perhaps more accurately, repurpose an old one. According to the Lincoln Memorial official history, *Phoenix of the Mountains*, this narrative came along courtesy of none other than Gifford Pinchot, famed conservationist and "Roosevelt Republican" who visited the school in the early 1930s when he was in his second term as governor of Pennsylvania. Pinchot had avidly read *Cudjo's Cave* as a boy and, when taken on a tour of the caverns, was filled with delight at the idea of finding, at last, the cave of the novel—like visiting Treasure Island.

Trowbridge's literary star had pretty much set by this time, but the fit between the story and the values of the cave's new owners was just too perfect to resist. Here's a progressive but pious tale, pro-Union, racially tolerant mostly, written into one of the nation's iconic landscapes. What better way to fulfill Lincoln's promise than to weave the values that informed Trowbridge's work into the bedrock of the community and thereby sweep away the vaguely debauched trappings of King Solomon's just as the campus swept away the spa and the Union swept away the Confederacy?

Thus, Cudjo's Cave opened to the public in 1934 and operated under various lessees until 1992; its souvenir stand and billboard-clad commercial entrance straddled US 25 as it wound toward the Gap loosely following the route of the old Wilderness Road. In the almost sixty years of commercial operation, tens of thousands of folks filed through to see the ten-foot-wide, forty-foot-tall Pillar of Hercules, the Capitol Dome, the Civil War graffiti, and the ballroom where Arthur's decadent aristocrats held their disreputable parties.

And it was all framed by the tale of Old Cudjo, the escaped slave who hid himself deep in the cave, who is believed to have died here though his body has never been found. Maybe, in the beginning, this was all framed as a re-telling of Trowbridge's story, but it didn't take long, I'm sure, for the story to morph into a "local legend" — despite being the creation of a man who never set foot here. In a forest of columns at a remote point in the tour, the guide would illuminate one speleothem from just the right angle, the shadows cre-ating the contours of a wizened face. And there he was, Old Cudjo, forever in hiding, a fictional character now written into the bedrock of the Cumber-land Gap by a trick of light.

And there he stayed for almost sixty years. Lincoln Memorial Univer-sity, now a going concern, eventually farmed out running the cave to various lessees. The infrastructure deteriorated; vandalism went unrepaired. And outside the cave, US 25 became more and more congested, the winding ap-proach to the Gap from the Tennessee side gaining a reputation as a danger-ous, slow, frustrating route. Cudjo's Cave contributed to that with its narrow band of parking on the shoulder and the ticket stand across the road from the cave entrance — a design from an earlier, slower time.

❖   ❖   ❖   ❖

By the late 1980s, the Gap, once celebrated for opening access to lands be-yond, had become an impediment to the movement of people and freight across the Appalachians. You could save time on the trip from East Tennes-see to central Kentucky by driving forty miles farther, taking Interstate 75 north from Knoxville. It looked like Cudjo's Cave would once again chart the descent of the Gap District into irrelevance. But there was another chapter of the rewriting of the meaning of this place to unfold, this time with the hand of the federal government behind it. And in a novel twist, the government's reworking of the landscape involves erasing a lot of its history.

Recognizing the historical importance of the place outweighed just about all its other uses, local and state leaders began discussions and plan-ning for a park at the Gap in the early 1920s, but since the task involved land acquisition coordinated among three states, the process was not quick. Finally, after more than thirty years following the first public discussions of an historical park at the Gap, the federal government in 1955 accepted the offer of over 20,000 acres acquired by Kentucky, Virginia, and Tennessee, and began the development of a National Historical Park that would be dedi-cated in 1959.

Ironically, as the park drew closer to becoming a reality, the traffic on US 25 through the Gap got worse and worse. The site of celebration of America's relentless movement was built around a dangerous nuisance for drivers.

From the park's point of view, it undermined efforts at connecting visitors with the history of the place—hard to envision another era standing at the Gap, with traffic chugging noisily by. Almost as hard as it was just to get out of the car and cross the road to see the monument marking the site where three states meet without getting run down by a truck.

But then came a solution to the traffic problem that also solved the park's public history problem: the erasure of vehicular traffic via the rerouting of US 25 through a huge, sleek $240 million tunnel. The tunnel's modernization of the infrastructure made available both opportunity (an influx of federal development money) and materials (clean fill dirt) for a peculiarly antimodern experiment.

As the tunnel went under the Gap, the National Parks Service expanded its holdings on the surface, acquiring Cudjo's Cave from LMU and consolidating its holdings along the US 25 right of way leading up to the Gap. In the 1990s the Parks Service began the process of giving the whole hillside, including both the inside and the outside of Cudjo's Cave, a thorough scrubbing, part of a larger effort to restore the entire landscape of the Gap to its "historic condition."

That's a term that sounds very definite and official, but on further inquiry, "historic condition" turns out to mean "more like what it was back between, say, the late eighteenth to late nineteenth centuries. Or so." The restoration attempts to offer visitors access to some pretty ephemeral stuff: feelings, associations, perspectives. Planning documents for the restoration project assert in carefully qualified prose, "The intent is to provide the opportunity for visitors to walk to the Gap along the Wilderness Road, to feel what it must have been like to cross the Gap . . . to see the landscape as it might have existed then, and to experience some of the thoughts and emotions of the pioneers." Precision work it isn't, but it has been an incredibly elaborate, ambitious project—on the frontiers, you might say, of public history, in its effort to preserve a historic landscape by physically deconstructing and reconstructing it.

So once the planning and the studying and the surveying were done, the next step was a $4 million joint project of the National Parks Service and the Federal Highway Administration that removed the now-vestigial roadbed of the old highway, along with any and all billboards or roadside structures of any kind, including the old Cudjo's Cave gift shop and ticket office. "We're more used to building roads than removing them," federal project engineer Jeff Schmidt told the press in 2001. "This is kind of a reverse cycle for us."

Then, using eighteenth- and nineteenth-century illustrations of the southern approaches to the Gap and a painstaking, fine-toothed archaeo-logical survey to sort out the skein of paths and roads and tracks and ruts, engineers placed the dirt from the tunnel project so as to restore the shape of the hillside to some simulation of its topography preceding the automobile age. Next, they traced a ten-foot-wide wagon road along the newly reformed slopes, which bury the US 25 highway roadbed to a depth of thirty feet in places. Finally, students from LMU planted 20,000 trees along the path of the deconstruction site—covering their tracks, as it were, through the very space they had helped develop.

The cave that LMU had once owned and administered had a special role to play here, a project within a project. The Park Service took control of Cudjo's Cave from Lincoln Memorial University in 1992, and work began to simultaneously upgrade and downgrade the old show cave armature. Parks Service employees and volunteers from the Pine Mountain Grotto of the National Speleological Society (NSS) devoted years of steady work cleaning out trash and (some, but not all) graffiti, removing handrails, monuments, and wiring. Now author Larry Matthews is content, in his NSS guidebook *Caves of Knoxville and the Great Smokies*, to proclaim that "the cave now closely re-sembles its original condition."

Throughout the project, park officials stayed on message, asserting that "park visitors were walking the newly-restored Wilderness Road in the foot-steps of Daniel Boone." "We're putting the pieces back together and re-creating as accurately as possible the first glimpse of the Promised Land," proclaimed park superintendent Mark Woods, evoking, consciously or not, Bingham's painting and its orderly Holy Family. "Past coming back to life at Cumberland Gap," declared the *Knoxville News-Sentinel*.

But any story involving time travel is bound to have some contradic-tions, starting with the irony that, when you stand on the new improved Wilderness Road, the ground beneath your feet was until as recently as 1996 deep beneath the Gap itself. As intriguing and ambitious as the premise of the project is, there's a lot you have to train your senses to ignore as you walk down the Wilderness Road today to have even the vaguest sense of what life was like here in the past. Most prominently, you have to disregard the sight and sound of busy traffic on the four-lane highway through the tunnel that made all this possible.

The whole idea of returning the cave to its "original condition" is even more vexing. What is the "original condition" of a cave tens of millions of years old? Are we talking pre-Cudjo's (prior to 1934)? Precommercialization (the 1880s)? Pre–white settlement in, say, the sixteenth century? Pre–human arrival, over 10,000 years ago? How would we know "original condition" when we saw it, if we could see it at all? Wouldn't its "original condition" be totally dark?

❖   ❖   ❖   ❖

The biggest puzzle here is how the attempt to make the past more available in many ways makes it less so. "History" appears to us as a narrowly defined zone that ended many generations ago, obscuring the fact that what we're seeing is actually a present-day definition of American heritage. Instead of reconstructing a meaningful, immediate, tangible past, this project—like Arthur's and Howard's before it—constructs a comprehensible past, but one with no claims on the present. It's not a revelation of the truth but an argument about what the truth of the Gap should be.

In other words, much of what's happened here is not restoration but redevelopment—a new version of the cave that's about the older versions of the cave. Lighting was removed so visitors now carry flashlights, but pathways and stairs have been upgraded to newer, safer, more durable designs. The roadside show cave landscape with its gift shop and signage is gone, but tourists still pay up to accompany a guide for the underground walk. Only now money changes hands not at the old roadside stand by the two-lane road but at the park visitors' center, demurely out of view just the other side of the new tunnel.

Once in the cave, visitors receive a tour that hasn't changed all that much, though it's given these days by uniformed park personnel: true to the terms of the genre, it's a mix of history and lore, some scientific fact and some tall tales, and of course a few illusions and a darkness demonstration, woven together by the story of the development and redevelopment of the cavern itself as a tourist attraction. Though the tale of the historical restoration process is now a part of that story, guides also still tell the story of how Old Cudjo, the runaway slave, took shelter in the cave—but now it's a "local legend," not the forgotten political fable of a Boston novelist. And sure enough, though the master lighting system is long gone, at a stop late in the tour, guides use flashlights to trace out the contours of his face. The novel that created him is all but forgotten; the cave that was his namesake has been erased from the map, but Old Cudjo escapes erasure again.

That's perhaps not what the Park Service meant when it said "historic condition," but it's appropriate that Cudjo, the fictional creation of an author who never even set foot here, retains a place in the local collective memory. The Gap is an area whose actual material history has been shaped and reshaped by mythology, by literature, by culture. To have a figure—a specter, almost—physically representing the presence of that myth is historical accuracy of a different order.

❖   ❖   ❖   ❖

Sorting out fact from fiction elides the role that the fictions play in shaping the facts. It's not factual to say that an escaped slave named Cudjo lived in Gap Cave, but it is factual to say that Trowbridge's fiction is part of a larger complex of stories, versions, ideas of this landscape, part of the cave itself.

The team that carried out the survey work, tracking down the routes of the Wilderness Road, figured this out. What it came to understand is that the Wilderness Road isn't any one thing but is a process, the mainstream ruts shifting and drifting around the hillsides and valley floor in response to weather and traffic and the gradual groupthink of thousands of travelers.

Just as various powers and interests have tried to make the Gap—the landscape, the people, the idea of it—into what they have thought it should be, the cave has been written and overwritten by these competing narratives, and all of them still linger in some way, restoration or no. If the pattern holds, someday this parks service restoration will be like another layer of graffiti, the remains of yet another attempt to rewrite the story of the Cumberland Gap.

Who knows what other fictions might shape the Gap? What new stories will we use it to tell? Examples are emerging: some clever literary detective work has determined that McCarthy's 2006 novel The Road begins its grueling post-apocalyptic journey at the Gap. Landmarks in McCarthy's text and on the road map correlate neatly to describe a route on Highway 25 south, down the mountain from the Gap to McCarthy's hometown of Knoxville.

This McCarthy novel opens with the father asleep in the woods, awakening from a dream of wandering in a cave (Gap Cave, surely?) with his son, "like pilgrims in a fable swallowed up and lost among the inward parts of some granitic beast." This cold, foreboding space is emblematic of the menacing, mysterious isolation facing the man and his son in McCarthy's vision of a place beyond our contemporary dream of plenty, looking back down the way we came and finding little but ashes. Finding, in other words, a new, no-longer triumphal frontier, defined not by the absence of civilization but its failure. But the Gap has always been a place of multiple, competing narratives. Perhaps Gap Cave can also help us see a way to avoid that fate.

FIVE

Total Darkness Demonstration

Sympathy for the Devil

❖   ❖   ❖   ❖

Even routine, ordinary darkness is harder and harder to come by these days, with streets and workplaces more and more brightly lit on a grand scale, while screens and even tiny diodes that never go out infiltrate our most personal spaces. It's a testimony to how profoundly the association between light and safety is wound into the everyday landscape.

The show cave is one of the only places people voluntarily encounter truly total darkness, to which your eyes will never adjust, because there is no visual information for them to process. So the total darkness demonstration is absolutely de rigueur. A show cave omits this element of the genre at its peril. A lot of the necessity of its inclusion in the tour derives from the fact that total darkness has got to be, hands down, one of the most menacing feelings you can experience, and a secure encounter with that kind of danger is just the kind of paradox that's possible in this underground theater of convergence.

Let's face it, in the contest of the darkness of the cave versus the light of the show, the show doesn't even stand a chance. Even the oldest show caves have been illuminated for less than a fraction of an instant of a moment compared to the epochs of darkness that have prevailed there. Geologic history makes it obvious, even certain that the cave will outlive the show. You can't help but remember, at some point in the total darkness experience, that this is what it's like in the grave. The cave's permanence reminds us that everything else dies. That kind of massive, patient, antithetical power, you're tempted to attribute to the Devil. You don't get to safely see it revealed every day, so you can't help but want to take a little closer look when the opportunity arises.

❖   ❖   ❖   ❖

You can trace routes all across the Southern Appalachians, the heart of the Bible Belt, by connecting the sites deeded over to the Devil through the power of place-naming. According to the US Geological Survey, in North

Carolina, Tennessee, Virginia, and West Virginia, the Devil is given possession of many dozens of places: Devil's Forks, Runs, Branches, Traces, Creeks, Gulches, Knobs, and Hollows. His belongings scattered across the terrain include the Devil's Pocket, Darning Needle, Tea Table, Looking Glass, Breakfast Table, Bench, Hopper, and Chimney. The Devil's Hole, Corner, Nest, Den, Kitchen, Garden, Stairs, Racepath, Woodyard, Tanyard, Courthouse, and (of course) Tater Patch form a network of his habitations and haunts. The Devil himself is dismembered like Osiris, with the Devil's Backbone, Neck, Nose, Elbow, and Gut scattered all across the upland South.

This naming isn't any great mystery: the main thing on display in places like these is a vast, brutal power. The jagged and sometimes treacherous terrain typical of these devilish places suggests a malevolent force at work. They're usually places where the bedrock is exposed in a way that is visually fierce and dynamic. Razorback ridges, jagged crags, and impassable terrain all sketch out the skeleton of an unkind demon.

But there's an element of humor here, too. The Devil often appears in his guise as a vain sophisticate, not just as a destructive brute. He appreciates a good Tea Table and owns a large Looking Glass. At the same time, he's pretty busy gardening, quarrying, tanning hides, as he ekes out a living out of the rough patches of an earth that is not only a magical mystery but also a resource to be developed. In that respect it's straight-up American pastoral, the verge where the lines between nature and artifice blur. In these devilish names, savagery and evil meet the Protestant work ethic.

And yet so often these bedeviled places are interesting and pleasant, downright civilized places to be. I'm kind of an enthusiast for them myself, having passed some good nights camping at the Devil's Looking Glass. This towering cliff in a bend of the Nolichucky River is mentioned in the accounts of the area's earliest Anglo-European explorers, supposedly a sacred site of the Cherokee. A favorite hangout when I was in college was the Devil's Marbleyard, a vast rock glacier filling a holler on the side of the Blue Ridge, creating a boulder-hopping playground hundreds of yards wide and tall. Drawn by the geologic novelty that gave it its name, lots of people come to enjoy these satanic sites, usually without any negative consequences for themselves or the land, beyond some litter and a few sprained ankles.

Yet for all their charms, Devil's sites are often the kind of places where somebody has, at some point, fallen and gotten killed, where signs warn you away from edges. Of course, for a certain kind of tourist those signs just serve as an attractor, not a deterrent. Even for those of us not destined to end up in a local news brief about the area man killed when he ignored the warning signs to get a selfie with the waterfall in the background, that whiff of danger is part of the appeal. Even when there's almost no immediate threat involved, there's still a sense of being in the presence of malevolent forces. This place has a sinister backstory: it's been trouble before and could be again.

These Devil's Whatnots around the southern mountains are kissing cousins to show caves, where a legitimate element of risk is part of the appeal of any trip underground. And like the Devil's places, even if there's little in the way of actual risk, there's nonetheless a sense of being part of a larger story of danger defied.

❖   ❖   ❖   ❖

That's why show caves that don't include some semblance of a total darkness demonstration are very rare. That moment when the lights go out is the purest distillation of the undercurrent of menace in the cavern.

I was a couple of years into this project when I collected an example of a darkness-free show cave. I was roaming well outside of my Appalachian home base, when I found myself at Inner Space, a cavern in Georgetown, Texas, twenty miles north of Austin. It's a 25-million-year-old cave in 75-million-year-old East Texas limestone, but it wasn't until 1963 that drilling for overpass construction on Interstate 35 revealed the existence of spacious rooms beneath this patch of Texas plain. Living creatures had access to the cave for the first time since sinkhole entrances filled in over 25,000 years ago. Then the living creatures in question were peccaries and ground sloths, sabretooths and mammoths, all now long extinct.

The highway workers bored a large test hole and took turns being lowered into the cavern on a drill bit to explore the expansive cavern. The cavers soon followed. Before 1963 was out, members of the Texas Speleological Society had mapped over 7,000 feet of lavishly decorated cave, passages lined with formations of all description. Almost as quickly, local businessmen formed the Georgetown Corporation and began development of a show cave infrastructure: insurance, permits, lighting, walkways, staff; construction, decoration, inspection, taxation; and thus a gift shop now sits atop a funicular railway. By 1966, Inner Space Caverns was open for business. It's a physical space that went from lying almost entirely outside of all human awareness for 25 million years to being a corporate revenue stream inside of three years.

And there I was on an October Sunday, in town for the wedding of a friend with a few hours to kill before an early-evening ceremony. I sat on a bench at a picnic table, watching kids pan for gold at a birthday party, waiting for my tour to be called.

Teenage cave guides in unisex Inner Space polos, khakis, and sneakers hung around the fringes of the birthday, helping move the mostly Spanish-speaking group of first-grade-ish kids and their parents and assorted well-wishers from the cake to the piñata to the miniature water tank and rough board sluices of the Inner Space Mining companies. There the kids, with varying degrees of enthusiasm, sifted through the provided buckets of soil looking for chips of gemstones and occasional flakes of actual gold amid the sand and gravel. Finally, the main event: the guides rounded up the whole operation and headed inside to ride down the incline railway and start their cavern tour.

At that time I had a four- and a six-year-old at home, so I was well briefed about kids' birthday parties. Back home in the Chicago suburb I call Kidtopia, the sites that host these events form the Birthday Party Circuit. My wife and I shipped kids off to birthday parties at bowling alleys, gymnastics studios, indoor playgrounds, laser tag, children's museums, trampoline parks, and racquet clubs. The particular activity is less important than the criteria that it be organized but not rigid, active but not rigorous, wholesome but not tedious, vaguely edifying, and above all safe as milk (with a soy alternative for the lactose intolerant).

I felt a little doubtful that a show cave could pass the Kidtopia birthday party litmus test. Back in the Appalachian Valley, all the show caves reverberate with the presence of folks who worked around the unsafe, crumbling edges of society: the runaway slaves, the Civil War deserters, the treasure seekers, gentleman explorers, and entrepreneurial promoters; the vandals and partiers and outlaws and frauds; scientists, mystics, eccentrics. There's none of that here. And—not coincidentally, I'd say—there's no encounter with total darkness, no taste of distilled fear. (Hovering parents, you may relax.)

That element of holy terror, the kind of reaction that made an 1876 writer visiting Weyer's Cave declare "if the interesting and the awful are the elements of the sublime, here sublimity reigns in her own domain," is absent at Inner Space. Instead, the visitor's experience is more like that of online reviewer Debra C. at insiderpages.com, who declares Inner Space "a wonderful place to go to get out of the house on a hot summer day" with a "Huge parking lot located on the interstate highway." "The tour guide was a bit silly but kept our children entertained," declares John W. "He gave his opinion on the formations and also filled us in with bits of history as well." Arturo C. adds, "Avoid the snack bar and souvenir shop if you can and it is a GREAT value." Inner Space, it seems, is a marvel, but not quite a wonder.

The fact that this cave was pristine when developers discovered it has somehow made it more "natural" but less "wild." Having been spared the smearing of the view by vandalism, resource extractive industry, and earlier layers of commerce and custom, Inner Space arguably offers a remarkably clear view of the deep, distant past of this place. There's no human clutter obscuring the record of geologic time, save, of course, the apparatus of the show cave itself, the lights that they never turn all the way off. The amount and variety of speleothems, and every one free of vandalism, are truly remarkable.

But part of the wildness of the Appalachian show caves come from an edgier kind of wildness that's all too human. Here at Inner Space, no human foibles or trauma besmirch the birthday-party-friendly clean and healthy experience. Somehow, the Devil is less scary when he isn't intervening in the affairs of humans; fact is, the serpent in the Garden didn't have a lot to do until Adam showed up. Debra C. delivers the final verdict online: "With the recent addition of gem mining, my kids always look forward to going."

It feels like an important cultural and social function of the show cave has been lost in this particular case, where the drama of creation meets the birthday party circuit. The cave showcases elemental forces at work but never brings them down to the human scale. The power is present here, but there's no sense of human agency in the vast, violent drama of change. Something crucial about the show cave experience has to do with being in the vicinity of something primal, perhaps something sinister, even macabre — especially when that specter takes human form. The show cave is the preserve of something dangerous that, on closer inspection, looks a lot like us.

❖   ❖   ❖   ❖

Perhaps the most important thing we learn at that moment on the tour when the lights go off is that we are in a place that is still quite dangerous. Lighting is a thin veneer on the surface of a place not made for us. But to really add that electric current of dread, it takes other people. The abjection of total darkness gives you a dose of an unfeeling, inhuman eternity. The awareness that there might be others lurking in that abyss adds a more metaphysical malevolence to that environment's grim, physical indifference. There's a pervasive sense that this is a place that could bring out the worst in others, and maybe even in ourselves.

Sympathy for the Devil

In the show caves of the Appalachian Valley, having that encounter with both human and nonhuman menace in a controlled setting is a big part of what folks are paying for, I think. Nobody in their right mind wants to be Eric Rudolph or Lester Ballard, but lots of folks would pay to catch a glimpse of where they were coming from.

Of course, in cave country, there's always ways to get it for free, if you know where to look. The National Speleological Society's survey of the Tennessee mountains I grew up in has so far documented the existence of over 10,000 caves of at least twenty-five feet in length. Most of those caves, however, can be found only by people who know exactly what they're looking for—cave enthusiasts "ridgewalking," as they term it, roaming around the countryside on foot, seeking likely spots for a cave opening. Still, a few caves in the area are widely known enough, and accessible enough, to become destination hangouts for all kinds of folks, not just the hard-core cavers.

Here the stakes get a little higher, the encounter with darkness a lot less regulated. This is the world of the reckless, amateur cave explorer, out for pleasure, not for knowledge, lacking anything resembling the seriousness of the speleologist. These caves are technically, I suppose, classifiable as "wild," but in practice it's wild more in the sense that a party is wild, not that an animal is wild. Unlit, undeveloped caves are just plain dangerous, and yet despite—or maybe because of—the actual threat of injury and death, they remain popular sites for outlaw culture, graffiti and drinking and fireworks and drugs, celebrations of the seamier side of the Appalachian experience.

Growing up in East Tennessee I joined my friends on a few occasions in exploring these DIY show caves. What we termed "party caves" provided a raw, irresponsible, and adrenaline-laced experience, a volatile mixture of the profound and profoundly dangerous. In the party cave, you can enjoy as much of a total darkness demonstration as you so desire. But if you're not careful (and if you are there at all, you probably aren't), you could find yourself stuck in a darkness demonstration that has no end. No guide is going to throw the switch for you; there's no switch to throw.

One choice cave for that kind of expedition is out in the woods just beyond the Johnson City limits, in the foothills of the Unaka Range. Carter Saltpeter Cave (I learned the name much later; at the time it was "that cave out by the Laurels") is about a half-mile back off a country road. As the name suggests, the cave was mined for saltpeter back in the nineteenth century, so it is not exactly a secret. In some ways crawling around in it is more like exploring an abandoned factory than it is communing with nature. Speleologist Thomas Barr, in his 1960 *Caves of Tennessee*, describes it as "a large and well-known cave, but very hard to find." You've got to know somebody to get there.

These days a prefab house with a long rolling lawn fills the site where once an overgrown pasture provided cover for small groups of enthusiasts discreetly cutting across private property, heading back up the hill to the open maw of the cave, a steep muddy scramble down and through a large stone archway into darkness.

❖　❖　❖　❖

One autumn afternoon about twenty-five years ago, the three guys I shared a house with, Patrick, Ethan, and Robert, and I were that party of enthusiasts heading nonchalantly but quickly up the hill, concealed by the still-dense brambles that swallow the well-worn path to the cave. We were four single guys in our early twenties, sharing the kind of house maintained by kids with brains and no money, getting by on graduate stipends and food service work and student loans.

We were like a B-team version of the A-Team: Patrick and Robert were the art jocks in work boots and thrift store topcoats, a matched set of sturdy, temperamental Irishman (Patrick) and gangly, florid Scotsman (Robert). Their art reflected their dispositions: Patrick abstract but muscular, Robert given to more lavish reworkings of mythology, personal and otherwise.

Ethan and I were more garden-variety grad school weirdos, covering the math and cultural history and social psychology in our little faculty as we tinkered on master's degrees. We were also kind of a complementary set, Ethan wiry and droll, the science officer, me more the loquacious walking dictionary, the cultural studies droid. In the movie adaptation of our lives, we were more like the ones who'd be back in the orbiter, advising the away team over the comlink.

Despite our delusions about our marketability in Hollywood as a crack team of Liberal Arts specialists, we all worked in food service, having glommed en masse onto cooking, cleaning, waiting tables, and generally hanging out at a local vegetarian restaurant. And we lived a few blocks from the regional university we all attended in some form, in a ramshackle house on the shabby side of a good neighborhood. Daily life included an ongoing cat-and-mouse game with an (often-justifiably) apoplectic landlord. We had to remain alert to surprise visits from this tense, bitter retiree named Horton, whose soaring blood pressure compelled him to bite through the butts of the Parliaments he chain-smoked.

Easily bored, as our kind tends to be, we were ever alert for a cheap thrill.

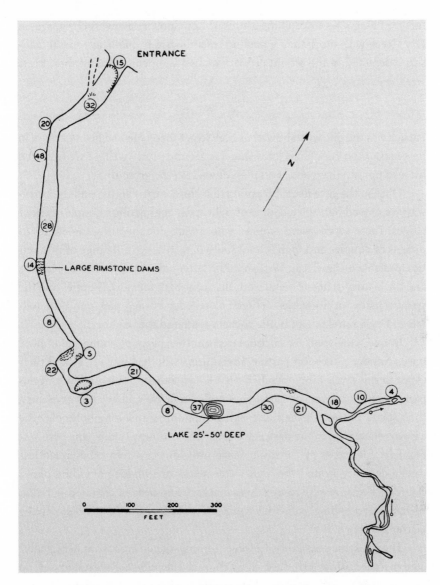

ENTRANCE

LARGE RIMSTONE DAMS

LAKE 25'-50' DEEP

0   100   200   300
FEET

Carter Saltpeter Cave, Carter County, 1955, by L. C. Johnson, L. P. Foster,
and J. W. Tamblyn. (From Thomas Barr's 1961 *Caves of Tennessee*,
Tennessee Geological Survey Bulletin 64).

Sunny weekends were prime time for rolling out to one of the stops on the
circuit of outdoor party spots scattered among our own stretch of Appalachian mountains. There was the Big Rock, a scenic overlook and sandy beach
on the Nolichucky River, just downstream from the aforementioned Devil's
Looking Glass; Beauty Spot up on Unaka Mountain, a ridgetop meadow per-

fect for flying kites or catching a sunset; Zep Spot, a narrow rocky gorge on Dry Creek with more than a passing resemblance to the heavy metal landscape depicted in the album artwork of Led Zeppelin IV. And then there was the cave.

◆　◆　◆　◆

Patrick was the one who showed us how to get there. He had been in there in his teens, often enough to know his way around pretty well, so we followed his lead up into the woods and then down into the ground.

Once in the cave itself, breathing that close, earthy air beyond the entryway, we moved through a couple of tight spots connecting a couple of wider spaces. These rooms were scoured with graffiti documenting the names of dozens of couples and high school football teams, the full range of profanities available in American English in the latter half of the twentieth century, and the history of heavy metal from Black Sabbath forward. Empties and the spent remains of fireworks—shreds of powder-burned paper and the telltale red twig remnants of bottle rockets—littered the confines.

In one wide spot, we encountered another party of young men, more bored Sunday afternoon partier/adventurers who had already staked their claim to this space. They perched on a ledge, already adding a few empties to the joint, bottle rockets surely not far behind. We said hey but gave them their space, passing through their pleasure dome into a long borehole. The cavern rolled away in the dark like a prehistoric subway tunnel. The path was regularly cut across by rimstone dams, walls of stone formed by relentless calcite deposits around the high-water marks of still, long-standing pools. Some of the dams were two or three feet high and needed clambering rather than merely stepping over, but we pressed on deeper and deeper beneath the Carter County hills.

The constant possibility, however remote, of getting lost in here generated mental static as I trudged along through the puddles, heaved myself up over another rimstone barrier. I remember asking myself, for the first time, are you inside or outside when you're in a cave? You can make a good case for either answer, I decided. ("You're inside the outside" is also acceptable.)

The Eagle Scout in me, though, was fretting over the fact that we were taking so few of the most reasonable precautions. That's part of the game: placing yourself in danger, defying common sense. Lacking any real enemies, we settled for threatening ourselves.

As a result, my baseline level of anxiety was pretty high. Some of it was just being in this kind of space without the benefit of the accoutrements of

Sympathy for the Devil

a show cave, especially that sense that somebody is seeing to your safety. Instead, other people present a vague threat and have left a legacy of malicious damage to the cave itself. I couldn't help but sense that the cave could have its revenge yet. Even in this easy-to-follow borehole, I could imagine crevices leading off to other rooms above and below, terminating in every case in absolute, pitiless darkness.

For our foolish and ill-equipped party that day, though, real danger remained only a threat. And the adrenaline that threat elicited was part of the reason for being there. My fears of getting lost never came to pass, and our collective need to just explore was met. In fact, we felt a sense of accomplishment that day when we found our way to the source of a small stream, where, crowded in the damp crawlway, we broke out the six-pack we'd lugged with us all the way to celebrate "discovering" the terminus.

It's an old impulse for roving bands of white boys to celebrate when you reach the edge of the map. I always thought of our little party when, traveling the valley, I'd pass by the marker in Swift Run Gap, Madison County, Virginia, noting the spot where, in 1716, Virginia's royal governor, Alexander Spotswood, and a group of his buddies who dubbed themselves the "Knights of the Golden Horseshoe" reached the crest of the Blue Ridge.

Spotswood's scribes reported that, after that momentous occasion, "We had a good dinner, and after it we got the men together and loaded all their arms, and we drank the King's health in champagne and fired a volley, the Princess's health in Burgundy and fired a volley, and all the rest of the royal family in claret and a volley. We drank the Governor's health and fired another volley. We had several sorts of liquors, viz., Virginia red wine and white wine, Irish usquebaugh, brandy, shrub, two sorts of rum, champagne, canary, cherry punch, water, cider, &c." I'm sure if they'd had bottle rockets they'd have littered Swift Run Gap with red sticks and powder-burned paper.

There we were indulging in our delusions of grandeur again, four damp guys sitting in the mud in a cramped little stream passage somewhere beneath Carter County, Tennessee, imagining we were partaking of a long-lived tradition. One thing we did have in common with the Knights of the Golden Horseshoe was that we looked forward to going back to our warm, dry homes at the end of the expedition.

Like most forms of play (case in point, recreational gem mining), ours was a reenactment of an obsolete form of work. We were only re-creating an exploring expedition for fun, not, like Spotswood's boys, firing the opening salvo of the new phase of an imperial landgrab and ethnic-cleansing project. They were coming to impose the grid, while we were taking refuge from it.

Budweiser tallboys would suffice in place of usquebaugh. We celebrated our achievement and went back home to face another week of work and school and life with a solid afternoon of interesting, atypical sights and sounds and some stories to laugh about for a long time to come—a more modest expedition, but in our own way, much more pure of motive. We just wanted to explore.

◆　　◆　　◆　　◆

Just as Spotswood's opening of the valley to white settlement would only temporarily sate the colonists' hunger for land, however, our expedition to the back of Carter Saltpeter Cave satisfied that restless need for edgy fun only for a time. A few months later it was early spring, and we were all shaking off the effects of dark winter days in a drafty old house. We'd been on particularly bad terms with Horton, as we engaged in a vicious cycle of us not paying him promptly and him never ever fixing anything. When we asked him to repair our baseboard heaters, which had been giving out one by one through February, he brought us a stack of secondhand electric blankets, which issued disconcertingly smoky smells when plugged in.

We had seen the fireworks of the first Gulf War pass by, and the surge of jingoistic patriotism and the spectacle of the first ever video feeds from smart bombs and helicopter gun sights was enervating. The alternative rock we listened to pivoted from its poppier origins in "college radio" to the early days of grunge as we moped through classes and projects and subsistence jobs like the Gen X slacker stereotypes we unwittingly fulfilled.

In this chilly damp season, Robert was also processing personal tragedy, the death of his mother, which had turned some of his romantic excess into something a little more nihilistic, both in life and in art. And he was going it alone, the rest of us never having experienced any such thing. Bound up as our kind tended to be with our own melodramas, we probably didn't give him the kind of support he needed.

Our lifestyle writ large needed a whack upside the head. A dose of cave adrenaline seemed like just the thing, and there we four were again, on the path through the now-withered thickets, into the trees and under the hill.

Things were pretty routine through the initial rooms and down the cave's main borehole, right up until we reached the pond. That rimstone-lined corridor eventually opens out into a domed ceiling above, and below, down a steep mudbank, a placid, round pond maybe fifty feet across. Shining flashlights down into the still and clear water revealed that the room

Sympathy for the Devil

was really an oval, the bottom dropping out steeply below the surface of the water, mirroring the domed ceiling above. Given the shadows and the optical tricks of the water, it was impossible to guess the depth, but I know that when we shone our lights on coins we tossed in the pond, we saw them fall and keep on falling.

Patrick had shown us the route across the pond the last time we were here, the previous fall. It would have been impossible for me to intuit it myself. On that last trip, after pausing to take in the scene at the pond and to speculate on what a good time you could have down here if you brought in a bunch of lights and guitars and pretty girls, we followed Patrick down to the edge of the water on the left side of the room. There he explained that we would follow a narrow ledge around the edge of the pond, from about 7 to 11 on a clock face, and climb the bank on the opposite shore where our passage continued.

The water reached about knee deep, and while chilly, the effect was not so shocking since the air and water were the same temperature, and the air so damp that already, we were used to our clothes feeling soggy. Because our journey to the end of the tunnel from there was not too long, and once we returned to the surface, it was just short walk to the car, and outside it was a sunny autumn late afternoon, we weren't worried about hypothermia. (Caver's Note: we most definitely should have been.) After the previous fall's successful outing, we were proud of ourselves for adding a mild but manageable challenge to the day, and seeing a part of the cave that few of the more casual visitors ever had the gumption to reach.

But the last time we were here was a warmer and drier time of year. This time, we could already tell that the cave had a little more water in it than before, as the water behind those rimstone dams reached almost knee-deep in places where just puddles lay in our path before. And somehow, even though the temperature of the cave is relatively constant, there was just a little more nip in the air—maybe just from the fact that we were already a little damp and chilly by the time we walked up to the cave entrance, or because our feet got wetter sooner. Now on this damp late winter afternoon, as we slipped into the pond at the start of the ledge, first Patrick, then Ethan, then me, then Robert, we each took a slight breath as the water gripped skin. Then we gasped again, more audibly this time, as it quickly got much deeper than it was before—up past my waist, and I'm a tall man.

I was in third place on purpose. Not exactly the most coordinated person in the world, I wanted to see Patrick and Ethan, both wiry and sure-footed, successfully negotiate the underwater ledge ahead of me. I would come along behind, having gathered as much data as I could for my own traverse. I would have trailed behind tall and lanky Robert, too, but he held the rearguard position in a death grip.

Like last time, my ongoing twinging of nerves and slight but constant worry was an accent within the larger complex of sensations coming from being in the cave. I was expecting it this time, and so it was maybe even a little less disturbing than the previous visit. Robert was having the opposite experience. Perhaps because of the amalgamation of tragic experiences he'd had since our last outing, in Robert's head, the anxiety had that day become, a dominant, almost solitary force, a single voice of screaming panic. It was a testament to his loyalty to his friends that he was there at all, because he was not happy from the moment we set foot underground.

You could always tell when Robert was really suffering because his presence, normally big, ebullient, and self-deprecating, suddenly evaporated entirely, replaced by an otherworldly solemnity. On that day Robert's suffering was intense and intensifying. By the time we reached the pond, he would make basic communication and follow directions but otherwise remained very nearly mute. About the only thing he said to me on the trip was to half-gasp, half-growl "I've lost my light!" when he dropped it in a shallow stream. He stared at it intently but uncomprehendingly until I grabbed the flashlight out of the water and handed it back to him. As we started across the pond he was ashen, completely impassive, as the water rose toward his chest.

What I hadn't factored into my little plan to stay in third was that, as they passed across the ledge, Patrick and Ethan generated clouds of sediment in the water. I hadn't noticed it so much in knee-deep water on the previous trip, but in three-and-a-half feet of turbid pond, not being able to see where I was putting my feet, or where they had put theirs, was a bit more of a problem. Feeling edgier still, I kept one hand on the cave wall, my flashlight lashed to my other hand, and I felt with my feet along the uneven, slippery, unseeable route.

Then there was a sound I'd never heard before: a single, reverberating CLOOP. It was the sound of glassy cave water closing over the head of my friend Robert. I looked around. Robert had slipped right off the ledge, perhaps taken a step and missed it entirely, and fallen slowly but inexorably, spinning gradually so that he was facing back toward the ledge as he receded into the pond. He had not called out, nor swore, nor waved his arms to resist the loss of balance, nor created a commotion of any kind. Instead he slipped into the water like a newly christened ship in a silent movie.

Sympathy for the Devil

Robert had fallen away from the silt cloud around our feet, and I saw his face just an inch or so below the surface of the water. It shone beatifically in my flashlight beam, while behind him, his flashlight tumbled down through the water, end over end, coming to rest by happy chance pointing straight up, illuminating the pond and casting the vague, dappled patterns of the now-rippling surface on the walls and ceiling.

I reached out and grabbed Robert by the shirt-front and pulled him back to the ledge. Emerging from the water into the newly illuminated room, he came to. Holy shit! we said to each other many, many times in the brief conversation that followed: Holy shit! Then, by the dying light of his submerged flashlight, we made our way across the ledge to our companions.

We didn't make it all the way to the terminus that day; even we could see that we'd played it pretty much to the limit. Forgoing the tradition of the explorer's toast, we hauled ourselves back to the house chastened, shivering, and spent in our clammy, cave-soaked clothes. We huddled around the space heaters we'd swiped from our parents' homes (cursing Horton for making the thefts necessary) and started drafting the oral history of this adventure. And home seemed like a much better place to be as a result.

❖   ❖   ❖   ❖

The trips to Carter Saltpeter Cave were never going to be the family-friendly, carefully risk-managed show cave trips of so many family vacations. No AC lighting, no pavement, no wisecracking guide, no safety equipment, no toy tomahawks in the gift shop for afterward. The emotional experience was much more assertive and complex. The implied threat that makes show caves harmlessly thrilling became a more clear and present danger, and the source of the threat was our own selves, the gear we didn't bring, and the baggage we did.

Whatever their risks and rewards, these trips weren't what any decent, seasoned cavers would call "caving." In fact, cavers have a term for what we were doing: spelunking. "Spelunking" is a word that non-cavers just love. Practically every time I have discussed this project with friends, colleagues, acquisitions editors, or family members, there's a moment where whomever I'm talking to will almost light up at the opportunity to insert the word "spelunking" into the conversation. Let's face it, it's fun to say.

Cavers do not like the word. I've never heard an explanation of this distaste, but I suspect it has to do with those same phonics that cause us civilians such delight. "Spelunking," with its unlikely jumble of consonants and thudding short /u/, sounds like a bunch of twenty-something housemates mucking around underground on a boring Sunday afternoon. "Caving" is so much more efficient and purposeful, with its bright vowels and crisp treble notes evoking preparation, knowledge, and a certain moral seriousness.

Or so I sense from a statement like this one in the *National Speleological Society Bulletin*, the 2006 edition of the eagerly-awaited annual "Cave Accident Report" issue. "'Cavers,'" the editor notes, "generally consider 'spelunkers' to be people who have no real knowledge or understanding of caves and caving safety, but who decide to enter a cave anyway, usually without proper equipment." A popular caver t-shirt puts it more concisely: on the front, "What's the difference between cavers and spelunkers?" And on back: "Cavers rescue spelunkers."

The Cave Accident Report helps educate its caver readership toward the goal of controlling, even vanquishing the element of risk underground, but it also provides an opportunity to heckle the spelunkers a little bit. The editors and contributors compile the statistics—four killed, seventeen injured, not including cave-diving accidents—and categorize the incidents in a concise catalog of human misery: "Lost . . . Flooding . . . Illness . . . Exhaustion . . . Stuck . . . Bad Air." Then each incident receives a brief synopsis and a line or two of pointed commentary from volunteer contributors.

Sometimes it comes across a little smug: "This could have been a self rescue with a caver with more experience," one author sniffs about a seventeen-year-old girl stuck in Clay Cave, West Virginia. Of a couple on a novice caving trip who couldn't make the ascent back to the entrance, the reporter notes, "Both Donald and Robin were reported to be overweight. That, the tight entrance, and their inexperience and exhaustion contributed to the problem. They also had no packs." Pity Donald and Robin, fat, packless, spelunking losers.

It can even get a little bit heartless: of the death by falling of an arrowhead-hunter in a pit cave in Missouri, the reporter snips, "Need it be said that people should not hand-over-hand down a rope without a light when they cannot see the bottom?" It feels like unseemly victim-blaming, except for the fact that in cases like this one, the victim really is to blame.

Like, I imagine, most of the guests of Carter Saltpeter Cave, Patrick, Ethan, Robert, and I were a Cave Accident Report punchline waiting to happen. The thing that's so infuriating about caver condescension is that, of course, they are right. Trips like the one I'm describing here aren't safe. They can too easily result in damage to the fragile cave biome, the wasted energy of an emergency rescue, not to mention injury or death for the spelunker. My little band of useless superheroes hadn't followed even the most basic

Sympathy for the Devil

guidelines for safe caving. We weren't carrying three light sources apiece. We didn't let someone know where we were going and when we would be back.

Spelunkers, I think, bring a kind of populist grudge to the whole enterprise. It somehow seems unfair to exclude ordinary folks from the underground experience. It seemed reasonable, somehow, to the two teens at Snail Shell Cave (Tennessee) — lost, the Accident Report notes, due to "several very poor decisions" — to explain themselves to their rescuers by saying that they "just wanted to explore," as if that's something we should be able to do. Even if it means that sometimes folks get hurt. Even if it means they hurt themselves.

❖   ❖   ❖   ❖

Cavers, on the other hand, are dedicated to the proposition that no one should ever get hurt. An injury-free underground would represent the triumph of their values, no packless losers clogging up the crawlways, only those with the training and the values to leave no trace of their passage. The ideal cave, in this view, is one with no record of human use at all, the venerated "virgin cave."

For the caving community, the threat of the human encounter with the cave is to the cave as much as to the humans. When they run off the spelunkers, cavers aren't just rescuing people, they're rescuing the cave from those who would deflower her. To a caver, Carter Saltpeter Cave is a veritable damsel in distress. The NSS and its many various sub- and affiliate organizations are always on the lookout for the opportunity to work with the landowner who has the risk-management misfortune to include a party cave among their holdings. The cavers will facilitate the construction of bat-friendly gates and even engage in cleanup activities in the cave, usually negotiating, in exchange, exclusive rights to exploration of the cave and an extra key to the bat gate. The caver community is the rare group of enthusiasts dedicated to making the object of their passion less popular.

The hard-core caver might see Inner Space, by contrast, as an opportunity lost, an acceptable compromise, but a compromise nevertheless. It's a shame to lose an untouched network of gorgeously decorated, fossil-filled caverns — so full of virgin cave it's practically a convent — to the birthday party set, but at least it keeps both cave and human visitor out of trouble. Still, the best-case scenario for cavers is one that holds the shuffling masses at bay, closing up the cave to the public forever. One usual item on the cave rehab checklist, as we saw in the case of Gap Cave, is the removal of the traces of attempted commercialization.

The cavers form a kind of priesthood that has sworn off that reckless, profligate element of risk. Their vocation trades foolhardy pleasures for a more disciplined, ascetic kind of satisfaction, rooted in devotion to something bigger and older and weirder than us. The spelunker's cave is a profoundly social place, whereas the caver's ideal is a cave that has never had human contact, which, ironically, as humans they can never achieve. It's their version of original sin. Leaving no trace at all, emerging unscathed: these are the highest forms of accomplishment. The high priests of legend are said to have the power to enter a virgin (cave) without defiling her.

Like any priesthood, its initiates live up to these ideals to varying degrees. Rare is the caver who doesn't have some story to tell featuring a dicey gamble undertaken, or a failure of training or protocol, or a brush with temptation that exposed the expedition to real danger. With the kinds of challenges these folks seek to undertake, there's no need to amp up the risk factor by cutting any corners. The cave itself is dangerous enough as it is: there's more than one seasoned, experienced caver included in the Accident Report.

Cavers' behavior underground is (ideally, anyway) as orderly and restrained as spelunkers' conduct is transgressive and disruptive. When cavers gain access to a new cave, the first order of business is to properly secure it from public attention. But then ritual and reason require that the cave be surveyed. Since the advent of modern surveying methods in the late nineteenth century, cavers have been dragging chains and sighting scopes through challenging subterranean landscapes, a task made much less strenuous with today's laser technology. Producing a truly masterful cave map requires cartography in three dimensions, cross sections and profiles, special notations for passage height, a complex mapping symbology for indicating types of formations, pits and slopes, the interconnections of passages and rooms totally ungoverned by plane geometry. Oh, and it needs to be readable in low light.

It's a project that is diametrically opposed to the spelunker aesthetic. For spelunkers, the cave provides a proscenium for little melodramas, transformed to fit the needs of restless, casually destructive people. The caver's survey, on the other hand, painstakingly represents the cave via a method that aspires to capture the cave exactly as it is.

This cartographic mission seems very rational and empirical, and it is in its methods, but in other ways it's almost mystical. Often as not, all this surveying doesn't serve any practical purpose; its scientific value is real but slight, more old-school descriptive science than a project of inquiry. Often as not, the only person who will even use the map for navigation purposes is the mapmaker him- or herself, since this mapping is being done by people who intend to make the cave less accessible to the world at large.

Cavers often guard their map collections very closely; even other cavers are held at bay. Published maps will often include the minutest details of a cave's interior but leave off the latitude and longitude of the entrance. The NSS *Bulletin* once published a reminder to its readers that they should leave written instructions for donating their map collection to the NSS — too many hidden caches of maps, they believed, were being lost to posterity upon the death of their owners. Most maps are intended to help people find their way someplace they've never been. Not these maps. These maps are the illuminated manuscripts of a mystery religion. The initiates have recognized the tendency of these places, through the way people use them, to become devilish, and their order therefore labors to keep it on the side of the angels, pristine and unattainable.

❖   ❖   ❖   ❖

What we're seeing here is a kind of continuum. There is a range of ways different kinds of people respond to the element of danger ever present in interactions between people and caves. And there are different kinds of caves as a result.

In this physical and metaphysical struggle, show caves inevitably fall somewhere on the spectrum between virgin cave heaven and spelunking hell. The spelunker loves the show cave's ready access to the social experience of hanging out underground but chafes at the sanitizing rules, the unrequited desire to see where that little hole goes. The caver can be cheered by the fact that the show cave is secured and protected but worry over the fact that hundreds of thousands of new people every year know where the cave is and might be interested in coming back under less restrictive conditions if the show cave operation, as so often happens, goes under.

A show cave's place on the spectrum is never static. Indeed, the history of any show cave can be seen as the story of the cave's movement back and forth along that spectrum, drifting back and forth between the angels and the devils on its shoulders.

SIX

The Legacy of Gene Monday

The Stories of Cherokee Caverns and Indian Cave

❖　❖　❖　❖

The push and pull between light and darkness, angels and devils, cavers and spelunkers is an essential part of the dynamic relationship between nature and culture that show caves bring to life, another set of conflicts and contradictions that the show cave artfully suspends. Down in East Tennessee, in the countryside surrounding Knoxville, are two almost-vanished show caves that dramatize this clash. These two caves mark out extreme ends of the spectrum. They are still show caves, but only just barely. One has gone over to the caver and the other to the spelunker end of the scale.

One was known in its earliest commercial incarnation (ca. 1929) as Gentry's Cave, for owner Margaret Crudington Gentry, whose Crudington forebears owned the land for generations. It has gone on to earn the distinction of the show cave operated under the most names. After Gentry's Cave came Grand Caverns, Atomic Caverns, Caveman's Palace, Palace Caverns, Caverns of the Ridge, and the entirely too wordy Cherokee Firesite Ceremonial Caverns. The spinner finally stopped on the nondescript Cherokee Caverns. A smallish but extravagantly decorated cave bearing evidence of human use dating to prehistory, it burrows into a bluff on the southern banks of the Clinch River near a crossroads called Solway, northwest of Knoxville near Oak Ridge.

The other has been known as Indian Cave since the white folks started arriving in the area. It opened for business as Indian Cave Park in 1924 and has operated under that name or something close to it more or less ever since. (Sometimes it's been hard to tell if it's in operation.) Indian Cave's vast entryway overlooking the Holston River in Grainger County to Knoxville's northeast opens onto a long, wide stream passage winding over a mile beneath the rolling hills of the valley bottom. Contemporary cavers have found tools and bones of Paleoindians, the far end of an almost unbroken chain of human occupation. Indian Cave has beckoned to travelers through the region as long as there have been travelers through the region. The intertwined fates of Indian Cave and Cherokee Caverns illustrate the struggles that take place over how and to what extent people should be allowed, even encouraged, to brush up against the cave's dangers.

❖   ❖   ❖   ❖

The fates of the two caves were joined in the summer of 1947. The precise date is a mystery, but it's some time around then when Gene Monday decided to take the family for a Sunday drive. Gene (full name Eugene Monday Jr.) was forty-three and a prominent Knoxville real-estate investor and property manager. He had taken over as the head of Gene Monday Realty upon his father's death the year before and was on his way to becoming one of Knoxville's leading property owners and philanthropists.

That day Gene Monday Jr. apparently decided he was going to buy not one but two show caves. When he and his family visited Cherokee Caverns — then known as Grand Caverns — the heirs of Margaret Crudington Gentry, who had passed away the year before, were looking to sell the cave operation. Monday found Indian Cave in a similar situation. Longtime operator Hunter B. Chapman, who also ran Shenandoah Caverns in Virginia, died suddenly in his apartment at the Shenandoah Caverns Hotel on May 21, 1942, at the age of seventy-four. When Monday closed the sale it was with Chapman's son Douglas, a doctor in Richmond, Virginia. Asked why he decided to do it, Monday told the local paper, "I stopped by on an outing with my family and just got interested."

You have to wonder if he had his own father in mind that day, out and about with his family, maybe thinking about bigger issues of mortality and eternity. And here were not one but two family businesses that had lost their patriarchs. Or maybe he was seeing through the eyes of a man who had become the leader where once he had been heir apparent and entertained notions of how to put his own stamp on his own family business, and here was a really distinctive angle, the kind of thing that could give you a hook.

Or maybe he was just having fun and seeing some legitimately cool stuff and enjoying the kind of beautiful day you can have tooling around the back roads through the countryside north of Knoxville, in the ancient grooves of the Tennessee River headwaters, the Clinch and the Holston Rivers, draining the northeastern highlands into the Mississippi watershed. It's a nice thing to do to this very day. But that day maybe Gene Monday did it and thought, you know, this is worth investing in.

Or, probably most likely, he had gotten wind of the caves being available, and planned his family outing around checking out the properties. Gene Monday was a successful businessman, somebody who knew how to get a deal done, the kind of guy who does his homework. This play seems consistent with a man of his acumen.

However, after periods of initial prosperity, both caves began to slide back toward the spelunker end of the spectrum, until today both caves are only sort of still operating, even though both are still owned by the Monday family foundation. No billboards guide you from interstates hundreds of miles away; no brochures greet you in the racks of gift shops and rest stops. Indian Cave and Cherokee Caverns are caves that have been to the brink, and their future course is being set now by caretakers who have radically different ideas about who should be in caves and under what conditions.

◆   ◆   ◆   ◆

Of course, I didn't know any of this as I stood in the sun at the end of an unmarked gravel driveway that I drove by three times without noticing, on a sunny spring afternoon in March 2007. I was waiting for cave custodian Jim Whidby at Cherokee Caverns. This was a new thing for me, going to a show cave that didn't advertise its existence, didn't meet me with a polo-shirted guide.

I had come across mentions of Cherokee Caverns after I started my research. I'd seen this cave listed in some old editions of Jeanne and Hal Gurnee's *Guide to American Caves*, though it was conspicuously absent from my most current version. (You can't do this work without picking up a few Gurnee Guides along the way.) I figured I'd learn something worth knowing if I followed up on the mystery when I was in the area for an academic meeting. A few Googles later, I had Jim's name from newspaper articles about the Haunted Cave fundraisers he'd put on at Halloween.

In the early 1990s, right around the time of Gene Monday Jr.'s death, Jim worked out an agreement with the Monday family to become Cherokee Caverns' custodian. In the intervening years, Jim has used the limited proceeds the cave generates to fund a meticulous restoration of the cave's pathways, bridges, and retaining walls. I caught up with Jim by phone at the print shop he operates in his surface life, and he very cheerfully agreed to come out and show me around.

Jim and I passed the afternoon shooting the breeze, talking caves with the zeal of two people who have a lot to say about the subject but rarely encounter somebody else who shares the depth of the enthusiasm. We enjoyed the first really nice days of the spring, standing by the shipping containers that had been retrofitted as a warehouse for maintenance supplies and all the gear for the "Haunted Cave" operation.

Jim opened up the container to show me around soon after we first shook hands. As pleasant as the day was, as I gazed into a metal box filled with carefully organized rows and racks of severed heads, skeletons, fearsome masks and torture devices, it occurred to me that maybe I should have let somebody know that I was coming out here.

As I got to know Jim Whidby, though, I quickly realized I had nothing to fear; everything here, up to and including the Halloween trappings, is dedicated to preventing danger for both the public and the cave.

Jim is in a lot of ways the caver's caver. A short, sturdy, bearded man, late fifties, he devotes a fair piece of his life outside the print shop to caves. He's a lifelong and award-winning member of the National Speleological Society, trained in cave rescue, a veteran surveyor, and a longtime vertical caver, rappelling into otherwise inaccessible wild caves.

He's also a speleohistorian and the owner of a huge archive of cave-related and specifically show cave materials. Despite what he's seen of what spelunkers, left to their own devices, can do to a cave, Jim doesn't have disdain for popular curiosity about caves, nor does he dismiss the idiot-proofed environment of the show cave.

Like me, he's semiprofessionally interested in the way folks think about caves, how they mix what little they know about the actual world underground with their beliefs and imaginings about it. Jim can talk in exhaustive detail about such subterranea as the history of Hollywood depictions of caves and caverns, having acquired copies of films and videos of all genres and eras, as long as they show a cave. And this despite his overall low assessment of the caves of the silver screen. The light's always wrong. But how could it be otherwise? It may be an unsolvable problem in a space where any light at all is unnatural.

Jim has practical experience with these lighting issues: he's let public television documentary crews, makers of car ads, even cable TV's Appalachian melodrama *Christy* use the cavern as a backdrop. He opens the cave to school and church and scout groups and occasional curious enthusiasts like myself. And the proceeds of the Halloween event pay the overhead (more or less). I admire the paradox that Jim's creation of a perfectly safe underground environment is funded by people's willingness to be scared there. Spelunker money spends the same.

The Halloween-filled shipping container and another one right beside it were the only structures standing at the end of the driveway. As Jim told me the story of the show cave, we leaned against his truck across the turnaround from a concrete pad that marked the former location of the restaurant, and beside it a ramp descending to the gate at the arched tunnel entrance to the cave itself. We looked at old pictures and maps and some articles Jim himself had written for the NSS *Bulletin* and the *Journal of Spelean History*. Finally, after Jim asked me if I wanted to go see the cave, he opened up the second shipping container.

In it was the Cavemobile, a little blue electric buggy complete with an NSS bumper sticker and an old caving helmet affixed to the hood. Yes, we were going to tour the cave in an electric buggy Jim used to haul concrete and gravel and handrails. It was like the slowest Disney ride ever: after we scooted down the entry ramp into the cave's foyer, we'd motor a few feet and then Jim would unfold another portion of the story of the cave, its rise and fall and restoration. The Cavemobile was an object lesson in how fully Jim had domesticated a show cave operation that had gone feral.

◆ ◆ ◆ ◆

The beginning of the Gene Monday era saw the cave at its zenith. The first major formation Jim and I drove up to bore this out. Piggybacking on the post–World War II fame of Oak Ridge as the birthplace of the nuclear war, cavern owners in the late 1940s renamed a huge dripstone column "Bikini Atoll." Viewed through that framework, it certainly bears more than a passing resemblance to a full-scale mushroom cloud. But this all came to pass in that brief window of time where atomic blasts signified national triumph, so as Atomic Caverns, modest Gentry's Cave donned a distinctive identity as the show cave of the new frontier.

Jim parked the Cavemobile in a large, low central room, where water percolating up through the thick clay on the floor over the course of millennia resulted in soft little conical formations called "mud geysers," a rarity in Appalachian caves. The overall effect—especially seen through that Atomic Age lens—is like a claymation rendition of the surface of another planet dotted with volcanic cones, straight from the sci-fi B movies that were beginning to proliferate.

And then, to this otherworldly landscape, on a night in 1948, Stardust came—Stardust the "trick horse," accompanied by the "World's Tallest Singing Cowboy," Homer Harris, a seven-footer who had to duck to maneuver. A house band from the stable of local country music promoter, entrepreneur, and politician Cas Walker's radio show backed Harris and Ray Myers, who was, the advertisements proclaimed, born without arms, and thus played his Hawaiian guitar with his feet.

Jim reaches into the bed of the Cavemobile, rifles a file folder, then pro-

Cas Walker's entertainers. Writing on top of photograph reads: "Taken in Atomic Caverns (200 feet) under ground 1948—Cas Walker's entertainers (standing by trick horse Stardust, Ray Myers, born without arms)." Lower label reads: "Atomic Cavern Ballroom Inside Cavern. Homer & Stardust & Cas Walker entertainers, Kelly Family, Ray Mayers, Hack Johnson * Pee Wee Whaley." (Photo courtesy of Jim Whidby)

duces a photograph from his archives: the cowboy and his horse, the neatly dressed musicians, children, family members, and Ray Myers, born without arms. It all looks so antiquated, almost vaudevillian now, but I wonder if, when that picture was taken, it all looked quite progressive. These performers were part of the still-nascent mass media, radio stars (if of a fairly minor magnitude) playing hit songs their audience might be familiar with from shows like the Renfro Valley Barn Dance, the Tennessee Barn Dance, the National Barn Dance, and the Grand Ole Opry. Soon they'd be seeing the likes of these performers on the new medium of television, advertising Cas Walker's chain of grocery stores. This encounter was with the faces and sounds of a new but broadly shared cultural experience.

And yet it was an intensely local experience, not least because it was happening in a space that could literally only happen here, whose very form speaks of the deepest forms of local history. The music they were hearing was grown from their local culture and experience, here in Roy Acuff's old stomping grounds. For that matter the whole Atomic Age could legitimately be said to have been born just over the next hill at the government's Y-12 plant in Oak Ridge, a place where local labor helped change the world in ways that today we're still trying to reckon with. Atomic Caverns was a place an ordinary person from Knox County, Tennessee, could stand in front of a calcite effigy of the nuclear explosion at Bikini Atoll, listening to a Hawaiian guitar that a man from Ohio is playing with his feet, feeling right at home.

A moment like this is, for me, the show cave in full flower, a dreamlike scene in an unimaginably ancient space named for the advent of a new era of human destruction. Performers and audiences and even an extraordinarily domesticated animal came together in a truly anomalous instant, one that fairly bristles with all the vectors of history and possibility intersecting there.

❖   ❖   ❖   ❖

But like many dreams of that day, it couldn't last. The Atomic Age theming failed to have a durable allure, just as in the culture at large, the terror of mutually assured destruction replaced national exceptionalism as the popular meaning of Bikini Atoll. By the mid-1950s the cave promoters were looking backward for their themes again, as new management began the Caveman's Palace era. Under the rest of its various, less-forward-looking names, the operation limped along until October 1980.

That's when a fire in a deep-fat fryer destroyed the 1960s-era restaurant, the gift shop, and an adjoining cottage. As Jim and I sit in the subterranean ballroom beneath the site of this catastrophe, Jim again dips into the file boxes in the back of the Cavemobile. This time he produces a clipping from The *Knoxville News Sentinel*, reporting that thirteen children were touring the cavern at the time, whose only exit led directly into the restaurant dining room; the lack of additional information suggests they must have gotten out safely. Gene Monday was quoted in the papers saying the damage was well more than$100,000, and he didn't know when the caverns would be able to reopen.

That's when the spelunkers really started to get control. Though the cavern was occasionally in operation, the show cave didn't draw in many customers, especially after Interstate 40 drew vehicular traffic several miles to the south. The staff, when there was any, tended to be itinerant caretakers living in a trailer on site. The sloping ramp and arched entryway that once facilitated tourists and school groups taking a harmless peek underground now paved the way for a new kind of development.

The Stories of Cherokee Caverns and Indian Cave

Jim's tour doesn't attempt to suppress this part of the cave's history; instead, it's part of the story he has to tell, that he wants to tell. Throughout the cave he points out the traces of the cave's neglect, abuse, and decay. Broken formations, some even featuring bullet holes, and motorcycle tire tracks in the deep mud floor of that moonscape room testify, Jim tells me, to the occupation of the cave by the Outlaws motorcycle gang back in the 1980s. In the room where Homer and Stardust and Ray Myers performed for the crowd, wherever the ceiling height allowed safe passage for a cycle and rider, those mud cones that once helped evoke a triumphal vision of the future now feature a fat off-road motorcycle tire track straight through the middle.

On the one hand, I feel the kind of truculent moral indignation that's typically reserved for litterers and other antisocial pests, an almost generic outrage at the senselessness of it all. But on the other hand, like an inappropriate smile, the strong sense rises from that spelunker part of me, that it would be pretty cool to ride around on a motorcycle in here. I don't tell this to Jim, who's already told me of the cases upon cases of wire brushes he went through removing all the spray paint.

The last real effort to redomesticate a cave gone feral came in 1988, when two veterans of the Lost Sea, Janet and Scott Dixon, gave it a go. They had some friends in the local caving community who saw an opportunity to use show cave development as a way to alleviate the damage being done to the cave by spelunking squatters. These cavers tried to give them a hand where they could; first things first, they fixed the gate. Then, they helped the Dixons get the first Haunted Cave events at Cherokee Caverns under way.

❖   ❖   ❖   ❖

That's the point where the pendulum started to swing back into the other direction, when the cavers arrived on the scene with their ethic of safety and sworn duty to protect the cave from people as much as the other way around. That's how Jim Whidby found his way into the mix. After the Dixons packed it in and Gene Monday died, Jim took the cave into a kind of receivership. For Jim getting some authority over a cave of his own was kind of a dream come true, one he thought he'd never get to live out. "My wife told me that she was ok with the caving as long as I never bought a show cave," Jim told me. "This is the perfect set-up: I get to work on the cave whenever I want, give tours when needed, and stay married, too."

Besides, Jim has found the perfect partner for this undertaking. He goes on and on about the amount and the quality of the work done by his helper Robert, who is deaf and mute, and is one of those exceedingly rare people with a genetically reduced need for sleep. Robert will put in a full day's work at his day job, then come home and have dinner with his wife and kids, family time after dinner, even lie down with his wife until she goes to sleep, then he's up and moving back to the cave. His very presence is a key part of Jim's plan to protect the cave and keep away the spelunkers, a silent, sleepless guardian in the night.

"Here's all you need to know about Robert," says Jim. "Robert had a toy when he was little, and the toy broke, and he went to his mom and said, let's fix this, but his mom explained it couldn't be repaired. Then Robert cried and cried and just threw an absolute tantrum, not because he didn't have the toy anymore, but because he couldn't accept that he couldn't somehow improve it, make it unbreakable."

When Robert comes to the cave, along with the routine maintenance and whatever upgrades they've planned, he also experiments with things like handrails. There's got to be a way to do it so they don't rust like metal, rot like wood, or get slimy (and, let's face it, look tacky) like PVC. There may be right now a sleepless deaf man underneath a hillside in East Tennessee hard at work on discovering the solution. At least until dawn approaches, when he locks up and slips back into his family bed, ready to start the daylight cycle again.

It is with obvious pride that Jim drives me along the wide, dry gravel thoroughfare they've constructed, one of the only wheelchair-accessible cave tour routes I've ever seen. In the back corner of the moonscape/motocross room, Jim and Robert have built low retaining walls around a dry, sandy plaza, where Boy Scouts sleep on overnight visits. Robert even thoughtfully included an outlet in just the right spot to plug in a big-screen TV and show movies. Slumber parties now reign in the former headquarters of the Outlaws.

❖   ❖   ❖   ❖

Properly fitted out, the caver mentality holds: we can brush right up against the subterranean world and come back a little better for knowing a bit more about the extent of our world, with neither cave nor caver any the worse for wear. Jim has brought something of the same ambition to restoring this show cave, converting it from a place of real lawlessness expressed in a landscape of casual destruction to a place where anyone can move in near-absolute safety—Jim has negotiated the encounter on everyone's behalf.

He's rescued this cave, domesticated it, not just by sealing it off, but also by making it perfectly hospitable. At the same time, Jim explains to me, he

The Stories of Cherokee Caverns and Indian Cave

hopes that, by making this safe space available—by invitation and appointment—for folks to satisfy their need for a dose of underground devilishness, he's protecting other, less-despoiled or less protected caves from exploitation.

Cherokee Caverns today is not so much a show cave as an exhibition cave, reclaimed from degeneracy to help educate non-cavers away from their spelunking urges. He's defending caves not only by providing something almost like a decoy but also by trying to use that space to teach people something that might make them handle caves they encounter in the future more gently, reducing the risk for both the cave and the visitor. He may even help them get the lighting right in a TV show sometime.

And he hasn't just helped people, he's helped the cave, too. If it wasn't for Jim, Cherokee Caverns might have been ripped a new entrance: in 1997 the Tennessee Department of Transportation proposed a route for a new Knoxville Beltway that would have cut right across the northeast end of the cavern, in one of the few areas that currently lies beyond Jim's meticulous tour trail. Commuters would have driven across a room Jim had protected from the public but used on occasion for NSS meetings—a secret caver sanctuary. Jim was able to use the cave itself to help thwart that plan by arguing for its historical significance and ecological fragility, a powerful argument for a reroute during public comment, and ultimately another route was selected.

Jim has taken an abused, defaced cave and simultaneously protected it from people and used it as a space to teach people, up to and including the Tennessee Department of Transportation, to value caves. Cherokee Caverns has become what a show cave based on caver values looks like. That cave is in no way virgin anymore, but it can still be on the side of the angels. That's more than a little ironic, given that it was religion that helped get the cave in trouble to begin with.

At the time of the restaurant fire, the cave was being operated by a small, independent evangelical church. For them, the cave could serve as a built-in recruitment mechanism, while the gift shop and restaurant supplied a gathering area. Come for a thirty-minute tour of the cave, stay for eternal salvation: now that's a business model. Funny that it all ended up as a flaming tunnel leading under the earth.

When we're back above ground, looking at the footprint of the gift shop and restaurant, now just cracked concrete traces in the clearing around the entrance tunnel, I speculate aloud that maybe Monday, sharp real-estate investor that he was, handed the cave over to a not-for-profit to get a failing business property off the tax rolls.

There's certainly nothing in Gene Monday's biography to suggest he would have any special religious beliefs about caves or even an evangelical bent to him. Gene Monday himself seems like a very typical upper-middle-class white Southerner in terms of his religious life. He was born a Presbyterian and died an Episcopalian, so his affiliations never left the mainstream. His philanthropic causes, which were both numerous and generous, tended to be pretty uncontroversial: social welfare programs through the churches, substance abuse recovery, and Boys and Girls Clubs, all wholesome, upstanding traditional charities. So could it be that somehow his thinking turned a little mystical, where caves were concerned?

❖   ❖   ❖   ❖

"Funny thing," Jim tells me. "I don't know if this is evidence for or against your theories. But this wasn't the only show cave he turned over to a small-time church to run. He also owned Indian Cave, which was also in some pretty dire straits financially, and it ended up in the hands of a Baptist Church. Mr. Monday must have always had some kind of idea of it as a spiritual place—there's always been a lot of religious stuff going on over there. In fact, the guy who runs it now claims to be a minister himself."

Well, this I had to see. Jim assured me that the cave was definitely worth seeing for myself and probably more or less open. It just depended on whether or not the caretakers, Richard and Betty Dykes, were in town. They hit the road for days at a time working the flea market scene, selling whatever they had at hand. The Dykes' phone number was included in a whole packet of material Jim had in the truck—an account of the cave he wrote for the Spelean History Association's journal, photocopies of some old brochures. True to caver form, he didn't want me going in there unprepared.

Jim also gave me detailed directions for finding the place, and as it turned out, I really needed them. When I called the number Jim had supplied, I got an answering machine message that consisted of a brief, angry retort to creditors, followed by a "memory full" message and a disconnect. So the next day I was reading Jim's notes as I was turning on progressively smaller and smaller country roads, down into the heart of the Holston River valley somewhere between Rutledge and Jefferson City, Tennessee.

Indian Cave is not a place you go by accident; it is not getting any, I mean any, drive-by tourist traffic. Like Carter Saltpeter Cave and its spelunker party-cave brethren, it's a place lots of people have been, for some a regular hangout, but you have to know somebody to help you find your way there. Indian Cave didn't turn up in any of my old Gurnee Guides, it maintains no website, and it doesn't have any brochures or signs, save a few stray relics nobody ever got around to taking down. It's not a place you just come across.

After being funneled down the hollers toward the river, I emerge into the sunlight in flat green bottom land, and my road, now one lane of gravel, ends altogether by the water's edge. To my left I see the low brick building I know from Jim's scholarship to be the visitor's center for the cave, partially enveloped in the grey leafless winter kudzu. A vast skein of vines had consumed pretty much the entire hillside, spilling down like a frozen waterfall. In some places shapes bulged beneath the vines—a shed? a car?—enough to make you wonder what else might be lying beneath the surface. You could almost sense that it was thawing, awakening in the first really warm sunshine of the season.

Even beneath the kudzu blanket I could still match the contours of the hillside I was seeing now to the photos in Jim's article, terraces that were once the site of a charming group of cabins. This photo was taken back in the late 1920s, when Hunter Chapman of Shenandoah Caverns was so taken with the spot he bought the whole operation. Chapman's son Paul and Paul's wife, Louise, managed the cave for the family, moving into a little cottage of their own on the hillside. I can see why: in the spring sunshine the river sparkles; the fields on the other side roll up a low hill, golden in the new spring warmth.

People have been seeing the appeal of this spot for a long, long time. For most of human inhabitation of this site, the river served as a highway. For all that time, this wide, flat shelf on the high side of the river, with a reliable spring and the cave's vast opening offering ready-made shelter, has made for a hospitable stop-off. From Paleoindians to the Woodland tribes that the first white explorers encountered here, the appeal was not just aesthetic but practical.

Archaeological records show indigenous settlements here over millennia, fishing, farming, trading on the river-highway by their side. Legend has it a Frenchman set up a trading post in the mouth of the cave itself in the early days of white settlement when the long-hunters would come poling along on rafts. More settled times would see the cave mined for saltpeter, the river diverted into a mill race. From the turnaround I can see a replica of the wheel in the distance beyond the main building, rapidly becoming a massive kudzu trellis.

River travel had declined when Hunter Chapman moved down here, but the site was still an intersection. A ferry connected segments of Indian Cave

Road, and brought not only traffic but also folks waiting at the cave while the small-capacity boat ran back and forth. (Jim's article includes a charming snapshot of Louise posing at the wheel of the ferryboat.) Chapman focused on capitalizing on Indian Cave's historical role as a gathering place. He made it the site of a joint Grainger and Jefferson County Fourth of July gathering that drew hundreds of celebrants, prominent area politicians and orators, and local boys made good. Plus, the handbill from the 1939 picnic that Jim included in my packet noted, "INDIAN TRIBE HERE . . . About 30 Indians, costumed, with ceremonies in Cave." Indian Cave had it all—sandwiches, baseball games, and even Indians in the Cave.

The cave itself was really classed up, too. The Chapmans fixed it up with a practiced hand from their superb work at Shenandoah Caverns. The old wooden bridges were replaced with poured concrete that survived the massive 1982 flood intact, if covered in a thick layer of mud. The lighting was state-of-the-show-cave-art, talent imported from the Shenandoah Caverns team to produce the cave's claim to fame on its handbills that it was "the largest electrically illuminated cave in the world," boasting miles of cable and more than 1,800 light bulbs.

The Chapmans oversaw the cave at its height, from the early thirties when they took over, up through World War II. Then wartime rationing hit Indian Cave's business as it did tourism nationwide. The ferry disappeared after the Tennessee Valley Authority completed Cherokee Dam upstream in 1942, the same year Hunter Chapman died, and the changing water levels no longer allowed safe operation. With modern US highways 11E and 11W running south and north of the river, there was little call for a rural ferry anymore anyway. As it was with Cherokee Caverns, the arrival of Interstate 40 along a vector considerably to the south was a crushing blow. Indian Cave was about as inconveniently located for modern car tourists as you could get.

In the midst of all these changes, which pretty plainly spelled doom for the cave as a business venture, in walked the normally level-headed, conservative Gene Monday Jr. He bought into the operation in 1947, when Hunter Chapman's heirs got out of the show cave business. This systematically isolated show cave never really caught on again. Indian Cave slid quickly into obscurity, and from there, spelunkerdom was never very far away.

From 1948, when Gene Monday reopened the show cave, through the '50s and '60s, the cave was leased to brothers Charlie and George Norton. The Norton brothers seem to have had about all they could handle just to maintain the status quo. The improvements they attempted didn't amount to much. Water from the cave spring was diverted into a small lake for fishing,

The Stories of Cherokee Caverns and Indian Cave

long since silted up, just a swampy, low spot today. An ill-fated effort in the mid-1960s to build a two-story motel came to nothing when the second floor burned; the rambling single-story brick structure that remained has served as gift shop, restaurant, church, concert, and professional wrestling venue while being patiently engulfed by the kudzu.

Cherokee Caverns may have the most names, but Indian Cave, despite keeping the same name since antiquity, may stake a claim for the most operators. The 1970s are kind of a lost decade in the history of Indian Cave; it seems to have been under very loose supervision. Later, as my research progressed, I was struck by how Indian Cave just sort of flickered in and out of the periodic local travel pieces — every few years somebody would write a puff piece about the area show caves, and only every now and again would Indian Cave merit even so much as a passing mention.

It was while Indian Cave was out of the public eye that it drifted toward less commercial uses. In the late 1970s, at about the same time as he let a church take over Cherokee Caverns, Gene Monday handed Indian Cave over to the New Beverly Baptist Church, which used it for gospel concerts and group outings and offered tours during events on a donation basis. Somewhere in here the lease passed from the church itself to a couple of different church members, still trying to keep it going as a gospel venue on a donation basis. The Lord, however, did not provide, and a business model premised on divine intervention hastened the physical decay. Just as at Cherokee Caverns, this effort to have the cave do the Lord's work left it vulnerable to the spelunkers' devilments. All through the late '70s and early '80s Indian Cave's reputation as a party place grew, the cave growing more feral with each break in the chain of supervision.

The cavers did what they could to intervene. In the early 1980s, an enterprising young man named Dan Osborne was in the area looking for work at the 1982 World's Fair. He took over as manager, despite his total lack of experience running anything, much less something as weird as a cave. The cavers took a liking to the new guy and probably sensed, too, that he represented an opportunity to protect the cave from its ongoing descent into spelunkerdom. Jim Whidby writes in his own history of the cave, "Jim wanted to see Dan make a 'go' of it and realized that as long as someone was living on the park grounds the cave would be better protected. For years the cave was experiencing a lot of vandalism and the grounds and the cave were becoming trashed and getting a reputation as the 'local party place.'"

When huge floods hit right after Osborne took over, Jim brought in the cavers to clean up, which turned, of course, into surveying and exploration, archaeological finds, all kinds of caver fun. (Though to show you what a dicey place it was, the beautiful Stone Age biface knife Jim's crew found was stolen from a display in the gift shop shortly thereafter.) The cavers recognized an opportunity for a mutually beneficial relationship. They helped Osborne organize Indian Cave's first-ever Haunted Cave, raising some much-needed cash to help the whole operation get through the fall and winter months, and helping to guarantee their access to the cave as well.

Alas, Dan Osborne couldn't make it work no matter what they did, and he was out within the year. A couple of management changes later and the cave had backslid right into sin again. That's when Richard Dykes came on the scene. He'd been working over at Cherokee Caverns when former Lost Sea employees Janet and Scott Dixon had made their last-ditch attempt to get that one back up and moving in 1988, and Dykes moved over here to Indian Cave with his wife Betty as soon as the opportunity presented itself.

He and Betty fixed things up once again, even generating a little press in the Knoxville papers about this latest spin on domesticating Indian Cave for tourist consumption. "It's getting harder and harder for families to go somewhere to see something from the past without it bankrupting you as soon as you get out of the car," Dykes told the *Knoxville Journal*, but he admitted that the cave could bankrupt them: "We're putting every nickel we've got into this place." Betty added "There are so many possibilities it's hard to say exactly what we are going to do. The important thing is to get it back open to the public." Gene Monday offered a guarded vote of confidence. "If they do good, and I believe they will, I want them to stay there."

Richard Dykes had an ace in the hole as a cave promoter, especially this particular cave, and that was his claim to the title of chief of the American Intertribal Association, an organization about which I have subsequently been able to find almost nothing save old listings as a vendor at few scattered powwows.

In fact, he had two aces, because he is also, by his own account, a licensed minister of the Universal Ministries church. In later conversations with Dykes, I'd learn that this group is based on integrating Native American spirituality and certain animistic beliefs into Christian theology, and, as it turns out, its world headquarters and seminary are right here at Indian Cave, in that low brick, kudzu-draped building.

❖   ❖   ❖   ❖

Richard and Betty have managed to keep Indian Cave precariously perched right on the edge of being handed over to the spelunkers, taking the whole thing about as far in the direction of wildness (human, not cave) as you can go without getting there. And they've been pretty adept with this balancing act, hanging in there for over twenty-five years now. Indian Cave as run by the Dykes embraces contradiction, the pleasures of juxtaposition: a folk-school workshop in flint-knapping or jewelry-making might be followed by a wrestling match, a gospel sing, and a visit from a Boy Scout troop. Unlike Cherokee Caverns, which became a kind of exhibit, a source of real knowledge and information about the cave wrapped in a redemption story, Indian Cave went the other direction, fully embracing the cave as a site of mystery and myth, the sacred, yes, but in full contact with the profane.

Surely that mysticism was part of the appeal to a group of Knoxville-based DJs and promoters in search of a truly unique venue for a rave. Perhaps the neotribalism of the electronic dance music (EDM) community similarly appealed to the Dykes; just as likely it was the idea that their checks would clear that got Richard and Betty to rent out the cave for a massive dance party.

The Rave in the Cave: it's still remembered today as a pinnacle of the early history of EDM in Knoxville, and it is surely the defining event of the Dykes era at Indian Cave. Not surprisingly, given the occasion, the Rave in the Cave is generally remembered somewhat inaccurately. Most folks who still remember that term automatically think of the final chapter in a series of events ending in the year 2000. Three times before that, promoter Nate Irwin brought performers such as Special K and DJ Slink along with tons of light and sound gear, and set up in the same vast entry room where gospel sings and powwows and haunted caves were also taking place. But unlike any of the other rituals around here, at least since the days of Hunter Chapman's Fourth of July shindigs, this one drew hundreds of participants.

By the fourth time, the locals had had enough, and their practical frustrations with traffic and noise were intensified, magnified into cultural and political and moral conflicts. Here in Grainger County, as pretty much everywhere, kids + music + drugs + sex = moral panic. That it was all happening in a cave was a force multiplier.

A little devilry has generally been tolerated in the cave, indeed, in caves in general—that's why we so often name them for the Devil. But on this scale, it seemed like full-tilt demonic possession. Something, it was collectively decided, had to be done.

What happened next is the locus of two very different understandings. Talking to the Knoxville scene paper *Metro Pulse* in 2003, DJ Slink (aka Heath Shinpaugh) described being terrorized by the people of Grainger

County: "It was a very ugly situation . . . [locals] didn't understand what [the rave] was for." Special K, real name Nate Wells, told of locals purposefully misdirecting attendees down dead end roads, waving shotguns at them from their porches, and even calling the promoters to threaten to blow up the cave.

A prayer team turned out to the rave site to sit in in silent protest. Other folks took more corporeal action, cutting down trees across Indian Cave Road, barring access for new arrivals and trapping attendees on site. "People drove eight to 10 hours to get to this event, and they were stopped by a bunch of crazy Baptists cutting down trees," Nate Irwin lamented.

But Grainger County sheriff Richard McElhaney saw the situation in something of a different light than the DJs. "We got a call about 8 pm Saturday that a bunch of rave people were coming in and a bunch of citizens had blocked the road to the entrance of the cave, and the rave people jumped out of their cars with baseball bats," he told the *Knoxville News Sentinel*. You might guess from his easy semantic distinction between "citizens" and "rave people" what followed: police roadblocks on every back road in Grainger and Rutledge County on the other side of the river. They arrested twenty-two kids for possession of marijuana and psychedelics and ended the era of the Rave in the Cave once and for all. True to form, when folks encountered a strange, exotic feature on the landscape, they attributed it to the devil. But it's the people that provided the real danger, to each other and to themselves.

Indian Cave settled back into its quiet routine of intermittent, informal operation, verging close enough to neglect that the place kept its reputation as a party spot. In 2001 two of the surviving Hunter Chapman–era cabins were destroyed in mysterious circumstances. But the place stayed secure enough that scout troops still came out, and church groups gathered, and the cavers came around now and again. Of course, the occasional Haunted Cave also drew a few new folks out to that lonesome bend of the Holston River.

❖　❖　❖　❖

And then there was me, ten years ago, sitting in my rental in the sun, looking ahead at the river, at the spot where once you'd descend the ramp to the ferry, now just a dead-end turnaround. I checked my cell: no service.

To my right was a mobile home attractively sited by the river, a kitchen garden plot freshly turned over behind it. Toward me, riding a lawn tractor, came a genial, rangy man I recognized from a photo in Jim's collection: Richard Dykes, proprietor of Indian Cave Village, chief of the American Intertribal Association, and minister of the Universal Ministries church,

The Stories of Cherokee Caverns and Indian Cave

in the flesh. I parked my rental car, a nondescript Toyota with out-of-state plates, and wandered over to meet him on the lawn.

I guess I was expecting someone a little more flamboyant, but Richard turned out to be just as low-key as he could be, maintaining the same pleasant grin the whole time we talked. He showed his age a little; his hair had receded but still had some sandy color in the gray. He seemed perfectly spry, carrying a little paunch but sinewy beneath, with strong hands extending from the turned-up sleeves of a plaid work shirt. I gave him the thumbnail description of my project, and summed up for him how I'd ended up there that day, that I was not just visiting show caves, I was studying them.

As soon as I mentioned Jim Whidby's name he good-naturedly waved me off, convinced, and said I was more than welcome to visit the cave. Normally, he said, he charged ten bucks a head, but since I was a writer he'd let me go on in there, no charge. Just head down the riverbank, past the building and the mill wheel, and you can't miss it. The gate was unlocked, and I'd find the light switches in the breaker box in the main room. "Enjoy yourself! Make yourself at home," Richard told me, and then ambled back over to the tractor to keep doing whatever he was doing when I arrived.

I stood there for a minute as he waved from the tractor, riding away. Wait, he's just going to let me go down there and have the run of the place? Part of me couldn't believe my luck—a show cave to myself, a chance to roam around it totally unsupervised. Part of me felt a little adrenaline surge, realizing that I was off the information grid, hundreds of miles from home, in a car that wasn't mine. Literally nobody had been informed as to where I was or when I should be back. My cell phone was a brick. And I was about to walk off by myself to a mile-long cave and find the light switch on my own, because a flea market vendor and self-proclaimed holy man told me to make myself at home. Was it all in the name of research? Or was the spelunker in me waking up from a long slumber?

I grabbed my camera and moseyed toward the visitor's center, documenting the scene. The building was cluttered inside and out, faded flags and rusty lawn furniture, old vending machines and the odd sculpture lining the exterior. The gift shop, locked up, had a lot of Native American–themed handicrafts and figurines lining the walls and the windowsills. It was unclear if they were on display or for sale, and a weathered sign soliciting donations for the Tennessee Native American Museum at Indian Cave Village didn't really clear things up either way. Nor did a holiday-themed model train layout taking up a couple of display windows. Writing on the big front window of a large common room proclaimed it the Universal Ministries Church, and a smaller cardboard sign leaned up on the inside of the glass noted the home of the Indian Cave School of Theology. Peering inside the darkened room, anticlimax: just folding tables and chairs, an American flag.

Still, I was feeling a little keyed up, alert to the possibility of unexpectedly discovering somebody else hanging around here, trying to affect a confident saunter, probably not succeeding. I took a lot of pictures, partly to document the place, and partly to look purposeful in case somebody was watching me. Down past the millwheel, steps vanished up the side of the hill beneath the kudzu, leading my eyes to where the scorched chimney of one of the Chapman cottages desperately struggled up through the vines like the last gesture of a drowning man. Then I saw the altar.

Rounding a bend just before you come to the cave's grand entrance, you can see straight ahead to where the trail concludes in a small paved plaza overlooking the river. There waits not just an altar but an entire chancel—communion table, pulpit, stone seats for presiding figures, all constructed out of river rock. But the furnishings are cracked and mossy, the plaza is thickly lined with fallen leaves, and here as elsewhere the relentless kudzu seems fixed on swallowing it up and breaking it apart. Right where you turn toward the cave entrance, the crowning touch, a huge concrete tablet like a giant tombstone, crudely inscribed with the Ten Commandments. I took a minute to process this. So I had stumbled onto a ruined temple, draped in vines, deep in the backwoods. How could this not end well?

Weirded out though I was, I still couldn't help but be struck by the majesty of Indian Cave's entrance. It's what cavers somewhat dismissively call a Hollywood Entrance, shorthand for a large, highly accessible cave mouth that attracts the kind of popular interest cavers usually seek to avoid. They'd rather crawl through a crack in an outcropping that no untrained eye would expect to lead anywhere. Indian Cave's entrance is definitively Hollywood: a massive vault a couple of stories high, draped with elegant if disheveled English ivy, which has somehow outfoxed the kudzu for this prime location. The lower third or so of this space is blocked by a natural wall, but a rustic-gothic stone arch fitted with a decorative metal gate provides access to the footpath leading to the cave's large, dim foyer.

A plastic sign on the gate sternly instructed: DO NOT ENTER WITHOUT GUIDE. I pushed, and the gate swung open. Once inside, the pavement and the light both started running out quickly. Fifty to sixty feet inside, the entrance hallway opened into a really large room, big enough, I'd reckon, for a pretty big gospel sing or a smallish rave. And I could easily see the appeal of the venue, the broad, naturally circular space graded level and surfaced

The Stories of Cherokee Caverns and Indian Cave

(albeit not recently, by the look of it) with crushed limestone. A brisk, flowing stream has been channeled around the perimeter on one side by a low stone wall, and a broad mantel over a stacked rock fireplace, complete with an ancient iron kettle, dominated another wall. A pathway broad enough to drive a small truck on vanished into the darkness away to my left, following the stream, while a wider opening to the right seemed to lead into another large room.

In the milky twilight that filters in from the entrance I could see a couple of picnic tables, some mismatched chairs, a trash barrel or two that could use emptying; the decorating theme from the office area apparently carried over to the cave as well. The wider opening to the right looked and felt really uninviting, but a steady breeze from the left-hand passage enriched that earthy cave smell and carried echoes of the stream gurgling and rippling in the distance. There was clearly a lot of cave ahead. But I had only one question in mind at the moment: Where was that breaker box?

I finally spotted it in the shadows behind me near the entrance path, once my eyes had adjusted to the gloom. OK, I told myself, let's do this: with a little bit of self-congratulatory ceremony, I threw the switch. Then I tried to figure out if it did anything.

The room on the right remained black as pitch, but peering back up that left-hand corridor I saw a dim string of lights, each bulb a lonely island of color, a widely spaced archipelago scattered along the path, leading further and further underground. The first light, a lone orange bulb, was still in the twilight reaches of the entrance, and the sun still shone faintly on the path beyond. From there I set out for the next stop a few dozen yards farther along, a green spotlight illuminating a wall of dripstone. Now the sunlight was pretty much gone, and the next and seemingly final stop, at least as far as I could see from there, was a pool of red light a couple of hundred feet further on, shining from its source on a pair of fluted columns descending from a fault in the ceiling.

This hop was longer and trickier—I was actively feeling with my feet now, working carefully toward the lighted destination, unable at this point to make out any details of the darkness surrounding me. More than once I stopped and thought, OK, this is stupid. But the path was wide enough and flat enough to get me over the hump, all the way to the beckoning red floodlight. Reaching it, though, I could see I was out of luck. No more electric lights, at least that I could see, and the natural light was long since gone. Not a prayer of talking myself into trying to go any further.

Fortunately, going back was actually easier than going in, working toward the sunshine, eyes fully dilated to collect any scraps of light they could get. Back in the main room, which seemed positively illuminated now, I tried to think of what else I could do here, not wanting to squander the opportunity to explore this bizarre space. But there was no way I was going to venture the pitch-black chamber that adjoined the entrance, and once I'd taken a few time exposures, I couldn't think of much else to do, so I moseyed back out into the sunshine and made my way back toward the car.

Right as I reached the car I encountered Richard Dykes again, walking toward the office with a weed whacker in his hands. "Well, whadja think? You didn't take too long in there." Did I detect a glint of amusement in that ever-present grin?

"I think I must have missed some switches," I said, "I only got just a few lights to come on, and I couldn't make it all that far without a flashlight." "What, you ain't got a light?" Dykes replied. Apparently I'd gone too spelunker even for him. "Come on down here to the office, I bet we can find you something."

He let me into the gift shop–museum–storeroom. Dust motes leapt in the streaky sunlight as we entered. "Here you go," said Richard, going through a drawer below the shop counter and producing a big old floodlight. "I used this'un a little while back when we had some scouts out here, I think the batteries are good." He switched it on; it had a wide beam but was already a little wan. "Better take this one, too," he added, handing me a penlight with a much stronger charge and a much smaller beam.

Well, it averages out to one solid light, I figured, and thanking Richard I headed back for another foray into Indian Cave.

Back in the big entry hall — the Rave Room, I'm calling it — I set out first to the right, the adjacent room. Turned out to be a big vault with the main branch of Indian Cave Creek running along the far wall to the point where it vanishes through a lower opening to emerge in the Holston River. It's a natural storeroom, and I wondered if this is where they kept the emergency rations and such back when Indian Cave, like so many show caves, was certified as a fallout shelter, with an astounding capacity of 9,065. Now, other than some stray garbage, the only thing it sheltered was an old refrigerator, sitting there with the doors hanging open next to some heaps of lumber and junk. I went over with my penlight to take a more detailed look inside the fridge. And in the freezer there was a human head.

I staggered backwards like I'd been shocked, even as I processed that this was a hairdresser's practice head, the stump of the neck painted with fake blood. Looking at the junk heap I saw that some of the lumber was

The Stories of Cherokee Caverns and Indian Cave

painted with Halloween iconography—spooky ghosts, jack-o-lanterns, and such—and tangled up in black crepe, and I realized this was all the ruins of the Haunted Cave gear. The contrast between this mode of haunted cave storage and Jim Whidby's neatly organized shipping container of horrors could not be more pointed.

That initial stunner set the tone for an even edgier second run at Indian Cave. In some ways it toughened me up a little bit: I only flinched a little when I glimpsed the guillotine. In that blackness between the lights in my earlier trip up the path, I'd been unable to see it sitting off to the side, but my flashlight beam found it on the second try. I guess once you've seen a severed head, you can't be too surprised when a guillotine turns up. Still, the bloody baby booties dangling from it did give it a real dose of Grand Guignol.

So, paradoxically jacked up and desensitized, I plodded along beyond the last of the light bulbs, swinging the beam of the big light Richard gave me methodically side to side, sweeping the path to avoid more unpleasant surprises. Soon the erstwhile haunted cave decor gave way to mostly just a sad, dilapidated cave. It never had all that much decoration to begin with, and what's there now is often badly damaged, and not even in much of an interesting way. In places it seemed like work was begun on removing the older show cave armature—wire pulled out, fixtures collected and stacked up, but then abandoned again. Clearly this project was not being conducted by a meticulous deaf-mute with a genetically reduced need for sleep. At one point, right beside the trail, what appeared to be the hollowed-out stump of a stalagmite about a foot across held a muddy bowl full of water. A dirty placard proclaimed, through missing letters, that this was the Fountain of Youth.

The path wound gently up the stream passage, fifty feet wide and always plenty tall for me to walk upright, crossing and recrossing the creek on charming arched concrete bridges dating back to the Hunter Chapman era. Every so often a hole by the trail clearly went somewhere—or so suggested the grooves and wear in the mud of generations of explorers, caver, spelunker, and otherwise.

I began to see occasional bats, scouting to see if enough insects had hatched out in the day's warmth to make it worth venturing out. In one space the ceiling held a dozen bats or more, circling the inside of the dome, zipping around its contours like they were in some kind of velodrome. When I stopped to watch them, they rustled past my head often enough to be disconcerting but not enough to be threatening.

In the next stretch of the cave I had occasion to explore even more thoroughly the fine line between disconcerting and threatening. Because that was where the voices began. The creek, much shallower and rifflier than it was back at the entrance, made a wide bend around the edge of a rounded, domed gallery, and about halfway across it on the path I heard the voices so clearly I stopped in my tracks: a younger woman with a lilting tone, a deeper interlocutor, generically male. I couldn't discern words, just the sound of sense, distant and indistinct over the creek's bubbling and chuckling.

"It is the stream, right?" I thought. "It's not somebody coming along behind me — several somebodies? — who got wind that somebody far from home, cut out of the herd, was up there (CORNERED) inside the cave?" Formulating a fully fledged conspiracy theory took me about two beats of my rapidly beating heart.

Overriding that impulse took quite a bit longer, especially since, as I stood there telling myself "It's the stream, it's the stream," I heard those voices again, and maybe some other voices, and it was hard to tell exactly where they were coming from or what direction they were moving. Finally, I shut off the light, partly to focus my senses, partly because I figured if somebody was following me I could at least gain the element of surprise. To my own surprise the total darkness felt good, reassuring, an equalizer. My eyes weren't helping me anyway. Listening deeply, carefully, I could convince myself that there was nobody coming, that this round room had some very cool acoustics, that the layers of watery music, an audio pointillist painting, were almost soothing. "It's the stream. It's definitely the stream."

I switched the beam back on, or tried to — it required a couple of sharp whacks before the light caught, and even then the beam was perceptibly yellower than it was when I started out. I had absolutely no idea how far I had come in the mile-long tunnel, but I felt confident I ought to speed it up a little. I settled back into a comfortably brisk walk, sweeping the path with the flashlight in rhythm, left right left right. And then the beam fell upon a baby.

Dead center of the trail. Sprawled there in old-fashioned bloomers. Eyes gazing sightless at the ceiling. "IT IS A BABY" screamed my mind, my central nervous system, my endocrine glands, and the deep memory of my species. "IT IS A BABY A BABY DOLL a baby doll jesus h christ a baby doll." Goddam haunted cave had one last surprise in store for me. Now I knew where they got the booties for the guillotine.

Do I need to say that was finally enough? Wielding the more reliable penlight, I made my way purposefully back to the entrance, turned out the lights, closed the gate, and headed for the car. When I got back to the office, Richard was parked in a peeling Adirondack chair. I gave him the flashlights and my sincere thanks for a truly unparalleled show cave experience. "Well,

The Stories of Cherokee Caverns and Indian Cave

The baby in the path, Indian Cave, 2006. (Photograph by the author)

didja see anything interesting?" Again, the amusement, like he already knows what I experienced.

Where to begin. "Do you ever hear voices in there?"

Richard's grin remained steady. "Oh, there are a lot of voices in there." Long pause. I ask him to go on. "Well, some of them might be what you call ghosts, but others, what I'd call it is that they are the ancestors, bringing us messages from other places. Are they dangerous? That depends on a lot of things, I guess, like what you bring with you." He paused again, as if remembering something, and chuckled to himself.

"For my money," I tell him, "It's not what you bring with you but who."

❖   ❖   ❖   ❖

What I realized at Indian Cave was that I wasn't scared of the spirits in the cave. I was scared of other people. The real threat in that situation was not that our shared supernatural fears of caves, the beliefs that lead us to name them for the devil and store our old guillotines there, were true. The danger comes from the fact that we bring those beliefs into the cave and make them self-fulfilling prophecies. What is it about these places that can make a normally level-headed, safety-minded English professor, husband and father, wander off underground, jumping at shadows without really facing up to the fact that the biggest menace is his own irresponsible behavior?

On this point the cavers are right: the only way to make caves safe is to keep the people out. The danger in the cave, the danger to the cave, comes with the people, so it's like the paradox that no one has ever seen a cave in its natural condition because its natural condition is unseeable. As long as there are people in a cave, they'll bring their own screwed-up dangers with them. The devil is us.

To understand this fact is to recognize that even the most darkness-free, birthday-party-friendly show cave is capable of harboring demons. The day I visited Inner Space in Texas, in fact, I got an object lesson in the cave's fallen nature. I finally reached the front of the line to enter the cavern. The wait time had increased, and the tour size had grown quite large, thanks to the special birthday party tour ahead of us, and the funicular trolley-car by which you descend into the cavern these days was approaching completely full. I handed my ticket to the uniformed staff member and stepped out of the Visitor's Center onto the platform.

As I paused and debated, at the staff's suggestion, whether I wanted to try to squeeze onto the train or simply walk down the steps, a minor commotion broke out at the far downhill end of the railcar: sharp tones exchanged, followed by the disarray of several people urgently working their way back up to the platform through the throng of fellow passengers.

A Middle Eastern man, late twenties, emerged from the car, followed by a woman his age and a boy of maybe nine, looking nervous and embarrassed: his family, it seemed. He sought and was met by the ticket-takers, blonde-haired teens, one male, one female, who instantly slid into a cool, terse mood known well to most service workers who have ever dealt with an angry customer on a really busy day. "Is something the matter, sir?"

Addled and struggling with the language a bit, the man blurted, "Those people." Gesturing in the general direction of the downhill end of the trolley, where I can see the silhouettes of people staring back indignantly. "I cannot be with those people. I want my money back." His t-shirt: a screen print of electric guitars finished with eagles and flags, and, in gothic lettering, "American Rock." He fumed; his whole body seemed tight as a fist. "They told me to go back home. I'm not a terrorist. I want my money back. Take these back," he said in a tight, even voice, thrusting forward the tickets.

The male guide moved into position to escort the man and family upstream against the crowd, beginning a litany of policies and practices that may or may not entitle one to a refund. "You can't send me down there with those people," the unhappy customer was saying, as he and his companions vanished back into the gift shop. I decided to take the steps. The girl who took the tickets clanged the trolley door shut, and the car rattled down the tracks of the incline railway, into the domestic darkness of Inner Space.

SEVEN

Adventures in Cave Development

Talking Shop at the National Cave Association

❖   ❖   ❖   ❖

In a by-the-book cave tour, right about now I'd be pointing out to you some key feature relating to the discovery, development, or operation of the cave. Maybe it's the point where the cave's first developers found their way into the big room, maybe it's a bridge built to replace the one destroyed in the flood, maybe it's some seismic or atmospheric equipment relating to ongoing research about how and why the cave is changing. At some point, show caves typically depart from the aesthetic of concealment that prevails at theme parks, calling your attention to the apparatus that makes your visit possible, and the history of how it came to do so.

In other words, show caves are always at some level about how there came to be a show in the cave. That's the final great dramatic irony of the show cave aesthetic: that the legitimate natural wonder before your eyes is also a legitimately amazing story of human exploration and deliberate transformation. It's simultaneously eternal and workaday. One of the great mysteries to me, that has perplexed and amazed me all the more as I've learned more and more about show caves, is that anybody goes to this much trouble.

Show caves are otherworldly by nature, but keeping them going involves a lot of plain old, everyday work. Paperwork. Physical labor. Bookkeeping. Management. Maintenance. And it's a terrible business model to start with, premised on something as unpredictable as human curiosity, built on something absolutely immobile, delivering something as ephemeral as a cocktail of emotions and sensations.

❖   ❖   ❖   ❖

One way to monetize the experience is to require visitors to exit through the gift shop. The typical show cave tour includes plenty of stories of the development of the show cave, from the earliest geologic history to the discovery to its current iteration of ownership, philosophy, aesthetic. But maybe the real story of what keeps the cave going is better found in the gift shop than in any floodlit crevice through which the boy pursuing his birddog or collecting his animal traps first found his way down from the surface.

Considering that each and every show cave is in fact unique, there's a surprising sameness to the gift shop merchandise, especially when you see a bunch of show caves in rapid succession, several summers in a row. Sure, each cave has its own logo, its own trademark images and money formations. But the actual thing those images are printed on, be it a mug or a tie-dye t-shirt or a leather coin purse, those all start to look suspiciously like they come from a common source. Everywhere you go you see not just the same geodes and minerals, imported from somewhere in South America, but the same store displays in which the stones are laid out. Even the pamphlets have a shared aesthetic and design vocabulary. Like an archaeologist finding cowrie shells and scrimshaw in a burial mound in Ohio, I begin to see the evidence of a broader trade network emerging.

Six years it took me, riding the backroads of Appalachia, cobbling together bits of information, chance contacts, terse messages, but I found it. It wasn't quite as I imagined: in place of some kind of Aladdin's Cave of knick-knacks, there was instead an elegant Georgian Revival facade, a restored vintage hotel lobby, and a short flight of steps through French doors into a sunlit ballroom. But I had found it, the source of the great river of kitsch, the node tying together show cave gift shops not just throughout the Great Valley but all across the country.

What I had found was the exhibitor's hall at the annual meeting of the National Cave Association (NCA), for a few days every year the epicenter of the show cave in America. In September 2011, the show cave owners, operators, and staff who form the NCA membership gathered in Luray, Virginia, the guests of the grande dame of the Virginia show cave circuit, Luray Caverns, and the Graves family that has owned the cave for three generations. Assembled at Luray's historic Mimslyn Inn to talk shop were 150 of the folks who actually make show caves happen, and I knew I needed to be there, too.

It wasn't an easy thing to find. Evidence of the existence of the NCA is everywhere — one thing it does is provide racks of handbills advertising all the member caves, conveniently positioned by the door in each member cave's gift shop. It's become a regular stop for me, kind of a scoreboard: "Seen it . . . Seen it . . . Seeing it tomorrow . . ." But in all this printed matter, there's precious little about the organization itself. Its website, cavern.com, similarly provides plenty of information about how to visit member caves, but it offers almost no opportunities for contacting the association directly.

It was kind of like finding a party cave: though lots of people knew it well, somebody had to show me the way there. It wasn't until I was pretty far along into interviewing show cave operators before somebody finally suggested that I'd be interested in the annual gathering and gave me the contact info for the NCA secretary and a link to the (unlisted) website for information about the Luray meeting. Emails went unanswered, phone calls unreturned. It started to feel a lot like my experience with the insularity of the caver crowd. Unlike the cavers, though, they didn't seem to mind if you go in the cave—that part is encouraged—but they really want you to stay on the path and not touch anything. Pay no attention to the man behind the curtain!

Despite the uncertainty, I made my travel plans, figuring that in the worst-case scenario, I'd spend a pleasant fall week in Luray, something I'd like to do anyway. Finally, I received an invitation by email from one of the meeting's hosts, John Graves (of the Luray Caverns Graveses), stating I'd be welcome to attend as his guest.

It was no problem wending my way from Dulles an hour west to Luray, a quiet Shenandoah Valley town in the process of transitioning from manufacturing and agriculture to tourist shops and restaurants, a destination for day-trippers from DC. I parked outside the hilltop Mimslyn Hotel, founded in 1931 and lovingly restored in 2005 as a part of that transition to a tourist economy. I breezed through the portico and into the gracious lobby, where a handful of conferees mingled amid its elegant appointments. But when I hit the registration desk for the meeting, it was another matter.

Misty, the nice young woman on duty there, was fitting me out with my program and some meeting swag when we were interrupted by an elaborately polite man whose beribboned name tag indicated that he, Bill, was on the staff at Luray and a member of the host committee. He intercepted Misty as she prepared to point out some schedule highlights and murmured, "Let me call Rod."

A few sidebars on the cellphone later, Bill came back and introduced himself to me, all practiced cordiality. "I am pleased to meet you, Douglas, and Rod and John Graves have both told me to say hello. The whole Luray Caverns family is so delighted to have you here with us. But there's a session or two on the schedule that aren't really appropriate for you to attend." He popped open the binder in my schedule and removed a few pages. "I'll just highlight the ones that it's OK for you to be at. We just need to be sensitive about proprietary information, and make sure our participants can

Talking Shop at the National Cave Association

have a free and open discussion," he chattered as he found a highlighter and skimmed down the listed events, "nope . . . nope . . . I guess the reception tonight would be ok . . . And please feel free to come along on all the outings and join us at Limair for our official welcome tomorrow night. So glad you're here!" He was all smiles beneath his mustache, and whisked himself away before I had a chance to react to my schedule getting bowdlerized. It was a classic southern social ninja maneuver, a completely obsequious way to be uncooperative.

Anyway, the Exhibit Hall was fair game, and it was even still open. I had arrived late in the day when the conferees were mostly all out on their own and the display tables were unmanned, so I had it all to myself. If you had to fit out a show cave and needed to get it done as quickly as possible, one lap around this room with your checkbook out would pretty much do it. Not just your gift shop merch, but your gemstone mining operation, surveying, environmental testing, insurance, photography and print services would all fall into place.

I wandered around dumbstruck, dropping representative free samples and brochures into a provided canvas bag. Given the mixed messages I had received about how welcome I was exactly, I couldn't quite shake the feeling that somebody was going to tell me to put it all back, that I could be violating some rule without even knowing it, that any minute the sentries would burst in to expel me from the treasury. When I had gathered enough swag to prove that all this was really here, I made good my escape.

Later on, though, while I wound down in my room at a B&B outside of town (the Mimslyn being fully booked for the meeting), I couldn't help but feel a little disappointed with my haul. I had found my way to the source, to the crucial linkage of all these caves, and discovered this system had a whole other level. Suddenly Aladdin's Cave seemed like only a flashy distraction keeping me from the real gold: the proprietary information, the magicians' secrets. Instead I had a bag of Chilean geodes, glow in the dark T-shirts, rubber band guns, and rock candy.

I thumbed back through the program and surveyed the list of sessions, all the insider talk I was going to be missing out on: the fiscal forecast, discussions of risk management and liability, marketing, environmental impacts. These sessions would have given me the stuff I need to form a sense of the state of the show cave business as a business. It seemed like the curtain was going to remain drawn across my view of what really makes a show cave work.

I'd traveled a trail to this place littered with the remains of feral, failed show caves and along the way I'd assembled a thick file filled with tales of financial ruin, and it looked like I was going to just barely miss a chance to see how the survivors manage to make a go of it. I was marked as an interloper right when I most wanted to blend in with the crowd.

Still, I'd come all this way, and the reception at the Mimslyn's rooftop patio sounded like an opportunity to at least get a few free drinks out of this thing, even if nobody would talk to me. I threw on a fresh shirt and a blazer and headed back into town.

❖　❖　❖　❖

Through the lobby I breezed once again, this time to the elevators up to the Skyline Terrace, whose rooftop patio made for a perfect gathering place on a warm September night. I was fashionably late, and while the interior dining room was deserted, the roof deck was crowded with conferees, along with the bar and a jazz trio. I angled for a spot on the rail, the better to survey the crowd, and near the bar, the better to add cocktails to the list of free stuff I'd claimed at this meeting so far.

Taller than most folks, I had a nice view of the attendee's heads: there were ball caps and cowboy hats (straw and felt) and floppy tourist sun hats and folks who wouldn't wear a hat to a cocktail party in a fancy hotel. Ages of the conference attendees ranged from late teens to ancient, racial makeup mostly but not entirely white, dress code from the upper end of business casual to T-shirts and shorts and sandals. The mood was the happy-awkward of folks who go way back but don't see each other very often. Lots of little bursts of delight at seeing someone again punctuated the cloud of chatter, infused with standards from the jazz band.

It was hard not to feel more than a little like a crasher: the crowd had the vibe of wedding reception. Like a big family gathering, it was at once an eclectic group but one that clearly had some common bond. There always has to be an overarching reason to bring together a group of people this arbitrary.

The patio was crowded enough that even if you were trying, as I was, to stay above the fray, you eventually found yourself in close enough proximity to someone that you'd really have to commit to not talking to them. Another guy about my age and similar jeans-and-blazer comportment was also drawing back to survey the crowd, and we found ourselves inside the must-talk radius. He was an environmental engineer from the Twin Cities and a caver, and he had become a kind of consultant to a cave in Wisconsin,

Talking Shop at the National Cave Association

helping the longtime family ownership give the operation an ecologically minded overhaul.

Sensing that rare opportunity to talk to someone interested in reflecting on what these caves mean, I sketched out my project for him, told him how I'd come to think of myself as a kind of a cultural speleologist. But this line of discussion seemed to rankle him a little bit. I seemed, I guess, unserious, and he got "cavier than thou" on me, as cavers sometimes will. "The important thing is that the cave gets people thinking more accurately about how the earth works, not the colored lights and the corny jokes," he said, shortly before seeing the people he'd been scanning for, and wading off into the crowd.

I watched an old man wending his way across the patio, leaning heavily on a cane as he stopped to chat with each person he encountered, whether he knew them or not. It was only a matter of time before he approached me, and he did, directly.

He turned and looked up from beneath the brim of his non-ironic trucker hat. I learned from his nametag that he was from a cave in the Ozarks that I'd never heard of. "I don't believe we've met!" I started to tell him my name, but he didn't wait for me to get a word in edgewise. I had the strong impression that he couldn't really hear me anyway. "If you want to buy a show cave, well, you just let me know! I can't wait to get out of this business. My kids and their kids, none of them want a thing to do with it. But they're no count."

I tried to toss out a follow-up question—this sounded promising. But he talked over me again. "I'll be around the meeting, let people know I'm looking to sell! I'm too old for this!" With that he turned to snag another attendee and began his announcement again.

So I had made it past the gates, deep into the heart of the network of contemporary American show caves, past the checkpoint at registration, through the easy distraction of the trade show loot. But it was starting to seem like people not only had no interest in talking to me but had little interest even in talking about show caves. The thing I kept overhearing folks talking about in scraps of conversation was zip lines—the "it" ancillary attraction this year. (Sorry, gemstone mining.) I was starting to feel rather stuck.

Just when I was thinking about backing out through the crowd and heading for home, I heard a voice I instantly recognized from my time underground. I turned to see Dr. Stan Sides, my speleology field school instructor and guide through the historic show caves of the Mammoth Cave area. Dr. Stan was the man who calmly got me unstuck in Bedquilt Cave. It seemed like a good omen.

Dr. Stan is a real raconteur and was in the midst of holding forth to a circle of folks from the younger and crunchier end of the conference spectrum, a group of bearded and long-haired folks from Wisconsin who came to caving through rock climbing and mountain biking. One guy was wearing a t-shirt that I coveted as only a cave nerd can, reproducing the cover of Thomas Barr's landmark 1961 survey, *Caves of Tennessee.*

"So what we finally had to do to that spot in Stan's Well" — a wild cave in the Flint Ridge system in Kentucky that bears Dr. Stan's name — "was to crawl in there with some microcharges in drinking straws. We drilled holes the size of a pencil and slid them in, and when we blew them it just shaved the edge of the rock off, nice as you please, just enough for us to get through with the climbing gear and the cable ladder." He had everybody nodding in admiration. Follow-up questions quickly got technical about the methods and the materials — fellow enthusiasts, talking shop.

I posted up on the outskirts of this conversation and when it dissipated I drifted in to say hey, along with several other folks who had also been lurking. I was not at all surprised to find that Dr. Stan is a popular figure in show cave society. As a founding member of the Cave Research Foundation, his caver bona fides are impeccable, of course, but he's also part of the ownership group that runs Diamond Caverns, just outside the Mammoth Cave National Park boundaries in central Kentucky.

Diamond is hands-down the most impressive private operation in that area, maintained with a caver's ethic for protecting both visitors and cave. It's also a classic of the genre, one whose history is interwoven with Mammoth and hence the whole legacy of American show caves. All this is well established on the Diamond Caverns website in an unusually detailed, carefully sourced essay on the history of the caverns, written by Dr. Stan himself, in his capacity as speleohistorian.

Dr. Stan greeted me with characteristic enthusiasm and showed me proudly to the new circle forming around him, announcing that I had got through Bedquilt Cave. Apparently these folks were all familiar with Bedquilt, because they looked my tall, stocky self up and down and seemed suitably impressed — with Dr. Stan, that is, since they immediately surmised I didn't get through under my own power. But I sensed nonetheless that I had broken into a new space, like a caver feeling a strong breath of wind coming from a newly discovered lead.

That feeling only got stronger when Dr. Stan introduced me around the circle, and I realized there was more accumulated show cave experience in this small circle of folks than I had ever seen in one place before. The

Diamond Caverns ownership group, several of whom were now gathered around Dr. Stan, were a show cave all-star team.

Next to Stan Sides was Gordon Smith, a tall, white-haired man with the good posture and confident air of a successful small-town businessman. That's an accurate impression: he has run a prosperous operation in Southern Indiana called Marengo Cave for a generation and participated in the NCA for many years. Beside him were Susan and Gary Berdeaux. Susan was the coordinating director of the National Cave Association, overseeing much of the organization's day-to-day business—I had her to thank for my request for information ever getting through to the Luray host committee. She was petite but with the kind of energy that gave the impression of a coiled spring. I'd see her a lot over the next couple of days racing about, taking care of some new minor mishap. Gary, her sturdy, bearded spouse, was the manager of Diamond Caverns and also a nature photographer, an ultralight aircraft builder and pilot, and (ergo) a specialist in aerial and subterranean photography.

Next to him stood his brother Wade, a little taller, a little wirier, clean-shaven; his areas of expertise more in motorcycles and ATVs. Wade's collection of antiques and historical objects, especially bottles, has given him a detailed working knowledge of such esoterica as the history of American glassmaking. Within this small circle, I was in the presence of one of the most eclectic skill sets I'd encountered anywhere. It wasn't just that they were all accomplished cavers and experienced cave operators—they did those things in addition to everything they worked at with the rest of their lives, from ultralight aircraft to cardiac care.

I was also in the presence of living history: the collected experience in this group connected directly to a broad and deep swath of the American show cave's story. Dr. Stan's expertise I was already well familiar with, having spent a couple of hours of lecture and many hours of caving every day for a week to learn what he knew about the history of the show cave in the Mammoth Cave area.

In addition to maintaining Marengo Caves, founded in 1883, Gordon Smith for a brief time helped run Wyandotte Caves, vast caverns in the bluffs overlooking the Ohio. Until they closed their doors in the early 2000s, Wyandotte was among the nation's oldest show caves, first opened for business in 1820 by the aptly named Henry P. Rothrock. Which means Gordon has run a show cave older than Mammoth Cave (which opened in the 1830s)—that's a small club. Fittingly, he is in possession of one of the two or three largest private collections of show cave memorabilia in the United States, holdings he envisions will become the core of the National Cave Museum. The completed museum is intended to be both a historical resource on show caves and an ancillary attraction for Diamond Caverns.

Gary and Wade, among all their other subterranean experiences, are the sons of Sonny Berdeaux, the owner of Endless Caverns from 1984 to 2006. Wade and Gary lived and worked around Endless Caverns for a good bit of their adult lives. From 1878 until now, that operation has seen some of the highest highs and abject lows. After making an initial $304,000 investment in 1984, the Berdeaux family enjoyed a productive twenty-two-year run and then sold the property for $2.6 million in 2006. If you have lived and worked at Endless Caverns, you are pretty much as fully initiated into the whole show cave phenomenon as a person can be (an idea I explore much further in chapter 8).

I had suddenly gone from a series of dead ends to leads unfurling in all directions. Listening to these guys talk shop was, for a show cave scholar, an embarrassment of riches, so much more substantial than my haul of free samples from the exhibitors. I had come upon a nexus of knowledge and experience and memory, as ephemeral as an intersection of cave passages is enduring. It was hard even to know how to start down any one of these routes, all of which appeared to lead to a lot more cave, er, a lot more information about caves.

❖   ❖   ❖   ❖

Then before I knew what was going on, the ring of the conversation opened up to my left, to include a woman already seated at a cocktail table just outside the group. As I turned to see who the circle had absorbed now, Dr. Stan called out a delighted greeting and crossed over to us. "Jeanne! I had hoped to see you here! Doug, this is Jeanne Gurnee. Jeanne, Doug here writes about show caves, too."

"Do you?" she asks me. "Please, sit down and tell me about it." I was looking at a trim, elderly, but active woman—the kind my Mom would admiringly describe as "very put-together." Omigod, I think, it's Jeanne Gurnee. No, seriously, Jeanne Frickin' Gurnee.

Now if you don't know a Tom Barr *Caves of Tennessee* t-shirt when you see one, you might not know why the sudden appearance of Jeanne Gurnee would flip my wig. I was looking at the woman who, with her husband Russell Gurnee, had spent over half a century in and around caves. After both Gurnees joined the NSS in 1951 as something that seemed like a fun shared interest for a young married couple, they commenced a lifetime of explor-

Talking Shop at the National Cave Association

ing wild caves; visiting, documenting, and writing guidebooks about all the show caves they could find; and combining those interests by developing show caves themselves or consulting on other people's projects. Jeanne continued actively pursuing their legacy after Russell's death in 1995, advising show cave development and cave exploration and faithfully producing new editions of the Gurnee guides.

The Rio Camuy cave network in Puerto Rico represents perhaps the Gurnees' most substantial accomplishment. In 1958, traveling among the limestone bluffs called mogotes in the northwest corner of the island, Russell and Jeanne found vast sinkholes opening onto flowing rivers at the bottom. While it's sometimes characterized as a discovery, what the Gurnees had discovered was a place that had been well trafficked over the course of centuries all the way back to the indigenous Taino people, and only recently forgotten by the outside world.

Over the next several decades the Gurnees led expeditions sponsored by the Explorer's Club (of which Russell was at one point president) and the National Geographic Society, surveying the vast cave system and its trove of archaeological, speleological, and cultural resources. Meanwhile they consulted with the US and Puerto Rican governments on the extraordinary logistical and environmental challenges of developing the caverns for tourism, from acquiring subterranean development rights to figuring out how to get the heavy equipment and materials needed to do the work to the bottom of a 300-foot-deep sinkhole, without destroying a big swathe of the side of the pit.

Helicopters and a hoisting crane constructed in the bottom of the sinkhole made possible the construction of a trolley that augers down into the sinkhole's depths. There the Rio Camuy flows out of caverns on the upstream side, and into the darkness of further caverns opposite. Through the bureaucratic, physical, and financial obstacles they persevered to create a unique, expertly designed show cave experience. They must have done something right: thanks to their decades of patient work, after they withdrew from the project in the 1980s, it became a national park and one of Puerto Rico's leading and most enduring natural attractions. Exploration and expansion of the public sections of the cave are ongoing, still building on the Gurnees' legacy.

Rio Camuy alone would be enough for me to be excited about meeting THE Jeanne Gurnee, but it's just one facet of what she has contributed to show caves writ large. The Gurnees didn't just make show caves, they influenced the way show caves are made. As president of the National Speleological Society, Jeanne Gurnee encouraged cavers to get past their native contempt for show caves and get involved in their welfare. She paved the way for the Jim Whidbys of the world to intervene on abandoned caves' behalf. She brought elements of her background as an environmental commissioner in her home state of New Jersey to introduce a stronger ecological ethic — an infusion of cavers' veneration of the untouched cave — to the way show caves present and, indeed, imagine themselves.

The NCA originally convened to do things like rally against Lady Bird Johnson's highway beautification projects on the grounds that billboards were their advertising life's blood. But the organization provided a forum for Jeanne and Russell to advance their environmentally aware version of show caving. The Gurnees were, along with several other NSS colleagues, early members of the NCA. If you ask her which offices she has held over the years, she replies, "All of them." And not coincidentally, the default setting of show caves today is to serve as genial outreach efforts in the struggle for environmental preservation and conservation. But the bedrock argument for this approach in the NCA is that maintaining a healthy cave makes good business sense, preserving and even intensifying its appeal.

Her work in this area culminated in the 1999 opening of Kartchner Caverns State Park, an intricately decorated cave beneath the Chihuahuan Desert of Arizona. For a quarter century Jeanne coordinated an effort, as she told the press, to create a cave where "everything that the caving community has learned about the preserving and showing of caverns is brought into use." An LED lighting system, a series of airlocks for climate control, trails designed for accessibility: the show here isn't just the abundant formations but the advanced design of the apparatus. It's an evolution of the way show caves traditionally include their own story as a part of the tourist narrative, bringing it away from self-promotion and toward science education.

Though she is not now formally affiliated with any particular cave, Jeanne remains an NCA member, the only one accorded the title "Advisor to the Board and International Liaison." She may very well have had greater impact than any single, living individual over the state of the show cave in the United States. Long before the era of customer ratings, the Gurnees installed themselves as arbiters of best practices in the field through the standards they set in their own work, the organizations they developed around common issues, and of course the guide books that reported their assessments to the world.

So there I was sitting in a crowded cocktail party across from arguably the single greatest repository of knowledge of, experience with, and actual influence over the course of the American show cave. She very pleasantly listened as I tried to give her my elevator speech on the book and nodded

Talking Shop at the National Cave Association

knowingly as she and I both began to realize my attempt to keep it brief was running out of steam and my anecdotes were getting out of control.

"Don't worry, it comes with the territory," she kindly interrupted. We commiserated on the breadth, both conceptual and geographic, of the whole subject of the show cave. She spoke in complete, concise sentences.

"I've just been trying to describe a small set of show caves," I said, "and I feel like I've been at this forever. I can't imagine how you feel, trying to understand so many more caves, and at such an advanced level. You seem so . . . coherent."

"Well, my goodness, this subject has kept me working and searching and traveling all around the world for over fifty years. I've been trying to understand show caves for longer than we've called them show caves. Do you know how we came to use that term?"

No, in fact, I did not. I suddenly felt quite exposed. All this reading and research, and I had never really thought about where the very name of the thing I was studying had come from — I had just acquired the usage without reflecting on it. And yet it's not a very widely known term. Whenever I'm talking to someone not named Jeanne Gurnee, I generally have to start off my elevator speech with a quick capsule definition of the term "show cave." I've come to think of it as a "term of art."

"Oh, yes, I was in the room when it was decided. At the international meetings in the early 1960s, we realized we needed a term that could translate well across languages and cultures. Many of the European cave operators, in particular those from socialist countries, strongly objected to the term 'commercial cave.' They saw themselves as preserving a public legacy. But they are still exhibition caves, whether or not they're operated for gain, so 'show cave' seemed a more accurate description of our shared purpose.

"When we came back to the US and brought this matter to the NCA, the holdouts were proud capitalists who fought for the term 'commercial cave,' but in the end we agreed it was useful because it also applied to the publicly operated caves like Carlsbad and Mammoth Cave. I have always felt that public, not-for-profit ownership represented the best possibilities for protecting the cave and promoting an understanding of caves as a resource and a matter of public interest. Private operations have too much incentive to cut corners where environmental best practices are concerned, and the consequences of failure for the cave are dire. I'm sure you know, it's a very difficult business. Oh hello!"

At this point a patient lurker took a slight lull in our chat as an opportunity to get Jeanne's attention, which set off another one of those little bursts of recognition. I had already gotten way luckier with my face time with Jeanne Gurnee in this environment than I could reasonably expect, especially given the myriad connections she had to practically everyone here.

"I'll let y'all get caught up," I said, and we both warmly assured each other we'd continue the conversation later. I didn't see her again. But this time when I got back to my room out in the country, I felt like I had really gotten somewhere. I'd made it to the stream level, pushed the survey deep into the heart of the show cave, where all the different leads started to come together: I had made it to the etymological source of the term "show cave" itself. I had found the connection that linked my little cave network into a broader global complex.

I really wish I had been able to go to those sessions. I'm sure I would have picked up some really nice footnote-able behind-the-scenes facts. But what I saw watching the folks who make show caves work made it clear that, once again, when push really came to shove, it's about the people at least as much as it is about the cave.

❖　❖　❖　❖

So, instead of learning about the trade by attending panels and presentations, I went with immersion. Having broken through into the heart of the gathering by way of Jeanne Gurnee, for the rest of my stay in Luray it seemed like I was involved in nonstop conversation with folks from all across the cave trade, and seeing the tradecraft being practiced at a very high level.

I started off the next morning with an on-the-record conversation with Eric Evans, the operator of Ohio Caverns and the president of the NCA. As we stood on the Mimslyn's broad porch, taking in the views of the rolling hills of the South Branch of the Shenandoah River, in summing up the NCA's current mission he confirmed for me the success of Jeanne Gurnee's reshaping of the organization. It's not about the money, it's about protecting the natural resource, was his go-to talking point. He balked a little when I referred to the meeting as a "trade show," arguing instead that it was more like a conference, dedicated to health of caves first and foremost, because healthy caves are a precondition to a healthy show cave trade. Probably a good thing I didn't slip up and refer to show caves as "commercial caverns."

Later I'd find myself sitting across from Eric's wife Janine on a field trip bus ride. She fleshed out his more philosophical view with a deep personal connection: they had met as Ohio Caverns guides when they were teenagers and had never left the caverns or each other. Later they took the opportunity to take over for the owners they had worked for. However much their current mission was focused on ecology and conservation, and their business operation is necessarily dedicated to staying solvent, the Evans's tie to Ohio Caverns is clearly a deeply emotional one.

And as eclectic as the NCA's members were as a group, this was their common bond: that their work with caves was not only a business but a personal relationship with their cave. In this sense, I realized, show caves do the same thing for operator and guest alike: they create an emotionally complex relationship among people and the earth. Many in the NCA, I further realized, knew this already. I began at last to find that deeper mode of inquiry into what show caves are and ought to be, the deep stream level.

A luncheon keynote speaker, Dan Cove, the director of Jenolan Caves in the Blue Mountains of New South Wales, west of Sydney, Australia, explored the show cave as a place where reason and emotion intersect. What show caves provide the opportunity for both their operators and their guests to do, Cove argued, is wed the environmental awareness to the peculiar emotional experience of being in the cave. Ideally visitors emerge with not just a better intellectual understanding of but also a deeper emotional attachment to an environmental ethic.

Cove was young and smart, and everyone agreed they loved his accent. What I was hearing was someone who came to show caves from the world of environmental science, making peace with the "show" part of the business. Cove has a degree in environmental science and graduate work in tourism management, but he's also a musician, even performing on piano in the Jenolan Caves House resort lodge. That element of colored-light vaudeville that the more environmentally aware among us sometimes find unserious, Cove was ready to endorse for its rhetorical value.

His talk's centerpiece was a discussion of Jenolan's creation of an audio tour of the caves in Klingon, the language of the Star Trek mythos's warlike empire. Sure, it's not exactly a lesson in earth science, Cove conceded, but in connecting the cave's story to other romantic narratives of exploration and discovery, and drawing in visitors who are already invested in these kinds of stories, we create an opportunity to see caves as a site of wonder and a resource for imagining our future.

Judging from the knowing nods around the room, it seemed like Cove struck a chord with a number of attendees. I wondered if I was seeing a kind of pendulum swing—the whole industry was born of show business, but the more ecological model now held full sway, or so it seemed. But here was someone coming out of the environmental education movement pointing us back toward the production, the performance, the artifice. Maybe a new chapter in the history of show cave aesthetics was opening, drawing back from the naturalistic, leave-no-trace ethic of the cavers, but in the service of a broader goal in the environmental movement—to get people to really feel a stronger affinity to the earth.

After the talk, the discussion turned toward the idea that there ought to be more general awareness of show caves as a phenomenon with a story of its own. Gordon Smith of the Diamond Caverns group spoke up to rally support for his pet project, a national show cave museum built on his own collection of show cave memorabilia.

"We need a place where people can appreciate our collective accomplishments," Gordon said, "and a central location for information about our history. You take this young man right here," he said, indicating me, "he's writing a book about show caves, and I'm sure he'd like to be able to have a lot of this stuff all in one place! Then he wouldn't have to come hang around with a bunch of old farts like us," he added, to amenable chuckles.

I nodded sheepishly as suddenly everybody looked at me. I hadn't expected to be called out like that in front of everybody, and I wasn't 100 percent sure this wasn't one of the sessions I wasn't supposed to attend.

Gordon was right that the idea of having a central depository of materials on the history of the American show cave definitely made my academic researcher heart beat quick. But what I was increasingly understanding is that being there, with them, was the information I was really looking for. From smaller moments of individual interaction, a larger portrait of a subculture began to emerge.

At a long, chatty luncheon in the sunny Mimslyn dining room, I caught up with Gary and Becky Barnett, the owner-operators of Bristol Caverns. Just a few miles from where I grew up, Bristol Caverns was my first show cave, thanks to Mrs. Brewer's second-grade field trip. The Barnetts were polite if not exactly overjoyed to squeeze me in at their two-top, but not because they were protecting any trade secrets. I got the feeling that this was a rare vacation for these folks, and they didn't want to spend too much of it on me when they could be talking to each other. It was sweet, actually.

They were both good solid East Tennessee people, and they both had spent their adult lives keeping this business going. They had grown up in Sullivan County right there around the cave, and he had been a guide and jack-of-all-trades there under the previous owner, taking over the whole operation from his old boss. It was Eric Evans's story again, and it was a story I heard several more times before the meeting was over. For so many folks here, what I came to think of as the NCA's rank and file, becoming involved

Talking Shop at the National Cave Association

in the work of show caves wasn't so much a conscious choice as a way of life that grew up around them. For a little while I had the chance to squeeze in alongside them.

◆　◆　◆　◆

And that's just what I did: I spent a big chunk of time over the course of the next couple of days riding around in motor coaches visiting show caves with the folks who make the show caves. In a lot of ways, the show cave crowd made for the worst tour group ever. Many of them knew each other and had catching up to do, so lots of side conversations rippled through the crowd. Running commentary, assessment, even critique bounced around. When asked for questions, they had lots of them, and they were oddly specific: How often do you have to regravel the walkways? What's your approach to dealing with cave algae? with lint? Do people have trouble with strollers on that hill? Anytime anybody stumbled or slipped, someone shouted "lawsuit!" They moved slowly but were surprisingly hard to herd, feeling at home underground and thus not as easily cowed into sticking with the group as your typical tourists would be.

But for all that, they were a very generous audience, looking to be impressed, finding things to admire. They ooohed and aaahed all the more sincerely and readily since they knew just what it took to make the spectacle happen. They took the time to appreciate the craft as well as the presentation and approached it all with the generous nature of colleagues rather than rivals or competitors.

The caverns we visited knew their crowd — they let folks linger over each phase of the tour much longer than any group of civilians I ever toured with. And they made sure to trot out a little something extra for the aficionados. If a major objective of this trip for me was more than satisfied by my time spent with the NCA rank and file listening to them talk shop, then another was fulfilled by the opportunity to see the host caves put their best foot forward.

Of course, we visited Grand Caverns, the eldest, among the most lovely, and so richly woven into history. In some ways this cave, now a publicly owned park with a strong conservation ethic and a modest, low-key ethos, was kind of like the unpretentious rank and file of the NCA. Shorn of grandiose illusions about the commercial and economic potential of the operation, it has an air of real hospitality, of a cave tended by people who care about caves, almost like a throwback to the days before Jed Hotchkiss arrived on the scene and the Mohler family passed the responsibility of offering tours from father to son.

After the volatile, utopian days of the Grottoes Company, the cavern went through a succession of local, family owners, until the final owner, Gladys Kellow, bequeathed the cavern to a regional parks authority, which in turn transferred it to the Town of Grottoes. As it turned out, fading ambition really suited this cave — not working for profit, the caverns has been able to put more emphasis on earth science and environmental health. No ziplines here; the only ancillary attraction is a community pool and a miniature golf course whose greens have seen better days. Perhaps because of the relative absence of hoopla, Grand has become a favorite of cavers, a site of active exploration. A tight muddy crawl (carefully gated, of course) leading to new discoveries that have dramatically expanded our understanding of the size of cave has become a landmark on the tour. It's a quiet, healthy operation, free from aggressive marketing and commercial come-ons, a low-key fulfillment of Jeanne Gurnee's argument about the virtues of public ownership.

The lagniappe on the tour here was, consequently, modest but no less special for that. You don't need to dress up the experience of getting to step over the rail and leave the tour route: it makes you feel like a VIP every time. Those of us who happened to be in the vicinity of the cave's manager, Lettie Stickley, got treated to a peek at a formation in a room that's no longer on the tour and a trip around back of a huge stalagmite to see some little-known Civil War–era graffiti. One sure sign you're running with an experienced show cave crowd: when we detoured off the lighted path, most in the crowd instinctively took out the flashlights they just habitually had in their pockets. You could see the show cave crowd light up, too, with the opportunity to get behind the scenes, to see Grand — the mother show cave itself! — as a cave you could imagine yourself working with, filled with hidden details to discover and develop.

◆   ◆   ◆   ◆

So by the time we got to Shenandoah Caverns the stakes for rolling out a special reception were pretty high, but Earl Hargrove, Shenandoah Caverns' truly singular owner, was more than equal to the task. He had a great cave to work with, first off, a property that came into its own under Hunter Chapman, the cave impresario who simultaneously ran Shenandoah Caverns and Indian Cave Village near New Market, Virginia, and New Market, Tennessee, respectively, from the 1920s to the 1940s. Unlike its mercurial sister cave, Shenandoah has been a consistent performer. From a cave revealed by demolition for railroad construction, Chapman built a solid, lasting attraction that never once fell into a feral state after he opened it for business in 1922.

Earl Hargrove took over the reins of ownership in 1966, jumping into the cave business with both feet, even though, as he often told people, he didn't know you could actually own a cave until the opportunity came along to buy one. Though he was new to the industry, Hargrove maintained continuity with the cave's past. He kept the current manager, Dan Proctor, on board, and his son Joe Proctor, whose middle name is "Earl" in honor of the owner, took over after Dan's death.

Perhaps as a result, the cavern has kind of a throwback quality that is immensely fun. You should expect no less from a cave that still bills itself (with tongue in cheek, surely?) the home of "Virginia's Only Cave Elevator Service." Shenandoah is a relative youngster among its show cave peers: without layers of former uses, its 1920s' car tourist aesthetic is preserved in an unusually pure form. It's the rare show cave that's only ever really had one shtick.

Fittingly, the showpiece speleothems tend to be great examples of a kind of formation found in a lot of caves: outstanding "cave bacon," for example, the ribbon formation striped with iron deposits that's a dead ringer for the real thing, especially when backlit. An exceptional "Capital Dome" — the name given to rounded, conical stalagmites nationwide — is luminous in blue, viewable from multiple points on the tour.

The money formation here is Rainbow Lake. It's a fine, maybe the best, example of the classic "rainbow lights" set piece, in which a formation (in this case a speleothem-encrusted tunnel containing a reflecting pool) is lit in different colors and combinations of colors and from different angles, bringing out different shapes and details and playing with the depth of field, before dramatically throwing on all the lights in culmination.

One of the great dividing lines of show cave aesthetics runs through the decision about whether to go with multicolored ("garish") or naturalistic ("boring") lighting. It's clear where Shenandoah Caverns comes down on this doctrine: all in on the razzmatazz.

That's understandable when you know who Earl Hargrove was. Up until he passed away in 2015, Earl Hargrove built an entire career out of pure artifice, an empire of appearances. He was born in 1929, and in the late 1940s, following high school and a stint in the Marine Corps, he apprenticed with his father, a successful Washington, DC, window dresser. His dad broke into the top tier, department store Christmas displays, in the high period of big downtown extravaganzas at stores like Woodward & Lothrop.

Young Earl evolved the operation along with the twentieth-century media, into the creation of parade floats, dramatic settings for inaugurations, dedications, speeches, and the like — any work that called for the creation of temporary simulations of monumental construction, the kind that would be in ever greater demand with the rise of the mass media.

Ephemeral visions of majesty became Earl Hargrove's unique stock in trade. The columns behind the phalanx of flags behind the dais filled with dignitaries could be papier-mâché as long as they looked plausible on television. His work on inaugurals and White House special events from Truman on earned him the nickname "the President's prop master." He even went his father an order of magnitude greater in his Christmas-decorating duties: Hargrove Inc., has managed the decoration and illumination of the National Christmas Tree for over fifty years.

Earl Hargrove was, in sum, uniquely overqualified for the show cave trade. Shenandoah continues to be a fine example of a cave maintained by someone as invested in the show as cavers like Jeanne Gurnee are in the cave. Shenandoah quite affirmatively owns the idea of spectacle for spectacle's sake.

Not only is the show cave unflinching in its loyalty to colored lights; the secondary attractions here put the show cave itself in the larger context of the Hargrove family business. Adjacent to the gift shop, in the Cavern Inn's upstairs is phase one of the Hargrove legacy project. "Main Street of Yesteryear" houses a wide array of reconstructed store window displays, their clockwork still bringing the toylands to life on command. Perhaps it's a touching tribute to Hargrove's father, perhaps a unique repository of a vanishing visual art, perhaps a way to monetize a bunch of stuff that was otherwise just taking up storage space. Probably all of the above, to varying extents.

Just down the hill from the cavern lodge stands a newer, corrugated steel warehouse building, iconically fronted by two statues. An old-school Emmett Kelly–style clown and a scale reproduction of the Statue of Liberty foreshadow the insane mix of patriotism and tomfoolery within. This warehouse is essentially Hargrove Inc.'s attic, where it keeps all the old parade floats.

But that description, while accurate, is completely inadequate. If Earl Hargrove took the family window-dressing business and evolved it into something much more vast and ambitious and spectacular, he did the same thing with the idea behind Main Street of Yesteryear. In its next generation, that concept became the warehouse-scaled American Celebration on Parade, "the world's only permanent indoor parade." And it was here that we were delivered when our tour of the adjacent caverns and department-store windows was completed. The motor coaches tooled down the lane toward the interstate and discharged the NCA membership and me at the front door, to experience the VIP treatment, Earl Hargrove style.

◆　◆　◆　◆

Arriving at the warehouse, the NCA conventioneers crossed the foyer, passed through an arched colonnade, and wandered into the midst of a vast technicolor freakout. Ducks in Edwardian schoolboy gear gazed in awe at an imperious Mardi Gras queen, serenaded by a band of busking pelicans, all rendered on a gigantic scale, the birds the size of people, the people the size of titans. Beyond the alabaster bust of the queen I caught glimpses of mythological beasts, birds of prey, and biplanes, along with a jovial family of polar bears. Lining the red carpet leading to the rear of the warehouse were a ten-foot-tall teddy bear riding a chopper, a sea monster pulling a chariot driven by Poseidon himself, an immense bald eagle, and an actual streetcar; hovering above them, suspended from wires, a spacewalking astronaut the size of Andre the Giant.

What we were seeing were the artifacts of Hargrove Inc.'s work as a supplier of floats to such top-tier parades as the Tournament of Roses and Mardi Gras. Mostly these were elaborate custom-built aluminum frames covered by a taut, synthetic fabric that could support the weight of a man. They were to the old chicken-wire-and-tissue-paper homecoming floats as the Space Shuttle is to the Wright Brothers' craft at Kitty Hawk.

To take it in all it once was to absorb a gust of pure artifice — as if the show biz element of the show cave trade could be distilled into its own separate essence, so pure it didn't even need the cave anymore. The rear portion of the building gave way from parade floats to inaugural stagecraft, the columns and bunting and podiums from the speeches and galas of presidents past, and nestled in this landscape of self-congratulation, the bar was open for business. It took me a second to realize I was looking at actual humans in black vests and bow ties and not some kind of audioanimatronics. Fortunately, the bourbon was real, as were the Asian-fusion-tapas snacks brought around by more actual humans as we filed in.

The mock grandeur of the entire situation made it feel like there was some nitrous oxide being piped in, and knowing something about what a careful event planner Earl Hargrove was, I didn't completely rule out the possibility. In any event, before the effect could wear off, here came Earl Hargrove through the crowd, cheerfully glad-handing and small-talking his way

National Cave Association reception, American Celebration on Parade,
Shenandoah Caverns, September 2011. (Photograph by the author)

through the arrivees with a good nature that seemed simultaneously artfully
honed and perfectly sincere.

Eventually my turn for a quick pas de deux with the host came around.
I hoped to make a play to disrupt his rhythm and see if I could get in a little
more of a chat with the man, or at least arrange one for later. But my social
skills were absolutely overmatched. My quick summary of my project received a few words of encouragement, and I was made personally welcome
by my host. However, my jabs at a little more detail about the life that resulted in the creation of this insane space where we both now stood ex-
changing pleasantries were quickly deflected to an assistant I had hardly even
noticed trailing in his wake.

The young woman wore a blazer and chinos, like the officer's version of
a cave guide uniform, her tablet at the ready with Mr. Hargrove's schedule
and notes, a Bluetooth earpiece linking her in to the broader support staff. "I
hear you are looking for some more information!" she cheerfully proffered.

"Yes indeed," I replied, "It certainly seems like there's a story behind how
Mr. Hargrove and all of this," I gestured around, "ended up out here by a cavern in a pasture in the Shenandoah Valley."

"Well, you just give me your mailing address, and I'll be sure you get a press packet that will fill you right in. And here is my card if you'd like to follow up with questions." A little information exchange and some taps on the tablet and we were finished here. For his last trick Earl Hargrove disappeared, from my ambit, anyway, without revealing even one of his tricks. But he left each of us a favor to take home that night: silk roses taken from the centerpieces of table settings at the Kennedy inaugural balls. Earl Hargrove's world, like the culture of the show cave, was one where no mark, once made, would ever permanently vanish—an improbable repository of the superficial and the ephemeral.

❖   ❖   ❖   ❖

The headliner of the NCA outings was, of course, our hosts' own Luray Caverns. There was no way to top Shenandoah with an even bigger, more elaborate spectacle, and though Luray has proved more successful over time, it couldn't pretend to Grand's historical significance. But Luray had its own kind of magic—a careful, artful, masterful romanticism—and the magicians here were at the top of their game, too.

Luray is, to all outward appearances, one of the most prosperous and impressive privately held show caves in the business. As many as 400,000 visitors per year at $24 a head pass through these caverns, the third-most-visited cave in the United States after Carlsbad and Mammoth, both of which are national parks. Their buildings and grounds are clean and classy and carefully maintained. Sure, they have their kitschy moments; homemade fudge and gemstone mining are in evidence. The antique car museum, "Toy Town" diorama, and garden maze bespeak a little more vaudevillian era, the remnants of the old "cabinet of wonders" sensibility that Shenandoah still makes its total stock in trade. (Since this visit, however, Luray has placed greater emphasis on local and regional history, a particular interest of Rod and John Graves, with the development of the restored farmstead called the Luray Valley Museum, included in your admission.) And lest one forget the first allegiances of this place to car tourism, the approach to the elegant stone lodge housing the cave entrance and gift store is dominated by a sea of parking lot.

Still, across the Lee Highway, a sunny sky over the massive Blue Ridge provides the picturesque backdrop for a carillon tower, and the rolling hills of the Shenandoah Valley bespeak a pastoral elegance, a little of Virginia's colonial dignity, held over from an earlier era when that colonial history could get away with being a lot more triumphalist and a lot more obtuse. In that sense, it's a self-consciously "classier" operation than most. Luray's proximity to the nation's capital has drawn enough dignitaries, including first ladies from Eleanor Roosevelt to Michelle Obama, to build a reputation as more than just a durable tourist trap. And I was getting the opportunity to see them roll out the red carpet, and conduct a kind of a master class.

The jocular pack of show cave folks actually fell a little more into line, paying a little extra attention. Murmurs of admiration swept regularly through the groups, not just for the bewildering beauty of Luray's lavishly decorated cave, but for the maintenance of pathways, the total absence of trash and discoloration around the lights, the invisibility of its wiring, the absence of vandalism.

A roving group of the show cave folks kept up a debate about the merits of prerecorded audio tours, a venture Luray had recently tried and abandoned. Generally the view was upheld that there were definitely some solid benefits: the efficiencies for your payroll, ease of scheduling (visitors could be sent individually instead of formed into groups — no waiting), and consistency of outcomes (no longer relying on the knowledge, enthusiasm, and improvisational skills of a teenaged seasonal worker for your quality control). But in the end, the human interaction with both the guide and the rest of the group was an important part of the experience, something isolation under headphones could never replace: the trade off, they figured, is a net loss. Plus, all agreed, keeping the batteries charged on those damn things has got to be a pain.

It's not surprising that a more traditional view would win out in this setting. Luray is the kind of cavern where the formations don't change names all that often: Titania's Veil and the Saracen's Tent are still just that, even though no one remembers what a Saracen is or why Titania was veiled (if indeed they ever knew). My personal favorite is the Fallen Column, a massive speleothem that fell over on the cave floor long enough ago that it now has an elaborate battlement of stalagmites along its horizontal length. Even constant change is ancient here.

Cutting-edge is not what people come to Luray for. I realized I was seeing essentially the same tour described by assistant state geologist William McGill in his 1933 survey *Caverns of Virginia*. "Terraced minarets, leaning towers, slender, graceful pillars and massive fluted step-growth columns project from the floor or rise abruptly from ponderous races of flowstone." Luray is a scene that can bring out the purple prose even from a scientist like McGill.

When we descended to the base of the majestic "Big Column," a uniformed staff member diverted us into a dimly lit side passage. "This room,"

The Stalacpipe Organ at Luray Caverns, 2005. (Photograph by the author)

she explained, "is not normally open due to flooding issues. It was once part of the candlelight tour but has never been electrically lighted. Tonight, we've arranged a candlelight illumination for our special guests."

We weren't able to linger, given the need to move several subgroups of our tour through, but I will remember that sight very happily, as one of the most purely lovely I've seen in all my work. The room itself was nothing that special, maybe fifteen feet wide and twenty-five high, but all around the irregular nooks and crannies of the room's walls, candles smoldered and glowed in the damp cave air, animating the shadows. It was like being inside a tiny organic planetarium. Later I learned, with the ironic touch I've come to expect of show caves, that when it was part of the tour, this chamber was called Hades.

From there we were whisked to Luray's climactic stop, the Stalacpipe Organ, one of the truly legendary, completely unique show cave features. I never tire of it. A multiple-manual organ console on a riser against a backdrop of draperies and stalactites creates an H. R. Geiger–meets–Captain Nemo spectacle in the heart of a magnificent gothic chamber. It was built by inventor Leland Sprinkle in 1954 and of course immediately proclaimed the World's Largest Pipe Organ (though I have since learned the technical term for the instrument is "lithophone"). The organ itself is wired to concealed electric hammers, each solenoid mounted on a speleothem producing at least a reasonable facsimile of the appropriate tone. The tour group gathered for patiently executed rendition of "A Mighty Fortress Is Our God," performed with an inevitability that evoked some ancient ritual.

The organ is now in self-player mode only, we were made to understand, though a recording of a recital on the stalacpipe by Naval Academy organist Monte Maxwell is available in the gift shop, and on YouTube you can see a video of none other than Fred Rogers playing "Won't You Be My Neighbor," which always makes me cry for reasons I don't quite understand. After a few remarks from the guide, we exited to the more ethereal strains of "O Shenandoah," a gentle xylophone arrangement punctuated by the random percussive snaps of falling water droplets. Something this eccentric, this elegant, made even people who work on putting on a show cave every day really pause and take stock.

❖   ❖   ❖   ❖

This exhibition of true show cave mastery was followed by a reception at Limair, the historic home of the Graves family on the grounds of the caverns. Limair was designed to be a sanatorium whose signature feature was a facility cooled and freshened by pure cavern air. Limair opened in 1901, complete with straight-faced scientific disquisitions on the bacteriological perfection of the purity of the air published in the popular science magazines of the day. With a show cave's zeal for superlatives, it was dubbed "the first air-conditioned house in America."

Probably its biggest health effects were a negative impact on the financial health of the whole operation, which was on the block by 1905. That is when Limair became the home of Colonel T. C. Northcott and his family. Colonel Northcott's newly created Luray Caverns Corporation acquired the cavern property, and it is still in the family today, by way of Northcott's daughter Katherine, who married a Graves. Their son, Theodore, became Rebecca Beall Jackson's husband in 1944 and a new generation of Luray Caverns leadership was intact. Ted and Rebecca Graves guided Luray confidently through a period of expansion when other show caves struggled and worked hard as civic leaders in Luray and as representatives of the show cave business. They served for years as representatives on tourist commissions and state boards and any other assembled body that took up business with relevance to Virginia tourism.

As we strolled from the cavern tour to the hillside mansion, attendees interested in issues of ventilation and air quality—a pretty large number of the attendees—eagerly flocked to the shed housing the fans that to this day draw 60 degree air from inside Luray through a tunnel into Limair's basement. A maintenance man pulled up on a golf cart and opened up the fan shed for the curious. I only speculated that Earl Hargrove was pumping in the nitrous, but I saw with my own eyes how the atmosphere at the Limair reception would be rich with the living breath of one of the world's finest show caves.

To enter the brick Georgian Revival mansion itself, one passed through a receiving line on the white-columned portico to pay one's respects to the matriarch of the clan. Rebecca Graves was arrayed on the porch in classic Southern lady style, small but hale for a woman of eighty-eight on a late afternoon in September, giving and receiving warm regards to and from all the attendees. Many of them were seeing her for the first time since her husband, who among his many roles was a past president of the NCA, had passed away a little over a year before, and took a moment to express sympathy or share a memory. Behind her, the tree-lined walk framed a view of the Singing Tower, tinted by the evening sun, itself a monument to a departed Luray spouse: Colonel Northcott had it constructed in 1937 in memory of his wife Belle Brown Northcott.

Mrs. Graves rounded out the tableau with a grandson of thirteen, who, she proudly reported to each guest as she squeezed his elbow, had earned the rank of Star scout. The Star scout himself bore the burden of his grandmother's pride with reasonable discomfort balanced out by genuine affection.

From there we passed through the foyer and into the parlor, where John Graves stood in front of the fireplace as if upon the bridge. He looked the part, gray temples, businesslike round glasses. Blue blazer and chinos and a dress shirt open at the throat were clearly second nature, perfectly cast against a backdrop of aged leather-bound books lining the cases against the far wall.

As the room filled, he gave a brief welcome speech, and a quick historical sketch of the house. Soon after the Northcotts moved in in 1905, the original sanitorium building burned to the ground. Colonel Northcott, not a man to be outdone, rebuilt Limair, but this time cast the entire structure in poured concrete, which was then clad in brick. He'd never again sift the embers of joists and beams. It seemed almost like a metaphor for the kind of persistence required to not only survive but thrive in the show cave trade for a century.

While John was holding forth, I found myself drawn to some framed pen-and-ink drawings on the wall that looked to date from the Jazz Age. As John finished, I found Rod Graves at my elbow. He's perfectly cast as John's kid brother; even though he has less hair he has a younger face and a more open demeanor. He seemed deployed at my side in the role of brand ambassador. He said he'd wanted to meet me since we share an interest in writing about regional history. Rod has worked on "Images of America" projects about the cave and the lower valley, part of a tradition, he notes, of the family being involved in other kinds of arts and culture. Many members of earlier generations spent time in creative pursuits out in the broader worlds, he explained, but they always came back to Luray eventually to contribute their range of experience to the show cave.

The house was like a private museum to the story of this family. The drawings I was looking at, and many of the other pieces on display were by various Northcotts and Graveses, including a sister of Rod's who currently lived in Montana, working as a potter. The house was always filled with music as well; Rebecca herself was a confident organist for her local Episcopal congregation, and another absent sister who now lives in France performed professionally in a bell choir. Suddenly the Singing Tower and the lithophone made more sense: one attraction that fills the underground spaces with music, and the other that projects music all about the valley above. It made sense somehow that those ideas were born in this place.

Indeed, what I was looking at here, I realized, was something not unlike American Celebration on Parade, the storehouse of a life lived in the deliberate pursuit of illusion, in the creation of images. But unlike Earl Hargrove's parade float Valhalla, this place bespoke a more human scale. This was the cultural, historical, human heart of a century-long show cave operation, like the show cave itself recording the layers and variety of human experience that brought it up to this point, encased in fireproof limestone, preserved by pure cave air.

❖   ❖   ❖   ❖

The time spent among the show cave folk, visiting some of Appalachia's, some of America's finest show caves, cast the whole industry in only the most positive light, once I had gotten past the protective veneer. As I rode back to the airport, I couldn't help but wonder what it was, exactly, that they didn't want me to hear.

After the incident at check-in, my pet theory was that they were concerned I might be there to start sniffing around about connections between show caves and the spread of white-nose syndrome. I wouldn't blame them, frankly, since white-nose syndrome poses something of an existential crisis, in the near term for the show cave industry and on a broader scale for life on earth.

"WNS," as it's known in administrative shorthand, is one of those things that's terrible on its face but gets even worse when you think even a little about its broader implications. In winter 2005–6, cavers in Howe Caverns near Albany, NY, discovered an entire hibernaculum of little brown bats dead and dying, each fallen bat's face frosted by a feathery white fungus. A survey of nearby hibernacula commenced immediately, and the grisly discovery was repeated in caves and mines around the region, with mortality rates in infected colonies running around 90 percent.

In the years since, the vector of infection has pointed straight down the Appalachian Valley, affecting not only the little brown bats but northern long-ears, Virginia big-ears, and endangered Indiana and gray bats. Scientists have determined that the fungus, at first taken to be a symptom of something else, is itself the cause. *Pseudogynmnoascus destructans*, as it is formally known, is held to be an invasive species, and a cunning one. Somehow it is perfectly designed for the caves of North America, loving the damp, but also the chill—it doesn't do well at temperatures above 68°F. As the fungus spreads it irritates the skin of the sleeping bats so that they prematurely emerge from their hibernating state.

If a hibernating bat isn't deeply entranced, its tiny heart races and its body burns fuel at an incredible rate, requiring thousands and thousands of insects each night to maintain. When bats wake up and can find no food in the winter air, the cold making their hearts work even harder, they quickly burn themselves up and die of starvation. A tell-tale sign of WNS infection is a confused-looking bat or two flying around a cave mouth in January daylight.

What's threatened is nothing less than the collapse of one large and significant link in the ecology of the entire continent. Bats can live anywhere from five to fifteen years, and they reproduce slowly, seldom more than one baby bat per year, so their ability to repopulate in the face of a catastrophic event is limited. Imagine all those insects—including an unfathomable number of mosquitoes—once consumed by those millions of bats year after year. Now all those bugs instead survive and prosper, the first stage of a chain reaction of events rippling, perhaps rampaging, through the entire ecosystem.

Clearly, no one is more horrified or dismayed by WNS than the show cave people, especially those in the tradition of Jeanne Gurnee for whom show caves are a place to put environmental beliefs into practice. But there's a deep current of a more practical concern at work here as well: WNS was discovered in a show cave, and its spread mirrors the map of show cave locations, and everybody is a little jittery about the possibility that an overzealous enforcement arm of some agency or another is going to shut down the show caves as a meaningless but highly visible effort at battling the syndrome's spread. Already the US Forest Service had closed all caves in the National Forests to recreational caving, despite the absence of some compelling evidence beyond an educated guess that cavers, carrying hidden spores on shoes, clothes, and gear, were a part of the chain of contamination.

Beneath that practical menace is an even more sinister, existential dread: What if show caves are spreading the fungus? What if these places born, above all, of a consuming, irrational love of caves, were killing them? What if all the quixotic, bizarre, occasionally fatal things these devotees of show caving had done in the name of getting Joe Schmoe to take a closer look at this magical space were actually damaging the caves, damaging the ecosystem, the world? Not even show caves are set up to withstand this kind of irony.

You could see where this might be an issue they wanted to keep in the family for the time being. When I inquired, during that initial check-in, after a session about WNS, it was pointedly excluded from my options. Still, as I rode around the valley with these folks I didn't feel like anyone was trying to cover anything up or be evasive when the subject came up, as it inevitably did. If there was some discomfort in the discussion, it was more in the sense that you don't like to keep bringing up Uncle Tim's lymphoma at the family reunion. There was a time for having a serious discussion about it, but nobody wanted to be reminded of it every minute.

A couple of times it came up in conversation that I had been told not to attend certain sessions. When it did, the cave person I was eating my box lunch with at the New Market Battleground or having a cup of coffee with after the keynote expressed surprise that anyone had any concerns. "I can't imagine what they thought you'd overhear that would scandalize you," said a nice woman from California. "The most controversial thing about those talks is how boring they are."

Later I'd learn something that might better account for that initial brush-off. On March 14, 2013, a freelance business writer named Ken Otterbourg landed the cover story of the *Washington Post* Sunday magazine with "The Rift," a behind-the-scenes look at the intense legal battles being waged by the Graves siblings of John and Rod's generation, which includes four sisters, all vying for control over the trusts that control the corporation that controls the caverns. "There is a sad and sedimentary quality to their fighting," writes Otterbourg, "layers upon layers of complaints built up over time—like the flowstone in the Caverns—then slowly fused into one solid and tangled block."

Local newspaper editor Chris Marston attributes the escalation of the legal dueling to the deaths of Ted Graves in 2010 and Rebecca Graves in 2012, less than a year after she introduced me to her Star scout on the front steps of Limair. "It was ready to unravel, and it unraveled faster than anyone imagined. . . . They are a wonderful bunch of people, individually, but do they get along? No. That is a soap opera up there."

There's no telling when Otterbourg actually began researching this story—it doubtless took a while to get through the several feet of wall space he describes in the Page County courthouse dedicated to the records of the Graves siblings' legal struggles. Those records were his only source of information about the siblings, who, when contacted, immediately lawyered up and refused all interview requests. I wonder if the Graves family might even have been on the lookout for a writer poking around—they command deep respect in the community to this day, and it's easy to see how word would get back if you were digging around. Could they have suspected that I was there to air their dirty laundry to the world?

So that tableau vivant in their parlor, a romantic poem to the eccentric but dedicated family business that makes it across the generations with prosperity, but also with a particular kind of dignity intact, that was really part of the tour. The Graves weren't giving away any more of their trade secrets than Earl Hargrove. Limair? that was a house on fire in a way that no amount of concrete can thwart.

Given what I saw of the genial fellowship of show cave operators, the way their business and cultural relationship with caves had shaped their personal lives, their emotional commitments, their lifeways, this was an undercurrent similar in tone if not in scale to the deeper fears of white nose syndrome: that the cave trade can take its toll on those emotional resources just as it can on the natural resources. Maybe it's reasonable not to want the world to know that even success in the show cave trade can endanger the delicate ecosystem of a family.

EIGHT

Natural Wonders, Inc.

The Stories of Endless Caverns

❖　❖　❖　❖

Of all the show caves and attractions we saw at the NCA meeting, one was conspicuous by its absence: Endless Caverns. Even though it's one of the most storied show caves of the Shenandoah, we didn't go there. Nobody currently affiliated with the place came to the meeting, even though it's just a half hour from Luray over to Tenth Legion, a quick hop to the other side of Massanutten.

It's too obvious an omission to be a mere oversight. If there's one show cave that fully sums up the possibilities and constraints that make up the whole history of the genre, it's Endless Caverns. In many ways, it's entirely typical, which of course means that one thing Endless shares with its peers is being extraordinary in its own unique ways.

The Endless Caverns origin story, two boys chasing a rabbit or maybe a dog venture into a heretofore unknown hole, is show cave boilerplate. Purely coincidence, I'm sure, that local farmer Ruben Zirkle's boys chased that rabbit into that hole within a year of Luray Caverns' celebrated opening in 1878.

Another prototypical aspect of the Endless Caverns story is that it is a tale of multiple financial failures, punctuated by periods of decline and neglect. Zirkle's Cave, which appears on maps from 1885 on as the much more marketable Endless Caverns, never even approximated Luray's reputation under its original developers. Russell Gurnee wrote in the *Journal of Spelean History* of a legendary incident in which Zirkle was approached by a delegation from the Smithsonian Institution, asking to explore and study the cave. Zirkle refused as he had never heard of any Smithsonian Institution, so the party continued over the hill to Luray, which they wrote up in awestruck tones for all manner of national publications.

By 1889 Ruben Zirkle was done; he sold off the place to a man named Horace Rosenburger, whose attempt at rebranding it "Silver Hill Caverns" was a complete bust and closed within the year. Over the course of the next three decades, Endless Caverns experienced a lengthy feral period, open on an appointment-only basis, or just left unsecured.

Then, in another set piece of the show cave story, the place received an important visitor: a stranger with a sense of adventure and access to capital, so taken with the spectacle he decides he must have the whole place for his own. In this case, the year was 1919, and the visitor was a certain Colonel Edward T. Brown. He had arranged a visit to the cave on a trip down south with his family. They were migrating from their home in New York, where, among other things, the colonel headed the prosperous Eastern Printing Company, to a household he maintained in Miami.

Like Hunter Chapman, owner of Shenandoah Caverns just up the road and Indian Cave in Tennessee, or Gene Monday, the Knoxville developer behind Cherokee Caverns and a later iteration of Indian Cave, the accomplished businessman fell so fully under the show cave's spell he couldn't be satisfied with just one cave. Colonel Brown bought Endless Caverns within the year and in 1929 added Melrose Caverns, a few miles down the Valley Pike at Lacey Springs, to his holdings in geologic oddities.

He called the fledgling landscape-tourism empire Natural Wonders, Incorporated. The collection was rounded out by something called the Sapphire Pool, about which I can find nothing, and the Cyclopean Towers, some peculiar cliffs now known as Natural Chimneys, right beside the crossroads of Mount Solon, Virginia, a stone's throw from Jedidiah Hotchkiss's home and school in Churchville.

Colonel Brown presided over it all from the historic 500-acre farm adjoining the Endless Caverns property on the flanks of Massanutten, moving his whole family and its domestic staff to the Great Valley when he closed the deal on Endless in 1920. There two more generations of Browns would stay to oversee the crown jewel of their family holdings for over fifty years.

Nothing in Brown's background anticipates he'd run off and join the circus. Born in Georgia in 1859, he was the eldest son of a distinguished white southern family with roots tracing back well before the Revolutionary War. He was a teenaged graduate (like Mr. J. W. Rumple, late of Shendun, Virginia) of Davidson College. Brown then "read law" in a private practice and passed the bar at age nineteen, another example of the kind of young professional supposed to populate the "New South" after Reconstruction and lead its ruling classes toward a modernized economic model.

His military rank was earned in the Army artillery during the fight in the Philippines to suppress resistance to the American occupation following the Spanish-American War—part of a new generation of southern soldiers, fighting for American expansion instead of Confederate secession. Before and after that, he practiced corporate law, started some businesses of his own, and became enough of a force in Democratic Party politics to become mayor of Atlanta for a term from 1890 to 1892, state committee chairman from 1900 to 1904, and a longstanding golfing buddy of Woodrow Wilson.

His political connections, cosmopolitan lifestyle, multiple homes and domestic servants, all attest to a man of considerable wealth and influence. Among all the various show cave entrepreneurs I've learned of in this project, Colonel Brown is unique in being so accustomed to the halls of power and privilege, so much a part of the establishment. He's probably the only one who at any point in his life could pick up the phone and call the president.

Maybe from his privileged vantage point he foresaw the first great flowering of car tourism that was to come in the 1920s and thought this could be a canny business move. Perhaps his social and political prominence and his financial prosperity gave him a level of permission to follow his bliss, and he was just ready to cash out of the fast track. That's an easy possibility to imagine if you've ever stood where the Endless Caverns farm looks across the tree-lined lane and sunny meadows and a rolling stream fed by the caverns' underground springs. It's a real-life pastoral idyll.

In any case, the show cave spell enraptured him. On August 21, 1920, his family acquired the Endless Caverns property from Rosenburger for $5,000, and the Colonel began one of the most careful, ambitious, and artful efforts at cave development I have ever seen. With typical show cave irony, it took a visitor to the area, a veteran imperialist backed by New York money, to create a landscape so sensitive to local conditions, to "build the site" in a way that honors the specific, unique setting that made it all happen in the first place. Under the Browns' leadership, Endless Caverns, like its owners, truly inhabited its surroundings, while paradoxically making it possible, even a little profitable, for strangers to pass through.

❖   ❖   ❖   ❖

Colonel Brown's caves are an example of what can be done with a show cave when one has ample capital on hand. Turns out the best way to become a wealthy show cave owner is to first be wealthy, then buy the cave. But for Brown, as for almost all show cave owners, it was clearly never just about the money.

What remains of his work suggests that part of the appeal for Brown was an element of master planning, an ambition familiar to the likes of his fellow engineers Jed Hotchkiss or Alexander Alan Arthur. But instead of trying to bring the land under the sway of his idea, he built the masterplan around the

The Stories of Endless Caverns

contours of the landscape, using its own vocabulary. The caves weren't just a decoration on a larger project; they were the larger project.

Unlike so many show caves whose launches seemed to be timed to coincide with economic catastrophe, Colonel Brown bought into the show cave market right as the first great wave of car tourism hit the Eastern Seaboard, and Endless Caverns lay right beside the Valley Turnpike, itself a travel artery since the paleolithic. Melrose, when it joined the empire, was even more centrally located: travelers had been wandering in and out of its natural entrance in the bottom of a sinkhole for millennia—or so claims one of the earliest written histories of the area, Samuel Kercheval's 1833 *History of the Valley of Virginia*. For once, the great constant of the cave business, location, worked to the cave business' advantage.

During the 1920s show caves surged into existence throughout the Shenandoah, as they did anywhere blacktop crossed karstlands. In 1920, only Luray and Grand Caverns attracted any significant number of tourists; a decade later, they had been joined by Dixie Caverns, Shenandoah Caverns, and Massanutten Caverns, as well as Endless. Melrose came into Brown's custody in 1929, when he leased the cave property from the family that had owned the land for generations, and opened for business in 1932.

Both Endless and Melrose received comprehensive makeovers before opening for business; together they show us the development of a very particular aesthetic, an understated, artfully organic elegance.

❖   ❖   ❖   ❖

When you see a lot of show caves, the difference in Brown's properties is conspicuous. I visited the surface of Melrose Caverns in 2007, which was at that time closed and unmarked. I didn't know then that Brown had anything to do with Melrose—I'd just seen the name on a topographic map and swung by on the spur of the moment while exploring the archives at nearby James Madison University.

The stone service station at the head of the drive was immediately recognizable though piled up with junk; the driveway, rutted but scenic. Prime Shenandoah pastureland now edged all the way up to the old lodge; cars in various degrees of repair, yard furniture, and toys grazed in front of the entrance to a couple of dingy-looking apartments built into the foundations, while the spacious great room above them stood empty and dark behind a broad stone portico.

Through the patina of neglect, I could still tell from the subtle care taken with the underlying design of the landscape and the architecture, even in its deteriorated state, that the same sensibility that produced the idyllic setting for Endless Caverns was behind it. The archives bore that hunch out the next day, as I pored over the handbills and postcards from both these caves, noting in the fine print below the tell-tale "Natural Wonders" logo that they were both from the same printer in New York—Brown's Eastern Printing Company.

As someone who's handled a lot of show cave promotional materials, let me tell you, Eastern turned out some top-shelf printed matter. Even the humble pamphlets were more clever than most, like the reversible double pamphlets: you see Endless Caverns on one side; then flip it over and turn it upside down, and it's a Melrose Caverns brochure. Flyers from the late 1920s featured striking expressionist paintings of all the Natural Wonders attractions; the artist, now lost to history, signed the work with the flamboyant initials "h.o.h." The beautiful engraved vellum keepsake book *Nature Underground: The Endless Caverns in the Heart of the Historic Shenandoah Valley*, now in the holdings of James Madison University's special collections, is easily the most artful gift shop item I've seen—gorgeous illustrations, both line drawings and photographic plates, and a narrative of the cave's formation and development written in prose of deepest purple, celebrating (a wealthy, white southern Democrat's version of) the heritage of the region.

A lush, carefully crafted romanticism similarly infuses the landscape design. Colonel Brown's properties are approached not by mere driveways but by direct yet picturesque lanes passing over elegant bridges, lined by large, healthy trees. At the end of the lane is not just a visitor's center, but a rustic, sophisticated lodge made from hewn local stone, quarried on the property.

At Melrose, the two-story hall, fronted by broad porches with rails of smooth, finished trunks, rises from the hillside like an ancient inn. The cave is entered through a passageway vanishing into the hillside from one of the rear wings. Endless Caverns features a broader single-story building, one wide room faced on all sides by generous porches, organized around a huge fireplace and air-conditioned by virtue of being situated atop the tour's exit tunnel. Adjoining covered galleries lead to the stone entry-hall built atop the gateway to the cave's chambers and the beginning of the tour.

It's an intensely southern place, but not in a typical way: it isn't so invested in plantation nostalgia. The vibe aspires to a feeling more ancient than all that. Given the way the bedrock is exposed in rills all along the side of Massanutten, the blue limestone buildings feel as though they just grew up

The Stories of Endless Caverns

there, with none of the red-brick Georgian pretensions of the fine houses that assert themselves in the sinuous lines of the valley bottom.

Even as the architecture bespoke an ancient lineage in a distinctly local idiom, as a part of a newborn branch of the fledgling tourist economy, the service strove to be absolutely au courant. At both caverns, Colonel Brown constructed combination visitors' centers and service stations out on the Valley Turnpike in that same locavore architectural style, to draw in weary motorists for whom the cave might provide a pleasant respite from riding along with the top down, a diversion while the cars were being serviced. Shuttle service up the lane was complimentary, of course.

At Endless, Brown sweetened the deal even more by carefully sculpting a campground in the holler beside the lodge, since tent camping (preferably with the aid of a driver and a valet) was de rigueur for the new touring class. For those traveling with black servants, Brown provided a matching blue limestone coach house with a cafe and lounge for waiting drivers. I'm justifiably skeptical, I think, of attributing any enlightened notions about race to a man who rose to prominence in the southern Democratic Party during the post-Reconstruction reassertion of white supremacy, but I have to admit, even if it's noblesse oblige, it's still more than the least he could get away with.

The "build the site" approach, combining high levels of craft with an ethic of sincere hospitality, carried over into the work Brown had done beneath the surface. A new entry tunnel conveyed visitors from the lodge directly into the heart of the cave at Melrose. At the more vertical Endless, rickety wooden stairs were replaced by carefully crafted steps carved from native stone. Paths were widened and flattened and oriented toward preferred views of signature formations.

Those formations were presented via what was then state-of-the-art electric lighting. Endless Caverns' promotional materials trumpeted the accomplishments of Phineas V. Stevens, consulting engineer of New York City, fresh off his triumph in the illumination of the Natural Bridge sixty miles up the valley, "whose genius conceived and whose ability perfected the plan of concealed wires and hidden lamps which removes from our minds all thought of the artificial and leaves us to enjoy the superb coloring and impressive architecture of these caverns in their natural state."

All this emphasis on keeping it natural makes Brown's signature collaboration with Phineas Stevens hard to figure. It's a massive ENDLESS CAVERNS sign on the side of Massanutten in the style of the Hollywood sign, as if a

The Endless Caverns sign on Massanutten Mountain, 2007.
(Photograph by the author)

name on a map had been literally written on the landscape. The (probably spurious) claim that it is the largest lighted sign in the United States still turns up in promotional materials. It's as artificial, as over-the-top, as the rest of the project is subdued and respectful, an almost imperial gesture. It's as if Brown recognized that no show cave is truly complete with some kind of jarring juxtaposition.

And in the ironical way things always seem to go around show caves, the very thing that made Endless stand out became the thing that made it an integral, defining part of the local landscape. The Endless Caverns sign on the mountainside above Tenth Legion is one of those landmarks you navigate by when you're a regular traveler in the valley, whether you live in that corner of Rockingham County or you drive by on Interstate 81, traveling from East Tennessee to Upstate New York. It's visible for miles around. Over the course of the checkered history of Endless Caverns in more recent times, the sign has been lit inconsistently, and each time the lights get switched back on, it's cause for local celebration.

Though undoubtedly the grandest gesture, the big sign wasn't the only thing Colonel Brown did to get the name on the map. Capital wasn't the only

The Stories of Endless Caverns

thing he had going for him in New York—Brown had social and cultural resources to draw on there, too. His son, business partner, and junior officer Major Edward M. Brown, became a member of the famed Explorer's Club in 1923, eventually becoming its president. (Thanks to Major Brown, there was a precedent for having a show cave man at the helm of the Explorer's Club when Russell Gurnee took office as president in the 1950s.)

As a sponsor of missions of discovery to the most remote corners of the globe, Major Brown reasoned, the club could and should execute a search for the end of a cavern heretofore presumed Endless—something that could be published by Eastern Printing Company's new subsidiary, Nomad Books, the official publishing house of the Explorer's Club.

In January and in May of 1925, Major Brown joined adventurers, journalists, and scientists on Explorer's Club expeditions into the lowest levels of Endless Caverns. On the second trip, the teams carried glass bottles with a printed message inside: "This bottle is placed at the farthest point penetrated by members of the expedition of the American Museum of Natural History and The Explorer's Club of New York, May, 1925. If anyone finds it and can carry it still farther, please report to the American Museum of Natural History." The note was signed by all the members of the party. The bottles have been moved just once since then, by a 1940 expedition that set out to do exactly that.

Now, this is a cunning bit of promotion on the Browns' part, some real expert-level show cave making. They got press: newsreels and photos of the expeditions made the national media. The 1925 outings included a pioneering woman journalist named Betty Larimore of the *Boston Post*, who wrote up the trips in a melodramatic style. Written accounts of the expeditions, initially reported in the club's journal, are still in print today in anthologies of Explorer's Club adventures edited by late club member George Plimpton.

In 1940, one of the Explorer's Club's best-known members was writer and radio broadcaster Lowell Thomas, who first gained fame as the embedded journalist on T. E. Lawrence's World War I desert campaigns. In the radio age Thomas's beat was tales of travel, adventure, history, and lore: key elements of Endless Caverns' brand and indeed of any show cave's. Thomas would prove a reliable ally of Natural Wonders, Inc.

Endless also got a certain kind of modern legitimacy, credentials from the cavern's association with such august company, being formally identified as a site of adventure and discovery by folks who should know. But the cavern also got something more enduring, even though the trips were completed without any real incident and generated no significant scientific knowledge. Endless Caverns got a great bit of narrative that has been a staple of their tours ever since.

Typically, the group lines the rail by the Bottomless Pit, a sinkhole in the back of the cave where these expeditions descended to the stream level. The guide gets to evoke for the group a mysterious space somewhere below their feet, a place only the elite explorers may dare. The iconic message in a bottle provides the perfect prop—it's easy to visualize, an emblem of the far reaches of experience, an artifact of people who have been a lot farther out there than you. Depending on the guide, on the day, you might hear that the bottles have never been found—our heroes' feat has never been duplicated. Or (more accurately) that successive generations have moved them farther along, but no end has ever been found. In this case, the cave is the hero of the story, its unknowability intact despite repeated efforts to control it.

One way or another, this stop on the tour is the title track: it's where Endless Caverns becomes not just a brand but a claim. It's high-level show cave artistry to make your superlative claim in the negative. Claiming to have the largest this or the widest that comes with an element of risk. Some spoil-sports in South Africa can find a larger underground lake than the Lost Sea, and all of a sudden World's Second Largest Underground Lake just doesn't sound as snazzy. But endlessness? No matter what happens, absence of evidence can always be presented as evidence of absence.

❖   ❖   ❖   ❖

Melrose Caverns would always be a junior partner to the great and ineffable unknown, but the cave lent itself to a different kind of spin that neatly complemented Endless's emphasis on the unknowable and the fantastical. Instead the lengthy history of human presence in the cave became the focus of the narrative, with special emphasis on the really extraordinary amount of graffiti left behind by soldiers from the many different armies that swept up and down the Shenandoah throughout the Civil War.

The money formation for Melrose wasn't some kind of spectacular flow-stone arabesque, but the Registry Column, a thick stanchion not far from the "Soldier's Entrance" in the bottom of a sinkhole, covered in its entirety with names and places, entire regimental rosters. Elsewhere what some might call vandalism became an important memento of the past; broken stalactites and a bullet-scarred pendant formation known as the "Soldier's Target" were occasions to imagine the cave a hive of human activity rather than the gateway to regions measureless to man.

The hook here was that these were real people, young men in the midst of life or death struggle whose legacy carries on all around us, and in the cave is recorded, for all intents and purposes, forever. If Endless traded on the unknowable, Melrose offered the possibility you'd see someone you know, someone from your town, maybe even from your family. In the earliest days of operation, when there was even the possibility that one of the signatories himself might be in the group, Endless Caverns advertised special tours for Civil War veterans.

The lodge became the site of a Civil War museum in the early 1930s, the permanent home of an exhibit Colonel Brown had acquired entire from another failing tourist attraction. Melrose's complementary role was complete: the cave of history, particularly Civil War history, paired with the cave that is older than history. It gave them more of a foothold with the Civil War tourism crowd that Endless, "discovered" so recently, didn't offer.

Melrose didn't make sense as a destination for the Explorer's Club, but that didn't stop the Browns from having Lowell Thomas down to the Shenandoah again in 1940, having already reported the last Explorer's Club foray in search of the end of Endless, to do a live radio broadcast from within the cave, in which Thomas celebrated it as "the only war memorial built by the soldiers themselves"—which if you think about it for a minute is complete nonsense, a real reach for a superlative. If graffiti is a war memorial, soldiers have built them all around the world for eons. (This kind of swing-and-a-miss may explain why Melrose was forever the junior partner.) Nonetheless, thus packaged, Melrose Caverns became a part of the broader synergy of the Browns' business network, the top of Natural Wonders, Inc.'s undercard.

At the same time as their Natural Wonders beckoned to out-of-towners, the Browns and their caves remained part of the fabric of the local community. Endless Caverns wasn't just a tourist operation; it was also a large working dairy farm, a water-bottling plant, and a site of beloved community festivals, pageants, and celebrations. During the Depression, the Brown family maintained the view that help was cheaper than machinery, so they provided basic work for many in the valley. But they never opened a full-service restaurant, because they didn't want to take business from the other restaurateurs on the Valley Pike.

Nowhere else have I encountered a project so coherent and fully realized as the Browns' Natural Wonders. It was asset-based development before the regional planners coined that term to describe taking something good about your place and making it a reason for others to come to your place.

When Colonel Brown died in 1933, he was the only show cave proprietor in the valley who could lay anything like a claim to operating on the level of his fellow colonel, T. C. Northcott, over the mountain in Luray. And he had his order of succession already lined up: his son, already fully initiated in the higher mysteries of show cave operation, assumed full command. Though separated by one officer's rank and a middle initial, Major Brown was a chip off the old block: a highly educated attorney and veteran of foreign wars (World War I this time) who found the show cave business a lot more fascinating than anything the printing or investing world had to offer. By 1937, when Major Brown officially incorporated, the stated property value was $66,230, a pretty good return on a $5,000 investment less than two decades before.

Having held on, even grown through the Depression, Endless was nonetheless no match for World War II, as wartime rationing ended car tourism for the duration, and the Browns' resistance to agricultural mechanization bit back on them when the farm labor pool all went off to war. Even without those rigid economic factors, you have to wonder if there's a market for recreationally confronting your worst fears when so many people you know and love are confronting their worst fears for real.

Endless and Melrose survived the wartime lull, though the rest of Natural Wonders seems to have dropped off the map by this time. Major Brown waged a successful campaign to keep Endless afloat throughout the 1950s, buoyed by a rebirth of enthusiasm for car trips, to very nearly reclaim the levels of popularity experienced by Colonel Brown in the 1920s. The farm converted from the increasingly mechanized and regulated dairy trade to more manageable beef cattle. The campground, shuttered during the war, came back to life, with more sites but the same emphasis on handling the Massanutten woodlands with care. Ever aiming for a slightly more cosmopolitan sector of the market than most, Endless became the home gallery of American impressionist William Starkweather, who did a faux-Lascaux treatment for the walls of the coffee shop. This should be the part where the sun sets on a contented, wholesome family institution, and they all live happily ever after.

But if you've read this far in this book, as you see the 1950s become the 1960s, you know to brace for impact with the advent of the Interstate Highway System. Major Brown, who even more than his father gave his life to the cause of this place-making project, did not quite live to see the opening of Interstate 81, for better or worse. He passed away at home in 1963, having lived there over four decades and raised his own children, Ed Jr. and Bliss, on the farm.

Major Brown probably foresaw the crisis, having launched an unsuccessful campaign to get an exit for Endless Caverns into the Interstate 81 master

The Stories of Endless Caverns

plan back during the planning stages. Up the road at Shenandoah, Earl Hargrove learned that you could not have your place-name on an exit unless you had a US Post Office. No problem for a man in the fabrication business: he had a reproduction vintage Gilded Age postal cage constructed in one of his shops and trucked down for installation in his Cavern Inn. A little bureaucratic rigmarole later, and Shenandoah Caverns had a zip code and, more importantly, its name on the exit sign.

For Endless, on the other hand, the advent of the Interstate hit them like a Mack truck. Edward Jr., bereft of the assistance of his military forefathers, did what he could to lead the Caverns out of this latest debacle, but drastic measures were called for. He jettisoned the ninety-nine-year lease on Melrose Caverns almost immediately, auctioned off the Civil War museum, and consolidated their position back at the original home base. Melrose Caverns would never again reopen as a working show cave, though a short-lived dinner theater once occupied the lodge, and periodically James Madison University students would rent the place from the Yancey family as a party barn. (At this writing, a successful National Register of Historic Places application has undergirded a reinvention of the lodge as an elegant event space rental — as usual with the show caves, the story of development is never over.)

The lonely little gas stations at the ends of the lanes of the last surviving Natural Wonders fell into disuse and disrepair, shorn of their opportunity to divert traffic off the mainstream. The campground began once again to disappear into the undergrowth. The sign was turned off. Gradually the decline began to affect the maintenance of the cave and the lodge itself. By the time they had braved the fuel crises of the 1970s, the Browns were finally ready to get out of the show cave business.

Bliss and Edward Jr. sold the cave property in 1979. They seemed to have found a buyer, Washington, DC, restauranteurs Tony and Sandra Lam, poised to continue the Cavern's tradition of aiming for a more sophisticated crowd. The Lams planned to use the lodge for an elegant, destination restaurant, "Le Chateau," taking advantage of the distinctive setting and Colonel Brown's organic architecture to create a unique dining experience.

Appearances, as is so often the case in the show cave trade, proved to be deceiving. The Lams opened their high-concept restaurant in October, and by December it was shuttered, collapsing even quicker than Alexander Alan Arthur's Four Seasons Resort. The condition of their relationship and their finances proved much more unsteady than expected. The legal fallout from the failed venture kept the property tied up for over five years to come, time during which the cave once again fell into a feral state, the buildings and grounds into further disrepair. A tree even fell on the roof of the lodge, punching a hole that let the elements in. Inside the cave, pathways silted up, wiring decayed, and the cave began its process of absorbing this latest intrusion.

◆　◆　◆　◆

Finally, in 1984, Endless Caverns hit the block in a foreclosure auction. For $304,000 Virgil "Sonny" Berdeaux, an entrepreneur and developer from Florida, acquired the entire Endless Caverns property. Sonny was a businessman—he bought the place with the proceeds of the sale of an RV park—but Gary and Wade, his sons, were serious cavers and cave divers who had successfully plumbed the depths of Florida springs that have taken many lives. Sonny turned a lot of the work of developing the cave itself over to his sons, who spearheaded a massive cleanup and overhaul.

For two years they worked, bringing the show cave back to life, exploring and surveying the cave with their colleagues in the NSS, making homes and raising families as Browns and Zirkles had before them. At the same time, they brought the show cave into the present day, creating a tour and an aesthetic in keeping with a more contemporary environmental, conservationist perspective, bringing the caver ethic of protecting and preserving the cave as well as the people in it, and reclaiming another derelict cave from the spelunkers.

But they had enough appreciation for the care the Brown family took with its work to keep it intact—especially that magnificent light and sound show, which is not only to this day still visually striking but now has added historical value as a beautifully preserved example of an older generation of cave showmanship.

The Berdeauxs understood that the way to continue the humane project Colonel Brown began was not to try to recapture or surpass its lost glory but to evolve it into its next stage. Endless Caverns might have been a less ambitious operation under the Berdeauxs, but the cave was again in safe hands, with people who loved caves for what they are. From their grand reopening on May 9, 1986, to the end of their regime, the Berdeauxs ran a solid, well-maintained operation—tours led by enthusiastic, well-trained guides who communicated the value of the cave not least through their clear affection for it.

The tour that I still remember as the best out of all I've seen came from a young woman in the employ of the Berdeauxs, in the last year of their time at Endless Caverns, which was the very first year of my research. I didn't know any of that then, and in fact didn't know anything at all about the Berdeauxs or the Browns or the whole story of the cave. But I did know what a guide who is really into it looks like, and the young woman leading the tour was the very image. She had a kind of a throwback Katrina-and-the-Waves thing going on with her sateen jacket and her Chuck Taylors, and she just brought a little extra delight to the cornball jokes and the trick questions. You can bet her darkness demonstration was on point. When a toddler on the tour inter-rupted her mid-spiel to ask what it would be like if the whole cave was made of chocolate, she paused, considered it for a minute, and said with utter con-viction, "That would be awesome."

When I came back two years later, the tour was still pretty much the same, but the guide situation had changed considerably. Now the tour guide was a blonde young man in an orange Endless Caverns polo and khaki pants who seemed like he might rather be working at American Apparel. The tour group was especially large, including many Spanish speakers, but after a few early "can everybody hear me's," he was content to just talk-yell his spiel to whomever was listening.

At some tell-tale moments he betrayed his own distaste for the sub-terranean scene even as he was dutifully good-natured about presenting it. We looked at a narrow crevice, and asking us to imagine crawling inside it as early explorers had done, he commiserated with the crowd, "I wouldn't want to do that, would you?" The total darkness demonstration was just long enough to say they'd done it. At several late stops on the tour our guide would open or close by letting us know that, just a couple more stops, and we'd be back on the surface. I did not get the impression that, if the cave were made entirely of chocolate, he'd think it was awesome.

When, to his apparent relief, our guide redelivered us to the gift shop, I noted an elaborate display on easels in the heart of the store. Various draw-ings and plats and plans outlined an ambitious expansion for Endless Cav-erns: yet another relaunch of the campground, this time on a larger and more invasive scale, fitting out all the old sites and many hundreds of new ones for access by the largest recreational vehicles and the electrical and water supplies they demanded. Around the base of the hillside sign, avenues of semipermanently installed "mobile" homes would create a pop-up cottage colony without all the burdensome permitting required to install a subdivi-sion per se.

A huge water play area of lakes and pools would now provide the center-piece of the camping experience. A huge corrugated steel building down the rolling hillside that was once Colonel Brown's dairy cow pasture would host a Moonshine Museum. A huge new amphitheater carved out of the lower pasture by the creek would welcome concerts and music festivals. It was like I left Bedford Falls and came back to Pottersville. What happened?

Turns out in 2006, Sonny Berdeaux had about decided he was ready to retire and right about that time got a nibble of interest from a group of developers fronted by a man named Larry Silver. From there things proceeded quickly to a deal that sold the caverns property to a small group of investors spearheaded by Silver for $2.6 million—almost ten times what he paid for it, and Sonny got to keep the farm homestead for his retirement, and Wade and Gary got jobs with the new management to help take care of the cave.

That was in May 2006; by July the new ownership was announcing the gigantic expansion plans I saw displayed in the gift shop that day, plans that would, if realized, radically rework life in the foothills of Massanutten. Suddenly the view from Sonny Berdeaux's front porch would be hundreds of land yachts cruising in and out on the country lane Colonel Brown designed for the tin lizzies of 1920. Suddenly weekends in this bucolic corner of Rockingham County would include parking and crowds and the noise of a concert venue.

The Berdeauxs had a front-row seat for what happens when you sell a show cave to a mall guy. Larry Silver's hallmark as a developer is creating omnitopias: places that could happen anywhere and everywhere else. Silver Companies have always been on the cutting edge of sprawl, getting its start dividing Virginia farmland into ranchettes, moving into apartment developments and strip malls and chain hotels, then hitting the big time with the monstrous shopping center Central Park, beside I-95 in Fredericksburg, Virginia, at that time the largest commercial retail development on the East Coast. (Self-promotional superlatives aren't just for show caves.) Larry's father Carl founded and grew the company, raising Larry to take the reins in adulthood, and everything went exactly according to plan.

Not factoring existing local conditions into the planning process is a trademark of the work Silver Companies: the kind of work they do always starts off with grading the site to a totally flat zero datum. Their development philosophy knows only one core principle: the extraction of value from the available space. No asset-based development here: the development is the asset; the place is just the base.

What the Silver Companies did not reckon with is that cave people are used to defending fragile places against heedless use and abuse. In this case that defense took the form of the rise of an organized opposition to the Silver Companies' plans. County approval processes, which the Silver Companies had probably thought were foregone conclusions, turned into highly contentious colloquia on the quality of life in the area and the value of its traditional

The Stories of Endless Caverns

and historical qualities, not to mention practical matters like the impact on local infrastructure and other hidden costs of large-scale development that would be redistributed among area residents.

The bad feelings reached an apex when a private investigator named Nic Carricino turned up around Rockingham County passing himself off as a researcher from Clemson University. His survey questions for local residents about the effects of development on agriculture, it quickly became clear to some of his interviewees, were thinly veiled opposition research about community members who had spoken out against Endless Caverns expansion. Local journalists didn't have much trouble connecting Carricino to the Silver Companies, and, their standing in the community diminished accordingly, Endless Caverns' new management found itself in confidential mediation with its neighbors.

Gary Berdeaux saw the writing on the wall first and shipped out to become the manager of Diamond Caverns for Stan Sides and his crew. Wade tried to stick it out with the Silver Companies for a time but couldn't bear the daily heartbreak of watching its heedless approach to reshaping this landscape.

"They were rapacious animals," Wade told me when I came to interview him at his home on a parcel of land adjoining the park that was not included in the sale. He has a collection of cavern memorabilia that was unceremoniously cleaned out of storerooms and thrown on the scrapheap. One incredible item is framed on his wall—an amazing work of cartography that focuses on a cutaway map of the cave in the foreground and morphs into a relief map of the Virginia landscape stretching to the east and north all the way to the Atlantic—the kind of masterful work I've come to expect from Eastern Printing Services. He's never had it appraised, he says in response to my unsubtle question, because he never intends to sell it. (Duly noted.)

Instead, Wade confers on me a cardboard box meant to hold Endless Caverns Butter from the Brown family farm. "Strong in Nutriment," it proclaims, "Rich in Vitamins, Improves Health." "There's no telling what they've thrown away up there that I never even saw. They were not interested in the slightest in what's been done in the past, just what they were going to do in the future."

His view of the rolling pasture leading up to the lodge was blocked now by a privacy fence. On the other side of that fence was the proposed site of their festival amphitheater, arrayed so that its public address system would be pointing directly at Wade Berdeaux's kitchen windows. "They weren't going to be content until they had driven all of us out of here and bought up our places for a song after they made it so our land was only valuable to them. But where was I going to go? My kids live here, my wife works here, my parents lived here."

The community managed to stop the worst of it, but it took its toll. Sonny Berdeaux had always looked forward to his retirement living right there on the farm, but you can't help but wonder if what he saw from his front porch just made him feel sick, the way it all went wrong. On March 27, 2008, Sonny Berdeaux died at the age of seventy-six.

Silver Companies didn't get their Moonshine Museum warehouse or their festival amphitheater, but they weren't deterred in their project to bring this peculiarly, uniquely local space under the banner of global commerce.

I mean that literally. The last time I visited Endless Caverns the flagpole in front of the lodge, commanding the splendid vista of the Shenandoah from the broad stone porches, was topped by an unfurling flag featuring the unmistakable logo of NASCAR. Their greatly enlarged, if not gargantuan, RV park, which did in fact get its water features, was now fully licensed and branded in the NASCAR family. Its marquee events were gatherings to watch the races on a monster screen erected in the campground. When I asked at the counter about a cavern tour (now available April through November only), the young woman behind the counter in the tell-tale orange polo said "Sure, I'll take ya."

It was nice to be the only one on the tour, and she gave me all kinds of leeway looking at things close up, taking pictures, asking questions. She was a lot more personable than my last Endless Caverns guide, but I couldn't help but be troubled by the fact that she liked working there because they just pretty much put her in charge of the cave, and nobody really bothers her about that, because they're all focused on everything going on over in the campground. Yes, that's nice, I said.

After our interview, Wade Berdeaux walked me down the hill below his house. In a lush little grotto on his property, a deep pool of crystal clear, intensely chilly water rises from a limestone outcrop, flowing out into a cattle pond and thence to the creek below. "Do you know what this is?" he asks. I think I do but I let him tell me. "This is the stream resurgence, where that creek on the lowest levels of Endless comes back to the surface. It's what all those expeditions were devoted to finding." The joke's on Larry Silver — they may have gotten everything else, but Wade Berdeaux still owns the end of Endless Caverns.

I have to say, I never thought I'd live to see it.

NINE

Last One Out, Turn off the Lights

The Show Cave's Afterlife

❖ ❖ ❖ ❖

When you've seen the end of Endless, the tour has got to be drawing to a close. But on this tour, we're going to stick around and see what happens when the gift shop closes and the lock clanks shut on the front gates for the last time — at least for now. In show caves as in soap operas, death is never a permanent condition. Given the penchant of caves for preserving a record of everything, it proves to be very difficult, perhaps even impossible, to ever completely stop the show.

Or so I found one summer, late in the project, exploring the southern end of the Appalachian Valley. I was just south of Soddy Daisy, Tennessee, driving north on Old US 27, heading out into the Mystic. Or so I hoped. Mystic Caverns was living up to its own claim to be "America's most Mysterious caverns." The mystery was, Where were they?

Old US 27 buzzed along the base of Walden Ridge, whose steep eastern escarpment forms the western wall of the Appalachian Valley in southeast Tennessee. (The newer, straighter divided highway version of US 27 swept along just to the east.) I branched off at a crossroads called Mile Straight, where the highway bends to the right and crosses Chickamauga Creek. Cribbing off the topographic map included in Larry Matthews's *Caves of Chattanooga*, I drove through an orderly little neighborhood, passed a church, and seemed to be on the right track when the road suddenly ended at a fence. I got out, examined the tall, solid board-over-chain-link construction, was duly impressed by the sound of very large, very angry dogs on the other side of that fence. I had to look for another way around.

Driving back down to Old 27, I found the far end of the fence. It parceled off a piece of land a couple of hundred yards wide that had been truly, thoroughly devastated from the highway up to the base of the ridge maybe a half mile away. It looked like someone had cut the timber, bulldozed the stumps, and now they were in the process of collecting and hauling off the rounded limestone river rocks exposed in the eroded soil. Bulldozers and bobcats sat idle near growing piles of stones, which I imagined would soon be cleaned and sorted and placed on sale in the Home Depot garden section.

As I clanged my rental up the packed-dirt road worn by the (de)construction traffic, a big pickup came down the other way. We gave each other the hi-sign as we passed slowly, him a beefy guy with a thick mustache and Oakley shades, a TV cop. True to formula, as I continued up the drive, I could see him in my rear view, turning around to follow me. Ahead of me was the source of the dog sounds: several pens of German Shepherds and a mobile home that, the signs said, served as the offices of a K9 training school. The driveway petered out into brambles and scrubby woods beyond the trailer, so I pulled into the parking area by the dog pens and waited in the car as the big black F150 pulled up alongside me from the opposite direction.

He was clearly sizing me up as I tried to explain quickly what I was doing there without sounding up to something. But he mellowed out at the opportunity to talk about the cave. Turns out he runs the dog business, training up security dogs on a contract basis. He was kind of amused when I asked if I could go see where Mystic used to be. "Oh yeah," he says, "the place where the gift shop and gate were is on up that trail just a little ways. They ain't much to see, though. When they quarried the rock out of there they collapsed the entrances to the cave.

"I heard they caved 'em in on purpose, on account of some kids who were up there tripping on acid, and a big rock in the entrance come loose and crushed two of them flat. They say there's still some of them under the rock—they just scraped out all they could to bury them."

I was pretty sure this wasn't true. But the destination I was after did have a pretty funky backstory. Mystic Caverns was the pure product of the blood, sweat, and tears of a young man named Cliff Forman, a sojourner of the show cave network. Mystic opened for business on February 18, 1961, but Forman had arrived many months before with not much more than a trailer full of equipment and the permission of the land trust that owned the site to start up a show cave.

Forman was a true-blue cave man, strong in all categories: a veteran explorer trained in vertical caving and cave rescue, and active in the NSS since he was a teenager. Now he had a cave of his own, and he spent countless hours, whole days and nights, digging out entrances, grading paths, stringing wire, and hanging lights. He ran completely out of money, had his car repossessed, even started sleeping in the cave as the weather turned cold. Neighbors looked out for him; a house full of squatters over by the creek felt sorry for him and had him in for dinner now and again.

Forman probably never thought there could be anything as hard as single-handedly developing a show cave until he tried to make a living with one. Somehow not everybody loved caves as instinctively and thoroughly as he did. So he tackled the problem the same way he did developing the cave itself: working tirelessly with whatever resources he had at hand. He made homemade signs from scrap wood featuring a big red circle and the admonition to "Follow the Dots" to America's Most Mysterious Caverns. He had turkey shoots, a giant buffalo on display. He even convinced a rambling eccentric named the Goat Man, a hirsute old timer who traveled this stretch of the Great Valley with his cart full of odds and ends and his namesake herd of goats, to set up his camp there for a time. Folks came to see the Goat Man, but not many paid to see the cave.

It took only six months for the wheels to come completely off Forman's operation. He handed the whole project over to a successor who organized dances in the cave but had his lease pulled when he failed to get insurance (just in case, you know, a rock falls off the ceiling and crushes some tripping teenagers). Not too long after that the quarry operation closed the commercial entrance, and the whole property began its transition into the brownlands it was that day I rode out there.

Forman, on the other hand, went on to pursue his devotion to show caves: he next developed Lost World Caverns in White Sulphur Springs, West Virginia, where he not only transformed a majestic breakdown chamber into a lovely self-guiding tour but expanded his repertoire of promotional tricks to include setting the world record for "stalagmite sitting." On September 3, 1971, he perched cave guide Bob Addis on a platform atop the twenty-eight-foot-tall War Club formation, and he didn't come down until fifteen days, twenty-two hours later. This feat didn't so much break the record as establish the record, since it had never occurred to anyone to do this before. Just to help generate a narrative, Forman proclaimed the old record to be seven days, twenty-three and a half hours.

Forman eventually left the War Club and the Lost World, too, migrating on up the show cave chain all the way to New York State, where he started up Ice Caves Mountain. Foreman may be another one of these cave apostles in the vein of Leo Lambert, seemingly in it mostly for the challenge of getting the thing up and running, designing the experience for others to follow (not to mention the opportunity to explore any time the spirit moves you).

NSS colleagues report that Cliff is still around today, a hale eighty-something living part of the year in Upstate New York and part in Hawaii, where he explores the local lava tubes, no doubt daydreaming at least a little about one more show cave score.

That whole history makes finding Mystic even more meaningful for me — it's like a lost early work of an accomplished show cave artist, some serious insider enthusiast stuff. Though insignificant as a business operation or as a natural wonder in and of itself, it plays a small but significant role in the history of show caves. I wanted to see it for myself.

Now, though, its day of being a strange little trickster space had decidedly come to a close. It was the landscape equivalent of the Giving Tree, minus the bittersweet conclusion. Scavenged stone cairns, cages full of bloodthirsty dogs, and then, up the jeep track, the bare earth turning to poison ivy and blackberry bramble, finally coming around the bend to the overgrown site of the quarry that took the place of the cavern entrance area, now a sunlit bowl filled with kudzu and creeper and tree of heaven shading an understory of abandoned appliances and empty motor oil jugs. And beneath that, shattered rock.

I poked around a little looking for an overhang or a crack that might go, but I was pretty soon plucking off ticks and thinking about how the terrain made for a cocktail of tetanus, copperheads, and ankle sprains. My ribs were still throbbing from a spill in Manitou Cave down in Fort Payne the day before, and I didn't need another research-related injury. I beat it back down the trail.

Back in the car I picked another couple of ticks off my socks and contemplated the possibility that I'd need to revise one of my main insights about the show cave: that unlike almost any other cultural project, it just can't be erased. Well, Mystic Caverns appeared to be thoroughly and completely erased. But reflecting on it, I decided it's more accurate to say it was trapped, like a tripping teenager under a giant boulder. Whatever remains that were still visible have been scraped away, carried off, buried. Something of it is still under the mountain, I reckoned; Cleopatra's Castle, the Giant's Pipe Organ, the Stone Bananas were still waiting there in the dark. But it sure looked like nothing was going to bring back America's Most Mysterious Underground Cavern. And thus it lived up to its name at last.

❖   ❖   ❖   ❖

As I was organizing that trip to the Chattanooga area that led me, eventually, out in search of Mystic, the name Manitou Cave popped up every now again. Manitou is a show cave in Fort Payne, Alabama, burrowing back into the base of Lookout Mountain, fifty miles south of Chattanooga. The sources I had found indicated it was a very pretty and quite historic cave: large passageways with ample speleothems; the money formation a huge heap of flowstone called the Haystack, which was yet another contestant for "the world's largest stalagmite." There is evidence of prehistoric habitation, Anglo-European graffiti going back to the War of 1812. The visitors center stands on the site of a Cherokee village called Willstown, a home of Sequoyah, the leader and inventor of the Cherokee alphabet, a town that was forcibly vacated in the Cherokee Removal of 1837. As a show cave it's another one in the generation born of the first generation of car tourists, flowing down from the upper Midwest via the newly created Dixie Highway to Florida's beckoning shores.

But all accounts agreed it was closed and had been for a while. Then for some reason I quickly checked again right before my trip, just seeing if it was worth venturing so far south. Sure enough I found some postings about going on a cave trip in the company of a local outfitter. My plan all along had been to stop the research at Chattanooga, but these were still technically in the Appalachian Mountains, in a southern branch of the Great Valley defined on the east by Lookout Mountain and on the west by Sand Mountain, broad, flat plateaus rather than mountain peaks, spreading and flattening into the piney woods of the Deep South. And all research rationale aside, the spelunker in me just couldn't resist the lure of getting in a closed cave. So I headed off to the southernmost stop on all my travels, True Adventure Sports at a little Alabama crossroads called Dogtown.

❖   ❖   ❖   ❖

It was blistering hot—94°F the car thermometer told me—when I pulled into the gravel lot filling up one corner of the intersection. The building stood alone in the middle of Lookout Mountain's broadening tabletop, serving as a check in and trading post for a campground nearby the Little River Canyon National Preserve, a rocky gorge and outdoor recreation destination a few miles north. As vans and boat trailers in the parking lot attested, True Adventure Sports also staged river and rock-climbing expeditions and, by arrangement with the cave's owner, a Fort Payne doctor who's looking to stay out of the show cave business if he can help it, has in recent years become the exclusive vendor for private guided trips to Manitou Cave.

I met Tyler, my guide, at the counter in the shop: early twenties, shaggy hair and chill attitude, sandal tan lines on his feet, the kind of ropy strong you get from hauling people (yourself included) over challenging obstacles. That day, though, he seemed bushed, and I couldn't blame him: the store had no AC and he'd been sitting there all day ostensibly running the register. Mostly he'd just been listening to the muted roar of the big pedestal fan in the corner, working furiously but ineffectively to generate a cooling breeze.

He roused himself, and I could see him start to transform as he picked through the house gear on one aisle: helmets, headlamps, an extra couple of lights, a first aid kit, water bottles, a ring of keys on a carabiner. His shoulders squared up as he filled up a sleek daypack and handed me a helmet and headlight. "OK, just follow me down the mountain, and we'll do us some caving. I'm in the black Chevy."

Falling into formation behind Tyler, I followed him east across the plateau, then we plunged abruptly down the steep mountain face on switchbacks, emerging from the woods abruptly into the valley town of Fort Payne. We took some worn side streets across the edge of town, through a working-class neighborhood along the base of the mountain. The road petered out at the mouth of a steep holler, where stood the midcentury modern visitor's center. It probably looked sleek when it was new, but the boards on the window and the disintegrating eaves emphasized its origins in another era. The yard had been mowed, but the flowerbeds were full of weeds, and the whole thing could definitely have used a fresh coat of paint.

Tyler hopped down from his truck and slung on his daypack. We headed into the trees, up the hill on a short steep trail, slabbing hillside up to a little shelf, where an alcove sheltered the door to the underground. Once at the cave door, Tyler had to execute a tricky maneuver, reaching through a hole in the metal armored door to open a rusty padlock out of sight on the other side. I stepped out to the edge of the shelf and surveyed the holler.

The mouth of the cove, where the cave spring resurges, was a turbid green bog. Beaver pond, I thought, and sure enough a beaver swam across the pond. Some old concrete pilings and metal wreckage pointed to an earlier time when a small suspension bridge made the trip to the entrance easier and a little more novel. The remains, though, were picturesque in their own way.

This is what it looks like, I realized, when you go on not a show cave tour but an ex–show cave tour. Already the show cave trappings were sinking into the landscape along with all the other obsolete human uses and, like them, leaving a distinctive mark for subsequent visitors. Manitou was new generation of attraction, combining the traditional trappings of the show cave with more current pursuits, a blend of adventure sports and ruin porn. This wasn't caving exactly—we were going into a well-known and well-traveled cave—

and this wasn't exactly spelunking. I had paid my admission, and I was under the care of a guide. Manitou was becoming something else still, maybe the thing that comes after show caves, as history stumbles on forward.

We got in and got used to the twilight, securing (but not locking!) the door behind us. Tyler grinned for the first time today; I could tell he was glad to be back in here, not least because of the sixty degree air after a day sweltering in Dogtown. Cooling, as it were, to the task, he started to give me a little more conversational version of the time-honored Intro Room speech: a little history of the cave and its development, then on to the basic cave formation principles.

I waved him off of that part, told him I had my speleothems straight, and was ready to see some cave. "Cool," said Tyler, and we started down a long and rapidly widening passageway into the heart of some really big cave. The broad main path, the handrails, everything was still in really good repair. Lots of light fixtures were still in place but, without any regular maintenance for many years now, not likely to work. Besides, the power had been shut off for as long as Tyler had been coming here. It all felt more like being in a closed show cave than being in a wild cave or a party cave.

In fact, though he laced it through a more conversational kind of interaction, I realized early on that Tyler was more-or-less reconstructing elements of the old show cave tour as we wandered along. In a lot of ways Manitou was by the book: named formations, shapes and shadows, Civil War smoke writing, saltpeter works from 1812, civil defense supplies from the Atomic Age, and fossils from the cretaceous. He even busted out a classic cave guide joke, one I'm sure that was used back when Manitou Cave was in its show cave prime.

Tyler paused on the path and said, "Oh hey, let me see if my friend is here." He explained that there was a big snail, a rare species that lived just in these Lookout Mountain caves, and he was usually in a little niche right around here. He shone his flashlight on the ceiling, about seven feet tall where we were, and sure enough, a big round mahogany snail shell was affixed there. "Check him out!" Tyler said, and I eagerly went in for a closer look. Come to find it's a big chert nodule. "Gotcha."

But the difference between whatever this trip was and the show cave tour became clear in one moment. I was looking over the rail at a big hole in the bank below. "I wonder where that goes," I said mostly to myself, as I have many, many times in the course of all these tours. It's probably one of the most uttered phrases by show cave visitors, and I'm probably one of many visitors to stand at this very spot and say the same thing.

"You wanna see?" said Tyler. He seemed pretty fully loosened and waked up now. "Let's do it." And swinging his leg over the rail, he clambered down the bank toward the waiting hole. I took a minute to appreciate that I was getting a show caver's dream come true, then I climbed over the rail and followed.

❖   ❖   ❖   ❖

We made our way down to the stream level, waded the creek, and climbed back up the bank to the tourist trail a couple of bends farther along. There we scrambled up a rocky promontory and into a narrower passageway with a rock shelf at about knee level. Tyler parked it there and broke out a water bottle; I did the same. He asked me if I wanted to cut the lights, to check out the total darkness. Did I. If the darkness demo was anything like the rest of the tour so far, my expectations were dialed up.

We put our stuff away and turned off the headlamps. Then, with no spoil-sports to ruin it with a phone screen, we just hung out in the dark. He told me about how, in order to be certified by their boss to take groups into the cave, they had to go all the way to the end of the commercial tour, a good half mile underground along a winding path with stairs and bridges over deep chasms, and find their way back to the entrance without a light.

"It freaked me out, thinking about it ahead of time," Tyler said. "But it turned out to be easier than I expected when the time came. If you go slow, feel with your feet, control your breathing, and above all use your memory, you can do it fine. You been in a lot of caves, right? You ever tried moving around in the dark?"

In this setting, that question struck me as about like being asked if I've ever flapped my arms and flown. As much as I love a good darkness demo, it had never once occurred to me to get up and walk around, and certainly not in an undeveloped part of a closed show cave somewhere beneath northern Alabama. That crossed a line I've generally maintained throughout this project between encountering danger and embracing it. Even that old spelunker in me never considered blundering around in the dark on purpose. So that's a no. "You wanna try it?" Well, what the hell.

"Alright. I'm going to move a little ways up this passage. You keep this shelf we've been sitting on to your right the whole time and you'll be fine. You'll be able to feel it about shin high the whole way. The path is pretty much level. If you climb up on anything you're doing the wrong thing. Alright, now listen to me go. Wait a minute or so, then follow." And with that Tyler's quiet footfalls went away to my right.

The Show Cave's Afterlife

The emotional complexity of what came next, after I sat and slowly counted to sixty, is difficult to explain. I rose with exaggerated care and started gingerly in the direction of Tyler's disappearing tread. On one level I was maniacally focused on my body, keeping my shin and my fingertips in constant contact with the flowstone shelf we had been sitting on, totally overthinking the need to avoid climbing on anything per Tyler's instructions. One train of thought was having a ridiculously detailed colloquy on what exactly constitutes climbing up on something. In another there was a note of paranoia, especially as the walk went on, as I wondered if I was being pranked. It got a lot easier to imagine that Tyler had quietly slipped back out to the main passage, or even the truck, and was laughing it up at that moment like he had just run a successful snipe hunt.

But there was also at a broader level a sense that I was getting a new perspective on a space that I was starting to feel a little bit inured to. A perspective that called on me to move beyond sight. This moment, I realized, was probably as close as I've come to experiencing the cave on the cave's terms.

As with all the show cave's pleasures, it was fleeting. Tyler's voice was suddenly close by my left ear. "You made it! How was it?" Truthfully, it was awesome. And then it was over, as Tyler switched on his light. I knew I was going to be underwhelmed by how small and safe the route of my epic journey really was. To my surprise I saw there was a pretty big sinkhole off to my left as I meticulously traced my way along to the right. Blundering off in the wrong direction could have had real consequences, a fact I pointed out to Tyler. "Yeah, but you didn't know that when you did it, and you got here just fine," he observed.

We climbed back down to the tourist trail, but soon departed it again to follow the paths of nineteenth-century miners into some remote sections of the cave. We eventually reached the end of the old works, where the ceiling dropped and the stream passage narrowed as it burrowed through the heart of the mountain. We were probably 800 feet below the top of Lookout Mountain now, Tyler told me, and still quite a long wet crawl from where this stream finally sumps.

We turned and started back. As I descended a short flight of steps carved into the clay a couple of centuries ago, my feet sailed out from under me, and I ended up on my back, an exposed rock jamming in between my ribs. For a minute I lay there trying to figure out why the cave suddenly turned sidewise. Then, realizing it was me that switched from vertical to horizontal, I took a quick inventory. Everything was pretty much intact, though that blow to my ribcage was definitely going to leave a mark in the near future, and left me gasping for air in the near term. In case there's any doubt, I can confirm a nineteenth-century mine is a hazardous workplace.

Tyler helped me to my feet and attended patiently while I got my wind back. "No, no, I'm good, I'm good," I replied to his concern. Adrenaline and injured pride conspired to give me the energy to fake it. "OK, I'm good, let's hit it." Fortunately for me, we were headed back to the entrance, but Tyler had one last trick in his super-guide bag. Heading back up the slope, the low-angle view afforded a nice view of a natural bridge about twenty feet long, crossing maybe thirty feet above the downhill side of the trail.

Tyler painted it with his flashlight beam: it was a featured formation in the old cave tour. I'd seen it in vintage colorized postcards online. "You wanna go walk across it?" And just like that he went ten feet up a steep bank like a spider, to a ledge leading to the bridge. Wet and tired, I tried to beg off, but Tyler just indicated to me where to set my feet to get up to the ledge. I'd come this far; here was one last chance to be able to follow that impulse to go off the beaten path. I knew I'd better take it.

I made it to the smooth, rounded lip of the ledge without incident, but I couldn't get any purchase to get my upper body fully onto the ledge proper. When I tried to push off my right arm, stars of pain shot through my rapidly bruising rib cage. Unexpectedly, I felt like I could slide backward. The situation started to take on a new urgency.

Tyler crouched by me nonchalantly. Seeing me scrabbling to avoid a six-foot drop back to the trail, he reached down, grabbed me by the belt, and hauled me bodily up onto the ledge, even though I probably had seventy-five pounds on him. Setting me down, he said, "Let me have your camera, man."

"It's the least I can do," I replied, handing it over.

"Naw, I'm going to go down there on the path and take your picture when you're out on the bridge. Just stop when you're out in the middle and look back down this way." I started cautiously up the ledge, and across the narrow isthmus of stone over the path below. Beyond the bridge, the tourist trail quickly rose to meet a ledge on the other side of the cave. Below me Tyler took one of the last pictures of this trip, and in fact one of the last dozen or so of the several thousand I took in the course of my field work. There I am on the bridge, smiling down on the tourist trail below. I'm helmeted for a reason, muddy, wet, more scared of heights than I'm willing to let on, and pretty banged up, but I've crossed over. I'm no longer taking the pictures of the formations — I'm in them.

❖   ❖   ❖   ❖

The Show Cave's Afterlife

Back out where the cars are parked by the old visitor's center, I poked around in the breezeway, which once separated the gift shop from the restrooms. The place had been pretty well gutted but on one bathroom floor there was a stack of mildewing pamphlets — for some reason, mostly for the Lost Sea. (Maybe leftovers from the NCA pamphlet rack?) On top of them was a stack of old paper signs for the cave, blue with yellow lettering spelling out Manitou Cave in an enthusiastic script against a backdrop of a mountain scene complete with generic American Indian. These signs were still dry, and I asked Tyler if anybody would mind if I grabbed one. "I can't imagine it," he said. "They'd probably thank you if you took 'em all and dropped 'em in a dumpster." One would be fine — it just didn't feel like the trip was complete without a little something from the gift shop.

❖ ❖ ❖ ❖

I was starting to exhaust all my leads. I reached the show cave trail's westernmost point after a day-long ramble around Sand Mountain in northern Alabama, taking in Jay Gurley's Cathedral Caverns and admiring the reconstructed Pleistocene village in the mouth of the Russell Cave National Monument. I wound through the mountains north, and descended the west side of the Cumberland Plateau at Monteagle, Tennessee. Where US 41 reaches the bottom of the hill, I hooked to the right on a country road across from a decrepit billboard pointing the way to Wonder Cave. Sure enough, the old welcome center sat by the rural road a mile or so back off the blacktop, weather-stained outlines still tracing the name of the cave on the front of the building where the metal letters used to be, as if to highlight the persistence of the show cave after its official demise.

I paused in front of the chained-off entrance to the parking lot to take a couple of pictures. The building was closed up tight but plainly still maintained; the grass was mowed and the shrubs were trimmed, and overall it was in a lot better condition than Manitou's old lodge. I looked around for a For Sale sign to provide me with the rationale for wandering up a little closer, playing the prospective buyer, but all I could find was No Trespassing. A couple of loose dogs wandered over to see what I was up to and the barking that relayed up the valley said they weren't the only ones in the neighborhood.

I sat in the car and considered my options, facing west, noting that the sun was past the yardarm and would soon be dropping to the horizon in earnest. Something just felt a little off, and I wondered if it wasn't the fact that, for the first time in all my travels, there weren't any mountains to the west; the horizon the sun was heading for was the rolling hills of Middle Tennessee. As tantalizing as the shuttered Wonder Cave was, I began to feel I was at last outside of my domain. Besides, I had somewhere I needed to be at sundown, a little bit of a drive back to the east, back over the ridge and into the Tennessee River gorge.

❖   ❖   ❖   ❖

I was headed for one of the most storied caves of them all: Nickajack. A massive horizontal limestone lintel framed the vast entrance to this cave at the foot of Sand Mountain's northern face, and for millennia a strong cave stream has poured forth into the Tennessee River. It's like Indian Cave on a grander scale, a broader entrance onto a bigger river, the kind of natural sanctuary along the water's thoroughfare that has attracted human attention for time immemorial. Indigenous people gathered there for many thousands of years, the last such gathering being the village of Anikusatiyi, founded by a displaced band of Cherokee known as the Chickamauga, led by a famous chief known as Dragging Canoe.

In 1794, however, white settlers attacked Anikusatiyi while many of the men were away, slaughtering the population of mostly women and children. The massacre was spearheaded by a man named Orr (sometimes spelled Ore, appropriately enough), who proceeded straightaway to set up shop at the cave with a tavern and a saltpeter works. Nickajack (which somehow descended phonetically from its Cherokee name) became a familiar landmark and regular stop-off for freight and passenger vessels moving up and down the Tennessee. By the time of the Civil War, Nickajack had become one of the largest saltpeter mines in the South, a strategic asset of great importance. When Union forces occupied the area in 1863–64, the military presence included a certain Brigadier General David Hunter Strother, whose alter ego, Porte Crayon, was quoted in *Harper's Weekly* relating the legends of the cave as a "resort of a gang of banditti," and that it "had now fallen into the hands of a worse and more desperate gang . . . the Confederate States of America. It had now—thanks to Grant and Sherman—fallen into honest hands."

The end of the war also ended the need for the cave's abundant saltpeter, and the next phase of its life began. By 1872, advertisements in the local papers testified that the cave was open for excursions, close by rail and steamboat stops at a crossroads called Shellmound. Nickajack became a staple of the early tourist culture of the Chattanooga area, when (as at Melrose) the folks lining up to see the Civil War graffiti could include some of the people who actually wrote it.

Entrance to Nick a Jack Cave Near Chattanooga, Tennessee, October 26, 1859.
(Drawing by David Hunter Strother ["Porte Crayon"]; courtesy of West Virginia
and Regional Historical Art Collection, West Virginia University)

In 1927 Nickajack made national headlines when the show cave's then-owner-operator, Lawrence Ashley, was "lost" in the cave. A massive search ensued, including reporters and stringers for newspapers across the country. These papers had discovered a public hunger for stories of cave rescue during the unsuccessful attempt to rescue explorer and show cave impresario Floyd Collins at Sand Cave in 1925. The effort to free Floyd from entrapment beneath a roof fall in a wild cave near Mammoth Cave in Kentucky erupted into an early version of a media circus.

Ashley's disappearance had a novel plot twist: he turned up alive six days later, wandering down a holler some eight miles away. His claim to have followed a family of wildcats to a narrow opening, then dug his way out with a trenching tool, could never be independently verified. In fact, Ashley himself could not lead others to the spot where he emerged. The stress and disorientation of his odyssey, he claimed, rendered him temporarily insensible.

The press left, and over time the tourists slowed up as well. As a publicity stunt, Ashley's disappearance achieved no discernible results. Nickajack was large and long but not particularly attractive—no decoration on par with Ruby Falls, to be sure. Not even the novelty of an underground boat ride or the intervention of Leo Lambert himself could keep Nickajack viable as a show cave. As proprietor in the 1930s in between gigs at Ruby Falls, Lambert scouted new routes for tours, including the site of Mr. Big, yet another candidate in the "World's Largest Stalagmite" pageant at sixty feet tall and seventy-five in diameter. But not even Mr. Big could save this operation, not when there was the much more lovely Ruby Falls right there where the roads to Florida met. Leo Lambert couldn't compete with his own finest creation.

So Nickajack had been lying fallow for some time when it had what may be its most famous visitor. The legend goes that in 1967, Johnny Cash, eclipsed in popularity by a new generation of country stars and seriously addicted to pills of all description, drove off from his farm outside of Nashville and kept going until he reached Nickajack. And there, where the women and children of the Chickamauga had been massacred almost two centuries before, he crawled back into the darkness of the feral cave amid the ruins of the mining and the tourism, and he waited for death.

Instead, in the darkness before dawn, Cash had a vision of the Lord saying to him that there was important work for him to do yet: "Get up, John." Crawling and feeling his way back to the vast entrance chamber, he emerged into the morning sun.

Depending how florid the version of this legend you're reading is, June Carter Cash is sometimes waiting for him at the entrance, and in some accounts his mother, drawn from her California home by a bad feeling, is there too. The most mythic renditions trace Cash's transformation into "The Man in Black," who "wears the black for the poor and beaten down" and "the reckless ones whose bad trip left them cold," to his encounter at Nickajack. It's like that total darkness rubbed off on him.

The exact location of that metamorphosis, like all good mythic places, is lost to us. Cash would never revisit or lead others to the scene of his redemption, because later in 1967, the TVA completed the Nickajack Dam and closed the floodgates, submerging all but the entrance hall of the cavern in the newly formed lake.

A thorough survey of the cave before its inundation lay to rest all the legends of dozens of miles of cave and other entrances, because the engineers needed to establish that the lake wouldn't drain out unexpectedly in some other location. The final tally was 3,500 feet of passage in the main branch burrowing into the foundations of Sand Mountain, and another 1,500 or so of smaller side passages, of which none are now accessible on foot. Catfish—gigantic ones, according to many accounts—circulate among the remains of the mining and tourist operations, in the space where Johnny Cash met his maker and found his mission. Back on the surface, approaches to the main gallery beyond that massive entry by boat are blocked by chain link fencing, protecting the endangered gray bat colony within.

Of course obstacles of that sort provide a perverse incentive for the spelunker, especially when they stand between the spelunker and a place so rich in history, legend, and myth, even when circumventing the obstacles involves scuba gear and truly incredible danger.

❖   ❖   ❖   ❖

On August 15, 1992, three divers entered the cave late in the night with spears in search of its reputed river-monster catfish. True to form, these submarine spelunkers found their greatest challenge in their own hubris. Trained for open water diving, they lost their bearings in the cave passages, lost their visibility in the silt they stirred up, then lost their cool and swam blindly in panic. Two divers guessed right and emerged in the entrance before their tanks ran dry, but a third, David Gant, swam the wrong way and by dumb luck emerged in a small air pocket in a dome deep in the cave. There he held on to a stalactite and slowly but surely exhausted the oxygen supply in the tiny chamber while his light went dead. Like Johnny Cash before him, Gant waited for death—but in conditions that made Cash's ordeal seem like a picnic.

On the surface, rescue squads alerted by Gant's companions despaired of finding him alive. Family and church members gathered near the mouth of the cave to stage a prayer vigil, poised to turn into a memorial—until a knowledgeable caver intervened. Buddy Lane, captain of the Hamilton County Cave Rescue Unit, struck on a "so crazy it just might work" plan. As dawn broke, Lane and his lieutenant, Dennis Curry, somehow managed to raise somebody on the phone with the authority to set in motion a drawdown of the entire lake: opening the floodgates at Nickajack Dam, absorbing the unscheduled release of millions of gallons in the lakes downstream and pumping the outflow into a massive reservoir atop Raccoon Mountain, and adapting the power-generating schedule all the rest of the way down the line.

The lake dropped fourteen inches, creating enough clearance in the cave passages to allow Lane and Curry to enter the cave without scuba gear. Their most important equipment was copies of the 1962 survey maps, which, as good cavers, they knew how to lay their hands on. Their knowledge of the size and shape of the cave passages allowed them to move quickly into the depths of the cave, despite passing through some spots where only the barest clearance between the surface of the water and the roof of the passage allowed them to keep breathing.

In fact, it was the last inch-and-a-half of lowered water levels that opened an airway to Gant's dome, where the exhausted, hypothermic, hypoxic diver was on the brink of unconsciousness and death, the darkness taking dominion. The tremendous rush of fresh air through the tiny but crucial gap between the water and the roof of the passage into the dome revived him. Fresh air was followed soon thereafter by the lights and the voices of Curry and Lane, calling to him.

The delirious Gant more than half believed he had died. He asked his rescuers, "Are you angels?" "We've been called a lot of things, but never that," came the reply. Soon the prayer vigil had transformed into a celebration as Gant was drawn from what was nearly his watery grave. Prayers had been answered in the form of Curry and Lane's courage and expertise and the Tennessee Valley Authority's technocratic command of the entire region's hydrology.

The "Miracle at Nickajack" became legendary among cavers and folks in the region more generally, the kind of tale that gets revisited in conversation and in the local media to this day. According to most accounts, David Gant emerged from Nickajack, like Johnny Cash, a changed man. Nickajack is a place whose backstory is rooted in genocide and banditry and war, and even in its run as a show cave was the site of hoaxes and failures. But it had now twice been the setting for legends of miraculous redemption—and also rendered impassable. The main resource Nickajack seems to offer these days is its deep, dark vein of irony.

And now I was arriving at the parking lot by the TVA boat ramp, where a boardwalk would take me out to an overlook. From there I could inspect from a safe distance the one show cave it would mean certain death for me to enter. The only thing that could help me in there would be divine intervention, and I wasn't about to bank on that, whatever the cave's recent track record.

❖   ❖   ❖   ❖

These days, the real show isn't inside the cave anymore, anyway. I was trying to be here at sundown because the main thing to see at Nickajack now is the bat flight, when the colony of endangered gray bats heads out on the nightly sortie to eat many times their body weight in flying insects. It's not exactly Carlsbad, but Nickajack is even now possessed of some remnant of its powers of tourist attraction.

So there I stood at the end of the boardwalk, looking in the cove at that legendary cave entrance, in the footsteps of such luminaries as Porte Crayon and Johnny Cash, though where their exact footprints actually were is deep

The Show Cave's Afterlife

beneath the lake's surface. I hadn't been standing there long when I heard more footsteps, coming down the boardwalk. It was such a beautiful summer night in the Tennessee Valley, it didn't surprise me a bit that I wasn't the only one drawn here at sundown.

Here came three college-age white guys, in T-shirts and cargo shorts and baseball caps appropriate for going out to see the bats. But instead of the cooler and fishing tackle you'd expect to round out the look, they were carrying with them a couple of tripods and a camera bag and a file box, and moving with purpose.

We said hey and, as I stepped back out of the way, they went straight about setting up a spotting scope and an infrared video camera, the view screen displaying a weird photonegative image of the hillside before us. Walkie-talkie messages blurted back and forth on the handset one of them had on his belt. The boats, apparently, were on their way, and sure enough, momentarily a couple of unfancy outboards with three or four people in each came around the point into the cove, one closer to the entrance than the other.

When their gear was all set up, I asked them what was going on. "Counting bats," was the reply. We introduced ourselves: two of them were summer interns with the Tennessee Wildlife Resources Agency, college students from Tennessee Tech, and the third a volunteer, also a college student thinking about studying to be a game warden. In a few minutes, when the bats started flying, the folks in the boats — a mix of TWRA employees, a couple of college-professor types, and assorted volunteers — would start counting bats, calling out their subtotals at predetermined intervals. Each team had a scribe who would record the numbers to cross-check their results later. It was a routine matter, they explained, to keep regular tabs on the size of the colony, since gray bats remain on the endangered species list, but white nose syndrome had given them some extra urgency, and they'd been keeping a little closer tabs than before.

The walkie-talkie announced that they were going to go into quiet mode since the flight would soon begin. The shadows were already deep in the cove, and a few tentative bats could already be seen among the swifts and evening birds still flitting about in the last light. As the darkness intensified, so did the flow of bats. The team on the platform watched the time closely on their phones, and in the depth of twilight, the count began.

"Twelve hundred," came a lone voice from the farther boat. Our scribe took it down on his clipboard. Shortly thereafter, the second boat called out "Eleven forty." At regular intervals the watchers in the boats — in a position, I realized, to be able to see the bats against the background of the sky—called out running totals. "Twelve sixty." "Thirteen twenty." "Thirteen fifty." "Fourteen forty."

I didn't quite understand their methods, but the whole scene was strangely meditative, the numbers surging higher, called out in the quiet, as the darkness intensified. The more bats there were coming out of the mouth of that cave, the harder they were to see. I couldn't help but try to will the numbers higher, to push the needle with my mind. As the numbers reached, then passed fifteen hundred, I could not so much see as sense the bats whipping through the woods around us as they hooked and darted up the lakeshore, feeding incessantly. Like shooting stars, by the time you fixed your vision on the sudden movement that bat was already gone.

One of the guys motioned to me to come take a look in the camera viewfinder. Across the inky backdrop of the hillside was a flow of bright dots almost like some kind of strange static. Each bat's furious beating heart made it show up as a little meteor streaking away into the night. The heat signature of the counters in the boats, now only vaguely visible with the naked eye in the gloom, melded into gleaming blobs on the bottom of the screen, stationary beneath the stream of bat-blips, dots, and dashes.

The count peaked at around 1,600, held there for a time, and gradually began to decline. The last few times they called the numbers out they were well below a thousand. When the numbers stopped it felt almost like waking up. They cross checked on the radios: the count was concluded. In the absence of that focusing chant I felt the urge to stretch and shake myself back to normal. The guys got the radio call from the boats: pack it up and meet back at the truck, so they set about breaking down the camera, chatting about where they might be headed next once they had dropped off the gear at the office.

I wandered back up the boardwalk, ready to pack it in, myself. I had a lot to think about. It was almost as if I had been present for this ancient, storied cave to transmit a message into the night, an encrypted stream of information that this team of careful readers, speleo-cryptologists, was making a group effort to decode. Their data-gathering—counting the bats with the naked eye from multiple perspectives—was elaborate but felt primitive. For me, stumbling on this scene unexpectedly in the gathering darkness, the whole thing felt as much ritual as science.

A little bit of solemnity was in order, though: what was at stake here is pretty profound. All they're trying to do here is keep a species from extinction at human hands. The gray bat's habitat was systematically destroyed by human development, and the species was placed on the federal endangered species list in 1976. Decades of dedicated conservation work of the kind I had witnessed here had helped stop the species decline and begin a promising recovery.

But with a total population estimated at only a few million at most, the gray bat was in a precarious enough condition before the advent of white-nose syndrome. Now this count had a new element of suspense: Would this team of readers encounter the same grisly disasters that bat counters discovered in hibernacula where the fungus had struck? Like the colony collapse among the bats' fellow fliers, the honeybees, the problem poses a broader ecological threat, that the loss of one species in the complex web of relationships would reverberate through the system in potentially catastrophic ways. All you have to do to convince someone that we need solutions for white nose syndrome is tell them about the effect a bat die-off would have on the local mosquito population, throwing in Zika and West Nile as needed.

Little did any of us know, we were witnessing the calm before the storm. In 2012 researchers discovered white nose among gray bats in Tennessee. In 2013 traces of the fungus were identified on bats in Alabama's nearby Fern Cave National Wildlife Refuge, the site of the single largest gray bat hibernaculum, home to over a million sleepers. It remains to be seen if the syndrome will be as lethal for the grays as it is for the little brown bats that have been its primary victims, losing over 20 percent of their population on the east coast since the discovery of the syndrome in New York State in 2006.

But the precarity of the situation has at least a little bit of a silver lining. If the bats go, they may take us all down with them. But maybe that means, that if we can figure out how to save the bats, we're on the right track toward figuring out how to fix everything else.

So many lies and hoaxes and crimes, so many myths and legends have issued from this cave. It's seen floods, ruins, mines, massacres, and the occasional miraculous redemption—yet the data that flows from it on tranquil summer evenings may be the most cosmically significant of them all. Perhaps Nickajack, for all its transformations, has one more miracle left in its depths: to teach us something we need to know about how to stay alive on this planet. It's easier to hope for such, anyway, on a beautiful summer night in the Great Appalachian Valley, enjoying the show at the cave.

❖   ❖   ❖   ❖

Or maybe we'll never decode what the bats are trying to tell us, and their nightly collective semaphore will just be one more record of a brief, transient life form on Planet Earth. The cave has plenty of them in there already. In the time frame that caves work on, what's one species more or less?

Though lost to us tourists forever, at least as we understand the term, all that stuff that Cliff Forman installed in Mystic Cave back in that long hungry winter of 1961 is still in there, and if caves teach us anything it's that one day everything inside it will end up being a part of that cave. Someday all those bits and pieces of show cave could end up a strange little fossilized pattern between layers of stone in a mountain range that doesn't exist yet. The wiring and the handrails and the signage, the fuse boxes and garbage cans, maybe even two kids crushed by a boulder: all will join the cephalopods and the gastropods and the stromatolites, trace fossils in the cave's permanent record. That's given enough time, of course, but what have caves got if not plenty of time?

Say what you will about the banality or the hucksterism of show caves; maybe they aren't exactly a high art. But one thing they've got over pretty much every other form of culture known to humankind is permanence. When you write on a cave, that is a mark that doesn't go away—we know this because half the stuff you see on any show cave tour is the markings left on the cave by previous cultures, previous ecosystems, previous eons. We know this because the earliest marks made by human beings have been preserved for us in caves. There might have been other kinds of art, older or more widespread or more highly regarded among these people, but we don't have any record of them: we still have the cave paintings. You couldn't get rid of every trace of a show cave if you wanted to, and we know this because people have wanted to, and people have tried.

I guess it depends on my mood as to whether this strikes me as nihilistic or oddly reassuring. On a night like that one at Nickajack, I went with the more hopeful message: this too shall pass. Defeat isn't out of the question, but neither is redemption. And in the end it sort of doesn't matter—it's all going to be part of the stone. But we still might have figured out some way to leave a mark, a track in the strata that really will endure, and is in fact the only thing that will.

The Show Cave's Afterlife

Epilogue

Valley of the Badasses

❖　❖　❖　❖

The show caves of the Great Valley, east to west, north to south, map out an area that's still a contact zone to this day. The western border of the Great Valley, in particular, is still a rough-and-tumble place. Driving west across Maryland toward the far side of the Great Valley, you can watch the last waves of commuter cul-de-sacs break against the fading northern stretch of the Blue Ridge. Splotches of sprawl blossom around Interstate 81, then you follow first the Potomac River, then the South Branch of the Potomac River, then the North Fork of the South Branch of the Potomac River, past the divider of Shenandoah Mountain, beyond the reach of limited-access highways. It's hard to remember you're about two hours from Dulles when you're in a place this rugged and remote. It feels like a throwback, holdout, opt-out space with its rough edges still intact.

There's something brawny, something kind of badass, about the whole area, in stark contrast to the Carolina High Country's rustic elegance or the more settled mood of the valley by the Blue Ridge. In the northern stretches of this western border, the last bands of valley limestone here are tilted up almost vertically from their collision with the coalfield shale. Erosion has left the less-porous strata jutting up in razorback ridges with sheer cliff walls — daunting, muscular terrain.

The stories that shape this place have acquired some of this attitude. A magnificent pair of outcroppings called Champe Rocks don't just sound tough: their backstory lives up to the name. Champe Rocks was once the property of Sergeant John Champe, given to him in a land grant in recognition of his extraordinary service in the Revolutionary War.

Champe sounds like a good fit with this landscape. His old commander, "Light Horse Harry" Lee (father of Robert E.), described him as "full of bone and muscle; with a saturnine countenance, grave, thoughtful, and taciturn — of tried courage and inflexible perseverance." Champe was such a complete badass that George Washington himself sent him on a secret mission to kidnap the traitor Benedict Arnold, an escapade that very nearly succeeded, and kept him under deep cover in the British Army until Arnold's command sailed for Virginia. Once they landed, Champe escaped back across lines and then walked home.

In truth Champe didn't live here long—he roamed around Kentucky and present-day West Virginia and died on the banks of the Monongahela—but this quartzite crag seems like an appropriate monument to this colonial action hero. Conflict is etched into this place's very bones.

Further up the valley is Seneca Rocks, another razorback outcrop, where no less badass an outfit than the Tenth Mountain Division trained here for warfare in the Italian Alps during World War II. It felt appropriate, somehow, that I had lunch at the sandwich shop across from the National Forest visitor's center in the company of two dozen members of a Pennsylvania motorcycle club. Motorcyclists abound in this valley; these winding mountain highways are a huge draw. They were all abuzz about the wipeout one of their members had earlier that day, and how certain stretches of this drive were renowned for claiming a victim regularly. While they were concerned for their friend, as I listened to them talk, it sure seemed like that element of risk was part of the route's appeal. Their whole outing was weirdly validated by the misfortune.

Across the way at the visitor's center, a trail leads to an observation deck on the shoulder of the exposed rock face. There, a tremendously large and wordy sign lectures you: "STOP: You alone are responsible for your safety! We know it is very tempting to proceed past this point BUT without proper climbing equipment you are putting yourself and your family/friends at risk."

The narration changes tone: "The top of Seneca Rocks is a knife-edged ridge less than 10 feet wide. Think about what would happen if you (or your child) slipped and fell . . ." The ghoulish ellipses give way to a more forceful, boldface tone. "Since 1971, 15 people have died at Seneca Rocks from falls. It's not worth the risk." This isn't some rinky-dink show cave, with its whispers of darkness and intimations of mortality. This place will just flat out kill you. Or maybe . . . your child. I was duly chastised, but it didn't stop the three teenagers who passed by me at the observation deck from heading on out the knife edge. I spent the rest of my stay on the deck listening attentively for the sound of people falling.

People aren't the only things that fall at Seneca Rocks. Sometimes the rocks themselves fall as well. For centuries, Seneca Rocks's own "money formation" was a pinnacle called the Gendarme, posted like a sentinel in a gap between twin peaks. You can see it featured in drawings by indefatigable geology tourist Porte Crayon. But on October 22, 1987, the Gendarme fell from his post in the night, a casualty of this landscape of bedrock struggle.

◆　　◆　　◆　　◆

If you're alert, other signs of conflict abound. On the drive from Seneca Rocks to nearby Seneca Caverns you pass, in fairly rapid succession, a plaque commemorating the Battle of Riverton, a Civil War cavalry clash; the grave of a Medal of Honor winner from World War II, Clinton M. Hedrick, whose headstone is large enough to reproduce the text of General Order No. 89, citing his gallantry as he perished in the fighting for Lembeck, Germany; and the tale of Hinkle's Fort, a blockhouse built in 1762 by the settler Hinkle, which became a fortification and refuge for the white occupiers of the area back when you had to be a pretty serious badass just to survive day to day. Dotted all along this valley and south all the way to the Tennessee line was a chain of forts and blockhouses developed and overseen by a young militia commander named George Washington in the 1750s, when this valley was the leading edge of white folks' expansion across the continent.

When I rode up to the top of Spruce Knob, the highest point in West Virginia at 4,863 feet, I parked by a durable homemade shrine to Fred La-lone Sr., 1930–2002, "USMC, A True Marine." Badassery is literally under-foot. Spruce Knob itself is an illustration of how hard this land itself and the people who have inhabited it have been put to it over the years. It's on a tall but relatively gentle ridge, whose windswept crest is covered with low-lying, scrubby woods—the stunted second growth of a vast hardwood forest that was completely removed by 1906. The rapid clearcutting unleashed mud-slides and general disruption on life in the Great Valley's western frontiers until it was tamed by the National Forest conservation programs. The fact that this solidly red-voting area is even habitable today is a tribute to massive Federal government intervention. Like many a cave, it's as much a postindus-trial landscape as it is a wilderness.

The show caves back in here continue this combination of amazing and tough. Smoke Hole Caverns, for example, is a good old classic hillbilly-themed roadside attraction. It's family owned and operated to this day, com-plete with an awesome Eisenhower-era sign practically on the shoulder of the North Fork Highway in a part of the valley known as Cabins, calling to the travelers about the cave and what the proprietors proclaim is West Vir-ginia's largest gift shop. The cavern features an abundance of decoration in-cluding some gigantic stone draperies that are the world's best something or other. But if Smoke Hole tops any lists, surely it's Most Awkward Names? What sounds like a crude euphemism actually derives from some much shallower caves in a deep gorge nearby, used by indigenous people as smokehouses and later arrivals as distilleries. Its very name, in other words, is about the earth as a workplace.

Seneca Caverns sits at the head of a long rolling valley, which was probably a spectacular view before the quarry, operated by the same company that owns the cave, opened up a big section of the valley to remove the rock underneath. Illuminate and mythologize it, or blow it up and haul it off: these folks are going to make money off this limestone one way or another. Still, it's fun to experience the tour in both caves in the company of big groups of motorcyclists from Ohio and Upstate New York, jostling and teasing each other and surprisingly jittery underground for folks who rode all the way here seeking thrills on mountain roads.

It's a place with scars, a place where things butt up against each other. The fly fisherman rides along behind the timber truck behind the motorcycle club, all passing by the quarry on the railroad in the valley resulting from the conjunction of two different geologic provinces. Stunning natural beauty gives way to factory farm, light industrial to ecotourism to resource extraction: from Seneca Rocks you can see a beautiful panorama of Wild, Wonderful West Virginia with a natural gas pumping station in the foreground.

❖   ❖   ❖   ❖

But when you ramble on down US 220, out of the Potomac headwaters, into a corner of Virginia tucked into West Virginia's eccentric borders, signs announce that you are now traveling the Sam Snead Highway. Suddenly, as you start to descend into the upper reaches of the James River watershed, the scruffy frontier gives way to acres upon acres of beautifully maintained golf course, with epicenters in the two remaining legatees of the high period of mineral springs resorts: the Homestead and the Greenbrier.

At the top of the valley you pass the Jefferson Pools, the grandsire of the curative waters industry that once proliferated throughout this district of bold, mineral-rich flowing waters. Archaic, octagonal wooden sheds protect warm, clear, aromatic pools a dozen feet deep where once arthritic and rheumatic plantation aristocrats, including the author of the Declaration of Independence, soaked their limbs.

It's the property of the Homestead now, however, so besides the occasional wanderer the clientele is mostly drawn from the golfing classes and their bored family members, transported here in logo-bearing shuttle buses up that emerald valley of groundskeeping. Golf courses are in many ways the opposite of show caves, creating a landscape whose appeal comes from the exclusion of most of its natural features and artificial enhancement of the ones that remain, using the most possible surface area for the benefit of the fewest possible people. Where show caves revel in irony and paradox, golf courses organize the entire landscape around a single, esoteric use.

In that sense Golf Valley shows signs of struggle as well: here the struggle of a monolithic economy to eliminate multiplicity. Once this was the heart of an entire region of resorts and inns started up by dozens of landowners; now of the two remaining, the Homestead is part of the Omni hotel global network, and the Greenbrier was owned by railroad conglomerate CSX until purchased by coal mine magnate Jim Justice, West Virginia's richest man and now thirty-sixth governor. These golf courses are the bizarro reflection of the mountaintop removal mining sites, linked financially and historically and philosophically, through a mindset that stops at nothing to bring the Earth under a logic of uniformity of purpose. Both the prosperity of the Greenbrier and the desolation of former mountaintops just west of here signify the power of a single story. The Golf Valley is in its own way an intrusion in the landscape as radical as Seneca Rocks.

◆　◆　◆　◆

When the resort properties abruptly end, the western valley quickly returns to checkered, battle-scarred normal. A few miles from the Greenbrier, right on the state line between the two Virginias, is an old, quiet show cave called Organ Cave. The show cave reflects the multiplicity of the place as the tour actually splits in two: a walk through some lower chambers, where mannequins in Civil War uniforms reenacted saltpeter mining tasks, and the upper section, which actually featured some decoration, though its namesake flowstone formation, the Organ, was just a big stone xylophone—a little underwhelming once you've seen Luray's Stalacpipe in action. The real takeaway point was what a hellish scene it would have been, digging earth for saltpeter, in the eternal night of a cave lit by lanterns and the fires under the vats purifying the nitrate to make gunpowder. As the guide points out, this was not duty that you sought out to avoid combat. It required its own brand of badass.

If you keep wandering down the road to the southwest you can swing by the federal women's prison at Alderson, where Martha Stewart did her time, en route to the tunnel that's the leading candidate for the site of John Henry's race with the steam drill. You'd be hard pressed to find a more pointed contrast in legendary American badasses anywhere. Add to all this some of the most legitimately beautiful rural and woodland landscapes you've ever seen. If someone asks me what's the prettiest place I've ever seen, I can answer quickly, it's the valley rolling away to the south and west of deceptively named Bland, Va. (I can see why they might guard their secret jealously.) How can any one story contain all this?

The southernmost show cave on this West and western Virginia ramble is Natural Tunnel, where the show is to see the cave at work: your visit is truly complete when you see not only the cave but also the train. An active rail line enters and exits the base of the ridge via a big borehole carrying Stock Creek down to the Clinch River. The "South Portal" on the down-stream side boasts a truly vast Hollywood entrance framed by an immense natural stone amphitheater, created by the collapse in some other epoch of what must have been a truly amazing underground chamber. When the train slowly and majestically emerges from the mountainside into the this deep stone arena, it's oddly moving.

A golf course does its level best to erase any evidence that it is causally connected to a mountaintop removal mine—even though when you are a golf course owned by Jim Justice, you are directly, causally connected to mountaintop removal. But Natural Tunnel wears it on its sleeve, or perhaps more accurately in its sleeve, as trains go up empty and come back full of coal from further up inland, beyond the limestone. The working landscape and the leisure landscape are one—and in public space, since Natural Tunnel, too remote to ever really be viable as a tourist destination but too singular to be left defenseless, is a state park. It makes sense that a place where so many of the area's versions and visions of itself come together would be public property.

Elsewhere in the 900-acre park there's a restored blockhouse—a part of the southern end of George Washington's chain of defenses. And it still kind of feels like, working your way down it, you're passing along the edge of something. To the east rises the spreading development patterns of car culture, a rising tide of asphalt pushing a scud of big box stores and chain restaurants. To the west, real physical devastation, not the slow-motion ecological disaster unleashed by the eastern sprawl. Mountaintop removal mines are visible from space. And when you poison the headwaters, the problems all roll downhill. If we're willing to treat the mountains themselves this way, is it that much of a surprise that the counties where MTR is widespread also lead the nation in opioid addiction?

I have an image in my files by photojournalist Earl Dotter of a Logan County, West Virginia, Walmart built on a "reclaimed" strip mine bench.

Epilogue

Walmart built on strip-mine bench, Logan County, West Virginia, 2005.
(Photograph by Earl Dotter)

The pyramidal stone wall that was once a mountain ridge looms in the background. The long, low Supercenter spans the orderly horizontal strata so they seem neatly stacked on top of it, overlooking a spreading sea of cars and blacktop. The striking visual composition underscores that they are all part of the same logic, one the architectural theorist Kenneth Frampton described back in 1983: "The bulldozing of an irregular topography into a flat site is clearly a technocratic gesture which aspires to a condition of absolute placelessness."

Appalachia is a region whose identity as a place, real and imagined, is undergoing profoundly dislocating experiences with all kinds of manifestations of the global economy, whether strip mines, golf courses, private prisons, or Supercenters. Unsustainable development, permanently scarring resource extraction, the effects of climate change, xenophobia, and ethnonationalism: the forces that aspire to placelessness seem in many ways to be firing up the social, cultural, economic, and political bulldozers right now. I don't know how it's going to turn out, nor does anybody else.

But I'm glad we're going to have show caves around while we try to figure that out. These pugnacious caves of West Virginia, scuffling, working, remind us that the show cave by its very nature aspires to the exact opposite of the Walmart or the strip mine. Show caves are some of the most placeful places you could ever hope to find. Like the civil defense supply caches that are a feature of so many show caves in the valley, the show caves themselves are a stockpile of the resources for placemaking. Wonder, reconsideration, and reflection. Inquiry and debate. The kinds of questions and queries that make people want to make things, whether they're books or maps or paintings or altars or lithophones.

The bulldozers are a powerful force and may yet carry the day. But it's reassuring, in the final analysis, to know that show caves can't be erased because they aren't even on the surface. Instead, lingering literally beneath our perception, is a space so bizarre and beautiful and illusory and menacing that, to this very day, somebody will turn up willing to take on the project of making its glorious contradictions available to everybody. Even though that project requires transporting boats to an underground lake, spelunking through the distant reaches of risk management and liability, corralling a seasonal workforce, stocking a gift shoppe, and accommodating your guests' random phobias and dilemmas while containing their impulses toward cave- and self-destruction.

Forget about the money—it was never about the money. If I've learned one thing, it's that the show cave is the worst get-rich-quick scheme of all time. There's got to be something more to it, if only to explain why folks keep literally throwing money and effort down a hole in the ground.

Show caves keep an idea alive: that in this world where increasingly we all draw into spaces and cultures and images and ideas with people like ourselves, we've still got a space that speaks to us of our place in a world, a cosmos that is always ever a lot of things at once. This space is preserved only by our collective, intuitive sense of our need for it, as manifest in our willingness to keep paying for it, year in and year out.

Show caves tell us the ordinary shapes of the ordinary world can have extraordinary underpinnings: the places we inhabit might not be nearly so homogeneous or undistinguished as meets the eye. We need more places that help us see our daily lives in a different light, that make us ask big questions and help us answer them in new ways, that get us to think about how we want to interpret the big network of connections that have brought us all to this very historical moment. We all need to learn to move safely through the darkness together, and somehow make it fun.

Acknowledgments

❖   ❖   ❖   ❖

Endless Caverns is in part my tribute to the freedom of inquiry and creative spirit of Columbia College Chicago. It's good to be part of an institution that supports this kind of project, and I am glad I have taken advantage of the opportunity. In addition to my colleagues all across this unique creative and intellectual community, I thank the English Department (led by chair extraordinaire Ken Daley), the School of Liberal Arts and Sciences, and the Office of Academic Affairs, which have supported the research and presentation of this work. Much of the travel described here was subsidized by Faculty Development Grants.

Along these travels I've been helped by a lot of folks who took the time to share their knowledge and experience. I'm sure this book would not exist were it not for Professor Ed Spencer, whose Field Geology class at Washington and Lee University in the fall of 1986 permanently expanded my awareness of our unquiet earth when all I was looking for was a lab section that met out in the woods. The Ham House Boys joined me on some key early explorations. I would never have found the intellectual resources I needed to do this work without the directions of Dr. Wayne Franklin. Flash forward two more decades: library staff in special collections departments at James Madison University, the University of Virginia, the Library of Virginia, the East Tennessee Historical Society, Massanutten Regional Library (especially Cheryl Metz), Virginia Tech, Lincoln Memorial University, and the Chattanooga Public Library deserve special recognition, as does Martha Wiley, the historian at Cumberland Gap National Historical Park. Cave owners and operators, cavers, speleohistorians, and all of the above patiently endured my interview skills and taught me much: Gary and Becky Barnett, Wade Berdeaux, Tyler Daniel, Richard Dykes, Eric and Janine Evans, Rod and John Graves, Roger Hartley, Gene Monday III, Gary Roberson, Stan and Kay Sides, Lettie Stickley, Jim Whidby, Jim Yancey, and the many rank-and-file members of the National Cave Association who allowed me to pester them at the 2011 annual meeting. Tony and Stewart Scales showed me around the subterranean spaces of Natural Tunnel State Park knowledgably and hospitably. A tip of the helmet to the whole gang from the WKU/CRF Karst Field School '08, even Darlene. Robert Lagueux read early drafts of this work and listened to me go on about it. Knoxville correspondent Ian Blackburn had the file I needed in his living room and the owner of the Lost Sea in his bar. Fr. Paul DeMuth's Holy Land was the perfect destination for this project to reach its conclusion.

To Mark Simpson-Vos and the good people at UNC Press, thank you for letting me be myself again. I hope your patience with a slow worker learning a new skill will pay off in the end. Sian Hunter deserves special recognition for encouraging me to think that this was something I could do. Phil Obermiller, Shaunna Scott, and Chad Berry provided firm, insightful feedback on an essay for their first-rate collection *Studying Appalachian Studies: Making the Path by Walking* (2015); this piece included some material that eventually became chapter 4. Jeff Biggers and Scott Huler read the whole thing repeatedly, carefully, sincerely, and constructively and helped me refine many facets of my approach to this work.

To the late Charles Kennedy: our acquaintance was brief but I feel like this work is invested with your spirit. Wherever you are, I hope there are hummingbirds. Godspeed, Professor Sidney Mathias Baxter Coulling III, who crossed the bar in 2016 with, I am certain, dignity and grace. Professor Robert J. Higgs rejoined the Oversoul as this project neared completion — a good and gentle man who changed my life.

To Franklin H. Alden Jr., aka Kavezookie: you've been my coinvestigator, interlocutor, engineer, arranger, and lyricist. Your role in the realization of this project cannot be overstated.

To my incredible family: know that I do not know what I would be without you all. Brothers and sisters, both biological and in-law, you're the only gang I want to be in. Richard and Sara Reichert, there's no way to measure the value of your generosity, not to mention your inside line to the Zuber Foundation. Harry and Janet Powell, Mom and Dad, your spirit of exploration and love of learning shaped all this project's best features, something I can gladly say of my life altogether. Please forgive any grammatical errors.

Pegeen, Charlie, Elizabeth, here is The Cave Book at last, that thing I've been wandering off and tending to for as long as any of us can remember. It is a modest tribute to all you've given me in the meantime. You are the center of my uncertain world.

Acknowledgments

Note on Sources

❖   ❖   ❖   ❖

Endless Caverns is a work of creative nonfiction. I've spoken to many people about show caves over the past decade, and I have woven many of their voices together here. As a rule, those who knew they were speaking to me as a part of this book project and explicitly gave permission, or those who spoke in some public capacity, have been identified by name. In all other cases, names have been changed or omitted. The precise wording of conversations, the nature and texture of events, is based first and foremost on my recollection. Any distortions in narration or description are attributable to memory's inevitable limitations and the constraints of my own understanding of my own experience. On a few occasions I have condensed or slightly reordered events for clarity or narrative consistency.

The narrative of this book is constructed from extensive reading and research as well as experience. In my reading in support of this work I have browsed a whole range of fields and approaches omnivorously, though historical and cultural studies of the Mountain South have formed the core of my diet. I have been especially inspired and informed by classic regional narrative histories like Robert Kincaid's *The Wilderness Road* (Bobbs-Merrill, 1947) or Wilma Dykeman's *The French Broad* (Henry Holt, 1955), and more recent work like Edward Ayers's *Southern Crossing* (Oxford, 1995), John Alexander Williams's *Appalachia: A History* (UNC Press, 2002), and Jack Williams's *East 40 Degrees* (Virginia, 2005).

The primary source for most of this work is of course the show caves themselves. Since 2005, I have visited thirty-six current and former show caves in the Valley and Ridge Province of the Appalachian Mountains, some on multiple occasions. My research area ranges from Sand Mountain and Lookout Mountain in Alabama and Georgia, northeast to the Catoctin Mountains of Maryland and the West Virginia Alleghenies. At each cave I made a careful assessment of the tourist areas, taking dozens of pictures inside and outside the cave, over 3,000 photographs in all. I kept both written and voice diaries recording my daily impressions and my accounts of my interactions with others.

To learn about the behind-the-scenes work of the show cave, I have conducted interviews with ten show cave owners and operators, including (among others) Wade Berdeaux, former owner-operator of Endless Caverns; Richard Dykes, operator, Indian Cave Village; Roger Hartley, owner-operator, Appalachian Caverns; Jim Whidby, caretaker of Cherokee Caverns; and Gene Monday III, son of the late Gene Monday Jr., owner of both Cherokee Caverns and Indian Cave Village. I expanded on this core of interviews via four days of conversation with a broad spectrum of folks in the show cave industry at the meeting of the National Cave Association, the research and commercial organization of the show cave business, in September 2011 in Luray, Virginia.

Though the caves in question lie outside my research area, my understanding of caves, caving, and show caves was greatly expanded by the field school course on "Commercialization of Mammoth Cave," offered by Western Kentucky University and the Cave Research Foundation, taught by Dr. Stan Sides, which I attended in June 2008.

I was assisted in locating show caves and their histories by a number of resources. *The Gurnee Guides to American Caves* are especially helpful; older editions, especially, helped me pinpoint several defunct operations. Larry Matthew's *Caves of Knoxville and the Great Smoky Mountains* (National Speleological Society, 2008) and *Caves of Chattanooga* (National Speleological Society, 2007) provide an eclectic range of very useful materials. William McGill's *Caverns of Virginia* (Virginia Commission on Conservation and Development, 1933) and Thomas Barr's *Caves of Tennessee* (Tennessee Division of Geology, 1961) have not only provided a wealth of information but also helped me understand the history and practice of speleology. My rudimentary knowledge of geology has been augmented throughout by Arthur N. Palmer's *Cave Geology* (Cave Research Foundation, 2007). A wide-ranging miscellany of information about many of the caves I am studying is found in the *Journal of Spelean History*, a publication of the American Spelean History Association since 1968. Online, "Showcaves of the World" (www.showcaves .com), a website maintained by German show cave enthusiasts, provides basic information about where the commercial operations are (or were).

Follow-up investigation of the history of the individual caves and their environs led me to significant repositories of historical documents, especially ephemera relating to caves (e.g., tourist brochures, promotional travel narratives) and vertical files collecting news stories about the caves and their operators. The East Tennessee Historical Society in Knoxville, Tennessee, and the Hamilton County (Tennessee) Public Library Local History collections in Chattanooga proved especially helpful. The James Madison University Special Collections department in Harrisonburg, Virginia, was especially helpful in reconstructing the history of Colonel Brown's work at Endless Caverns, as was James Sterling Trelawny's 1993 M.A. thesis, "The History of Endless Caverns," in the university archives. On the Web, Appalachia College Association–Digital Library Association's Collections and the Virginia Tech Library's online Special Collections have provided important resources, especially historic image files. The University of Virginia's Small Library is home not only to a wealth of show cave ephemera but also to many of the materials I consulted about the history of the Grottoes Corporation, including volume 2 of their correspondence. The other volume can be found in the Library of Virginia in Richmond, also the home of the records of the Virginia Geological Survey. The Massanutten Regional Library in Harrisonburg, Virginia, supplied a wealth of information about both Melrose and Massanutten Caverns, especially the documentaries they made inside both caves. The archives at the Cumberland Gap National Historic Site provided research support for my discussion of Gap Cave, including planning documents for the historic landscape project. Any errors of fact that remain in this volume today are solely the responsibility of the author.

Index of Caves and Caverns

❖   ❖   ❖   ❖

Appalachian Caverns, 24
Atomic Caverns. *See* Cherokee Caverns

Bedquilt Cave, 1–5, 133–34
Blowing Cave. *See* Forbidden Caverns
Blue Grottoes. *See* Melrose Caverns
Bristol Caverns, 142

Carlsbad Caverns, 139, 149, 190
Carter Saltpeter Cave, 89–97, 98, 99, 112
Cathedral Caverns, 27, 185
Caveman's Palace. *See* Cherokee Caverns
Caverns of the Ridge. *See* Cherokee
    Caverns
Cherokee Caverns, 7, 10, 102–11, 114, 115,
    116, 117, 159
Cherokee Firesite Ceremonial Caverns.
    See Cherokee Caverns
Clay Cave, 98
Colossal Cavern, 1, 3, 5
Composite Caverns, 16
Craighead Caverns. *See* Lost Sea
Cudjo's Cave. *See* Gap Cave

Diamond Caverns, 134, 135, 136, 142, 173
Dixie Caverns, 161

Endless Caverns, 10, 19, 26, 136, 158–74

Forbidden Caverns, 49–51, 56, 58, 60, 62

Gap Cave, 9, 62–63, 65, 67, 68, 71, 77–83, 99
Gentry's Cave. *See* Cherokee Caverns
Grand Caverns, 8, 31–34, 39, 44–47, 87,
    143–44, 161

Grottoes of the Shenandoah. *See* Grand
    Caverns

Howe Caverns, 155

Ice Caves Mountain, 177
Indian Cave, 10, 26, 102–4, 112–25, 144, 159,
    186
Indian Cave Village. *See* Indian Cave
Inner Space, 86–88, 99, 126–27

Jefferson City, Tenn., 112
Jenolan Caves, 141
John A. Murrell Cave. *See* Gap Cave

Kartchner Caverns, 138
King Solomon's Cave. *See* Gap Cave

Linville Caverns, 58–61, 62
Lost Sea, 11–15, 19, 23, 109, 166, 185
Lost World Caverns, 177
Luray Caverns, 46, 70, 129, 149–54, 158, 161,
    168, 199

Mammoth Cave, 3, 5, 133, 134, 135, 139, 167
Mammoth Cave–Flint Ridge Complex, 3,
    4, 5, 134
Manitou Cave, 178, 179–85
Marengo Cave, 135
Massanutten Caverns, 28, 161
Melrose Caverns, 26, 159, 161–63, 166–69
Mud Glyph Caves, 18, 28
Mystic Caverns, 175–78, 194

Natural Tunnel, 200
Nickajack Cave, 26, 186–94

Ohio Caverns, 140–41
Organ Cave, 199

Palace Caverns. *See* Cherokee Caverns

Raccoon Mountain Caverns, 26
Rio Camuy, 137
Ruby Falls, 19, 25–27, 187–88
Russell Cave, 185

Sand Cave, 187
Seneca Caverns, 198
Silver Hill Caverns. *See* Endless Caverns
Skyline Caverns, 19–20

Smoke Hole Caverns, 197–98
Snail Shell Cave, 99
Stan's Well, 134

Tennessee Caverns. *See* Raccoon
   Mountain Caverns
Tuckaleechee Caverns, 19

Weyer's Cave. *See* Grand Caverns
Wonder Cave, 185–86
Wyandotte Caves, 135

Zirkle's Cave. *See* Endless Caverns

Index of Caves and Caverns

General Index

❖   ❖   ❖   ❖

Addis, Bob, 177
"Adventures of Porte Crayon and His Cousins, The," 33–34
Alaska Gold Rush, 73
Alderson, W.Va., 199
Ament, Matthias, 31
American Association, Limited, 68, 71, 72
American Celebration on Parade, 147–49, 154
American Intertribal Association, 116
American Museum of Natural History, 165
Andrews, N.C., 54, 60
Anikusatiyi, 186
Appalachia, 6–7, 10, 16, 24, 29, 49, 50, 54, 56, 60–61, 66, 70, 88, 129, 154, 201
Appalachian Mountains, 4, 8, 56, 57, 66, 179
Appalachian Trail, 53, 60
Appalachian Valley. See Great Appalachian Valley
Arnold, Benedict, 195–96
Arthur, Alexander Alan, 68–74, 76, 77, 78, 82, 160, 169
Arthur, Tenn., 73
Ashley, Lawrence, 187
Atomic Age, 106, 108, 181

Barnett, Becky, 142
Barnett, Gary, 142
Banks, Nathaniel, 35–37
Barings Bank, 72
Barnum, P. T., 66
Barr, Thomas, 89, 134, 136
Barren County, Ky., 1, 3
Bats, 123, 155; gray bats, 190–93

Battle of Cedar Creek, 38
Battle of Cross Keys, 37
Battle of Port Republic, 37
Battle of Riverton, 197
Beauty Spot, 91
Berdeaux, Gary, 135, 136, 170, 172–73
Berdeaux, Susan, 135
Berdeaux, Virgil ("Sonny"), 136, 170, 172–74
Berdeaux, Wade, 135–36, 170, 172–74
Bingham, George Caleb, 65
Bishop, Stephen, 5
Blackburn (Grottoes Co. receiver), 45
Bland, Va., 200
Blount County, Tenn., 50–51
Blue Ridge, 37–38, 39, 52, 58, 85, 93, 149, 195
Blue Ridge Parkway, 19, 53, 58, 60
Boats, 12, 14–15, 71, 114, 166, 187, 189, 191, 202
Boone, Daniel, 63, 65, 68, 71–72, 81
Boston Post, 165
Boy Scouts. See Scouting
Brown, Bliss, 168–69
Brown, Edward M. ("Major Brown"), 165, 168
Brown, Edward M., Jr., 168–69
Brown, Edward T. ("Colonel Brown"), 26, 159–67, 170–72
Brucker, Roger, 3–4

Cabarrus County, N.C., 42
Cabins, W.Va., 197
Carillon. See Singing Tower
Carricino, Nic, 173

Carter County, Tenn., 92, 93
Cartography, 100, 173. *See also* Maps
Cash, Johnny, 188, 189, 190
Cash, June Carter, 188
Cave Accident Report, 98–100
Cave art, 18, 194
Cave diving, 98, 189
Cave formation, 16–17
Cave Hill, 31, 37–39, 41, 43, 45
Cave Men, 25–28, 34, 176
Cavemobile, the, 106, 108
Cave rescue, 98–99, 105, 176, 189–90
Cave Research Foundation (CRF), 3, 5, 134
Caverns of Virginia (McGill), 150
Cavers. *See* Caving and cavers
Caves of Chattanooga (Matthews), 175
Caves of Knoxville and the Great Smokies (Matthews), 81
Caves of Tennessee (Barr), 89, 134, 136
Caving and cavers, 2–3, 5, 86, 89, 97–101, 102, 109, 111, 115–16, 118, 120, 126, 130, 133, 134, 135, 137, 138, 142, 144, 146, 155, 156, 170, 176, 180, 189–90
Central Park outlet mall, 172
Champe, John, 195–96
Champe Rocks, 195–96
Chapman, Douglas, 103
Chapman, Hunter, 26, 103, 113, 114, 117, 118, 123, 144, 159
Chapman, Louise, 113–14
Chapman, Paul, 113–14
Charleston (S.C.) earthquake, 68
Charlottesville, Va., 31
Chattanooga, Tenn., 11, 19, 25, 76, 178, 179, 186
Cherokee Dam, 114
Cherokee Removal, 13, 179
Cherokee tribe, 13, 15, 85, 179, 186
Chickamauga Creek, 175
Chickamauga tribe, 186, 188
Child of God (McCarthy), 50
Christy (TV show) 105
Churches, 14, 23, 26, 36, 39, 105, 111, 112, 115–16, 118, 175, 189
Churchville, Va., 36, 159

Civil defense supplies, 13, 14, 181, 201. *See also* Fallout shelters
Civil War, 10, 34–37, 57, 59, 63, 65, 66–67, 73–74, 76–77, 78, 87, 144, 166–67, 186, 197, 199
Clinch Mountain, 63
Cobb, Bradford, 27–28
Cockrell, G. B., 71
Cold Mountain (Frazier), 56–58, 60
Cold War, 12, 23
Collins family (Linville Caverns owners), 59
Collins, Floyd, 187
Colossal Cave (game), 5
Cove, Dan, 141
Creationism, 17, 23–24
Crowther, Hal, 5
CSX, 199
Cudjo's Cave (Trowbridge), 66–67, 71, 82, 83
Cumberland Gap, Tenn., 62–63, 65
Cumberland Gap (topographical feature), 9, 62–83 passim
Cumberland Gap National Historic Park, 9, 81–83
Cumberland Plateau, 185
Curry, Dennis, 189–90
Cyclopean Towers, 26, 159

Darkness, 8, 10, 16, 21, 22, 24, 28, 29, 30, 33–34, 46, 59, 65, 67, 82, 84–93 passim, 102, 121, 124, 127, 137, 182, 188, 190, 191, 192, 196, 202. *See also* Total Darkness Demonstration
Davidson College, 42, 159
Davis, Roy, 14
Deliverance (Dickey), 50, 57
Democratic Party, 160, 162, 163
Development, 5, 16, 17, 22–25, 30, 34, 37, 42, 52, 53, 70, 72, 74, 80, 82, 86, 108, 109, 137, 149, 160, 161, 162, 167, 169, 172–73, 181, 193, 200, 201
Devil, the, 84–85, 88, 117, 118, 125–26
Devil's Looking Glass, 85, 91
Devil's Marbleyard, 85

Dixie Highway, 179
Dixon, Janet, 109, 116
Dixon, Scott, 109, 116
DJ Slink (Heath Shinpaugh), 117–18
Dogs, 129, 158, 175, 176, 178, 185
Dogtown, Ala., 179, 181
Dotter, Earl, 200
Dragging Canoe (Chickamauga chief), 186
Dulles International Airport, 11, 130, 195
Dykeman, Wilma, 70
Dykes, Betty, 112, 116–17
Dykes, Richard, 112, 116–17, 118–19, 122, 124–25

Eastern Printing Company, 159, 162, 165, 173
East Kentucky Land Company, 71
East Tennessee, 10, 12, 18, 50, 62, 89, 102, 110, 142, 164
Electronic dance music (EDM), 117
Emigration of Daniel Boone (Bingham), 65, 67, 81
English Mountain, 48–50
Evans, Eric, 140
Evans, Janine, 140–41
Explorer's Club, 137, 165, 167

Fallout shelters, 122. *See also* Civil defense supplies
Forman, Cliff, 176–78
Formations. *See* Speleothems
Fort Payne, Ala., 4, 178, 179, 180
Four Seasons Resort, 71, 72, 76, 77, 169
Frazier, Charles, 56–57, 60
Fredericksburg, Va., 172
Freedmen's Bureau, 74
French Broad, The (Dykeman), 70
French Broad River, 52–53
Front Royal, Va., 19, 37

Gant, David, 189–90
Gap Associates, 68
Gap District, the, 62, 63, 66–67, 71, 77, 79
Gas City, Ind., 25
Gatlinburg, Tenn., 48, 49, 52, 53

Gebser, Jean, 54–55
Gendarme, the, 196–97
Gene Monday Realty, 103
Genre conventions, 6, 8, 13, 15–16, 19, 30, 48, 82, 84, 134, 158
Gentry, Margaret Crudington, 102, 103
Geologists, 31–32, 36, 37, 42, 150
Geology, 58, 63, 84, 88, 128, 198
Georgetown, Tex., 86
Georgetown Corporation, 86
Gift shops, 7, 10, 14, 16, 20, 28–29, 51, 58, 80, 82, 86, 97, 108, 111, 115, 116, 119, 122, 127, 128–29, 131, 146, 152, 162, 171, 172, 175, 185, 197
Goat Man, the, 177
Grainger County, Tenn., 102, 117, 118
Grant-Lee Hall, 77
Grant, Ulysses S., 74, 77, 186
Graves, John, 130, 149, 152–53, 156–57
Graves, Katherine Northcott, 152–53
Graves, Rebecca Beal Jackson, 152–53, 157
Graves, Roderick ("Rod"), 130, 149, 153, 156–57
Graves, Theodore ("Ted"), 152, 157
Gray bats. *See* Bats
Great Appalachian Valley, 10, 18, 20, 24, 32, 38, 48, 52, 60, 62, 63, 87, 89, 129, 155, 175, 177, 179, 193, 195, 197
Great Depression, 14, 25, 167, 168
Great Smoky Mountains. *See* Smokies, the
Great Valley. *See* Great Appalachian Valley
Greenbrier, The, 70, 198–99
Grottoes, Va., 30–31, 46, 144. *See also* Shendun, Va.
Grottoes Company, 38–39, 41, 44–46, 144
Grottoes Hotel, 43–44
Guide humor, 20, 49, 181
Guides, 1, 4, 5, 10–22 passim, 28, 33, 34, 39, 44, 59, 62, 79, 82, 87, 89, 97, 120, 126, 133, 140, 142, 150, 152, 166, 170, 171, 174, 177, 179, 181, 184, 199
Gulf War, 94
Gurley, Jacob ("Jay"), 27, 185
Gurnee, Jeanne, 136–40, 144, 146, 155
Gurnee, Russell, 136–38, 158, 165

Gurnee Guides to American Caves (Gurnee and Gurnee), 112, 137–38

h.o.h. (artist), 162
Haggard, H. Rider, 71
Hamilton County Cave Rescue Unit, 189
Handrails, 4, 81, 106, 110, 181, 194
Hargrove, Earl, 144–49, 153, 154, 157
Hargrove Inc., 146–47
Harney, Will Wallace, 56
Harpers, 32–33, 68, 186
Harris, Homer, 106–7, 109
Harrisonburg, Va., 30
Harrogate, Tenn., 63, 70
Harrow School, 76–77
Haunted caves, 104, 109, 116, 117, 118, 123, 124
Hedrick, Clinton M., 197
Hell's Half Acre, 68, 78
High Country, 48, 52–54, 60, 195
Hillbillies, 14, 49, 50, 197
History of the Valley of Virginia (Kercheval), 161
Holler, Cato and Susan, 60
Hollywood Entrance, 120, 200
Homestead, The, 198–99
Honeybees, 193
Hotchkiss, Jedediah, 31, 36–43, 45, 70, 143, 159, 160
Hot Springs, N.C., 53, 60
Hovey, Horace Carter, 42
Howard, Oliver Otis, 73–77, 82
Howard University, 76
Humor. *See* Guide humor
Huntsville, Ala., 27
Hypothermia, 59, 95, 190

Illusion, 6, 8, 14, 16, 17, 19–20, 22, 30, 33, 34, 52, 53, 62, 82, 154
Indian Campaigns, 76
Indian Cave School of Theology, 120
"Indian Legend," 21, 49
Indians. *See* Native Americans
Interstate highways, 6, 14, 28, 46, 53, 79, 86, 87, 104, 108, 114, 164, 168–69, 195

Intro Room, 8, 16–17, 23, 49, 181
Irwin, Nate, 117

J.J. (Lost Sea guide), 12–14
Jackson, Thomas ("Stonewall"), 35–37
James Madison University, 30, 161, 162, 169
Jefferson Pools, 198
John Henry, 199
Johnson, Denis, 54–55
Johnson, Lady Bird, 138
Johnson City, Tenn., 11, 48, 89
Justice, Jim, 199–200

Keezletown, Va., 28
Kellow, Gladys, 144
Kercheval, Samuel, 161
Kincaid, Robert, 68
King Solomon's Mines, 71
Klingon language, 142
Knoxville, Cumberland Gap, and Louisville Railroad, 71–72
Knoxville, Tenn., 26, 48, 50, 71, 79, 83, 102–3, 116–17, 159
Knoxville Beltway, 111
Knoxville News Sentinel, 70, 71, 72, 81, 108, 118
Kyle, George, 13

Lacey Springs, Va., 159
Lalone, Fred, Sr., 197
Lam, Sandra, 169
Lam, Tony, 169
Lambert, Leo, 19, 25–27, 177, 187–88
Lambert, Ruby Eugenia Losey, 25–26
Lane, Buddy, 189–90
Larimore, Betty, 165
Lascaux, France, 18
Le Chateau, 169
Lee, Henry ("Light Horse Harry"), 195
Leeds, Maine, 73
Lee Highway, 46, 149
Letterbook of the Grottoes Corporation (vol. 2), 41, 43–45
Library of Virginia, 31

214   *General Index*

Lights, 7, 10, 12, 14, 16, 19–21, 29, 32, 49, 82, 88, 121–22, 124, 133, 145–46, 150, 164, 176
Limair, 131, 152–53, 157
Limestone, 12, 24, 25, 26, 34, 58, 63, 65, 86, 121, 137, 154, 162, 163, 174, 175, 186, 195, 198, 200
Lincoln, Abraham, 76–77
Lincoln Memorial University (LMU), 77–79, 80, 81
Lithophone. *See* Stalacpipe organ
Loch Willow Academy, 36
Logan County, W.Va., 200–201
Lookout Mountain, 19, 25, 179, 181, 183
Luray Caverns Corporation, 152
Luray Valley Museum, 149

Madison County, Va., 93
Main Street of Yesteryear, 146
Maps and mapping, 5, 8, 31, 36, 37, 71, 76, 82, 83, 86, 93, 100–101, 106, 156, 158, 161, 168, 173, 175, 189, 195, 202
Marion, N.C., 58
Marlborough, Duke of, 68
Marston, Chris, 157
Massanutten Mountain, 158, 159, 162, 163, 172
Matthews, Larry, 81, 175
Maxwell, Monte, 152
McCarthy, Cormac, 50–51, 56, 60, 62, 83
McElhaney, Richard, 118
McGill, William, 150
Meteorite crater, 63, 70
Metro Pulse, 117–18
Michael, Van, 14
Middlesboro, Ky., 62, 63, 70–73, 77
"Mighty Fortress Is Our God, A," 152
Mile Straight, Tenn., 175
Mimslyn Inn, 129
Mineral springs resorts, 7, 32, 52, 53, 198
Mohler, Leonard, and family, 31, 34, 37, 44, 143
Monday, Eugene, Jr. ("Gene"), 26, 103–4, 106, 108, 109, 111–12, 114–16, 159
Money Formation, 19, 49, 50, 145, 166, 179
Monongahela River, 196

Monteagle, Tenn., 185
Moonshine Museum, 171, 174
Motorcycles, 7, 109, 135; motorcycle clubs, 109, 196, 198
Mountain South, 7, 8, 53, 54, 66, 70
Mountaintop removal mining (MTR), 199–201
Mount Solon, Va., 26, 159
Myers, A. A., 76–77
Myers, Ray, 106–7, 109

Nantahala National Forest, 54
NASCAR, 10, 174
National Cave Association (NCA), 10, 128–57 passim, 158, 185
National Cave Museum, 136, 142
National Christmas Tree, 146
National Forests, 54, 56, 156, 196, 197
National Parks Service, 79–81
National Register of Historic Places, 169
National Speleological Society (NSS), 89, 98, 99, 101, 105, 106, 111, 136, 138, 170, 176, 178
Native Americans, 54, 56, 76, 113, 114, 119, 185, 186. *See also* Cherokee tribe; Chickamauga tribe
Natural Chimneys. *See* Cyclopean Towers
Natural Wonders Inc., 26, 159, 162, 165, 167, 169
Nature Underground: The Endless Caverns in the Heart of the Historic Shenandoah Valley, 162
New Beverly Baptist Church, 115
New Market, Tenn., 26, 144
New Market, Va., 26, 144
New Market Battleground, 156
"New South," the, 39, 42–43, 70
New South Wales, 141
New York, N.Y., 26, 28, 39, 159, 160, 162, 163, 165
New York Times, 33, 66
New York Tribune, 66
Nickajack Dam, 188, 189
Nolichucky River, 85, 91
Nomad Books, 165

North Carolina Geologic Survey, 58
Northcott, Belle Brown, 152
Northcott, T. C., 152–53, 168
North Fork Highway, 197
Norton, Charlie, 114–15
Norton, George, 114–15

Oak Ridge, Tenn., 7, 26, 102, 106, 108
Obama, Michelle, 150
Old Cudjo, 67, 78–80, 82
Old US 27, 175
Olympic Games (1996), 54
Omni hotel network, 199
Orr (frontier militia leader), 186
Osborne, Dan, 115–16
"O Shenandoah," 152
Otterbourg, Ken, 156
Outlaws (motorcycle gang), 109–10

Page County, Va., 157
Panic, 2, 33, 96, 117, 189
Panic of '93, 43, 72
Party caves, 89, 99, 130, 181
Philippine Insurrection, 159
Phoenix of the Mountains, 78
Photography, 16, 52, 131, 135
Pigeon Forge, Tenn., 49, 52–53, 58, 60
Pinchot, Gifford, 78
Pine Mountain, 63
Pine Mountain Grotto, 81
Plimpton, George, 165
Porte Crayon. *See* Strother, David Hunter
Potomac River, 37, 195
Powell Mountain, 63
Powell Valley, 63
Proctor, Dan, 145
Proctor, Joe, 145
Pseudogymnoascus destructans. See White-
   nose syndrome

Quizzes, 19

Raccoon Mountain, 26, 189
Rationing, 114, 168
Rave in the Cave, the, 117–18

Recreational vehicles ("RVs"), 10, 170, 174
Revolutionary War, 195
Richmond, Va., 31, 37, 38, 45, 103
Ridgewalking, 89
Road, The (McCarthy), 83
Rock formations. *See* Speleothems
Rockingham County, Va., 164, 172, 173
Rogers, Fred, 152
Rogers, William Barton, 31–32, 41, 44
Roosevelt, Eleanor, 150
Rosenburger, Horace, 158, 160
Rothrock, Henry P., 135
Rudolph, Eric, 54–56, 57, 59, 60, 61, 89
Rumple, James Wharton Walker, 31,
   42–46, 159
Rutledge, Tenn., 112, 118

Sam Snead Highway, 198
Saltpeter, 13, 89, 113, 181, 186, 199
Sand Mountain, 179, 185, 186, 188
Sapphire Pool, 26, 159
Schmidt, Jeff, 80
Scouting, 11, 13, 14, 92, 105, 110, 117, 118, 122,
   153
Seasonal labor, 12, 15, 150, 202
Seneca Rocks, 196–97, 198, 199
Sequoyah (Cherokee chief), 179
Sevier County, Tenn., 50
Sevierville, Tenn., 48, 50
Shale, 63, 195
Shellmound, Tenn., 186
Shenandoah Herald, 44
Shenandoah Mountain, 195
Shenandoah River, 46, 140
Shenandoah Valley, 10, 19, 31, 41, 46, 47,
   130, 149, 158, 161, 174
Shenandoah Valley Campaign, 35, 38, 166
Shenandoah Valley Railroad, 39
Shendun, Va., 39–46, 70, 72, 159. *See also*
   Grottoes, Va.
Sherman, William Tecumseh, 73–74, 186
Shining Rocks, 56
Sides, Stanley D. ("Dr. Stan"), 1–4, 133–36,
   173
Silver, Larry, 172

Silver Companies, 172–74
Singing Tower, 149, 154
Small Library, 41, 45
Smith, Gordon, 135–36, 142
Smith, Russell, 32
Smokies, the, 12, 14, 19, 48, 63, 81
Soddy Daisy, Tenn., 175
Southern Appalachia. *See* Appalachia
Southern mountains. *See* Appalachian
    Mountains
Spanish-American War, 159
Special K (Nate Wells), 117–18
Speleothems, 9, 16–20, 31, 37, 41, 46, 49,
    59, 62, 79, 86, 88, 106, 109, 138, 144, 145,
    150, 152, 163, 166, 177, 179, 181, 184, 199
Spelunking, 97–105, 108–11, 114–16, 119,
    123, 170, 179, 181, 189, 202. *See also*
    Caving
Spotswood, Alexander, 93
Sprinkle, Leland, 151
Spruce Knob, 197
Stalacpipe organ, 151–52, 199
Stalagmite sitting, 177
Star Trek, 142
Stardust (trick horse), 106, 109
Starkweather, William, 168
Stevens, Phineas V., 163
Stewart, Martha, 199
Stickley, Lettie, 144
Stock Creek, 200
Strother, David Hunter ("Porte Crayon"),
    31–38, 43, 45, 186, 196
Sulawesi, Indonesia, 18
Sweetwater, Tenn., 11
Swift Run Gap. 93

Taco Bell, 55, 59
Ten Commandments, 120
Tennessee Department of Transportation,
    111
Tennessee Native American Museum at
    Indian Cave Village, 119
Tennessee River, 26, 103, 186
Tennessee Tech, 191
Tennessee Valley, 12, 191

Tennessee Valley Authority (TVA), 114,
    188, 190
Tennessee Wildlife Resources Agency
    (TWRA), 191
Tenth Legion, Va., 158, 164
Tenth Mountain Division, 196
Texas Speleological Society, 86
Thomas, Lowell, 165, 167
Tora Bora, 61
Total Darkness Demonstration, 21, 33, 59,
    84, 86, 89, 171, 182. *See also* Darkness
Tourists, 4, 15, 20, 21, 25, 38, 54, 71, 82, 108,
    114, 143, 161, 179, 187, 194
Townsend, Ellen, 58–59
Toy Town, 149
Trail towns, 53
Trowbridge, John Townsend, 66–67, 71,
    76, 79, 83
Turner, Frederick Jackson, 65, 67
Tyler (Manitou Cave guide), 180–85

Unaka Mountain, 89, 91
Uncanny, the, 8, 13, 15, 19
U.S. Forest Service, 156
U.S. Geological Survey, 42, 84
U.S. Marine Corps, 145, 197
U.S. Post Office, 169
Universal Ministries Church, 116, 118, 119
University of Virginia, 31, 41
Upstate New York, 36, 164, 177, 178, 193,
    198

Valley-and-Ridge Province. *See* Great
    Appalachian Valley
Valley Turnpike, 161, 163
Virgin cave, 5, 99, 101
Virginia Geologic Survey, 31
Virginia Illustrated, 33

Walker, Cas, 106–7
Walker, Thomas, 65
Walmart, 200–201
Warner, Charles Dudley, 68
Washington, George, 17, 195, 197, 200
Washington Post, 156

Western Kentucky University, 3
Western North Carolina, 48, 52, 56, 60
West Nile virus, 193
Weyer, Bernard, 31
Whidby, Jim, 7, 104–12, 115, 119, 123, 138
White-nose syndrome (WNS), 155–56, 191, 193
White Sulphur Springs, W.Va., 177
Wilcox, John, 3–4
Wild cave, 11, 13–14, 134, 181, 187
Wilderness Road, the, 67, 68, 78, 80–83
Willstown, 179

Wilson, Woodrow, 126, 160
"Won't You Be My Neighbor," 152
Woods, Mark, 81
World War I, 53, 165, 168
World War II, 28, 106, 114, 168, 196, 197

Y-12 plant, 108
Yellow Creek Valley, 70, 71

Zep Spot, 92
Zika virus, 193
Zirkle, Ruben, 158, 170